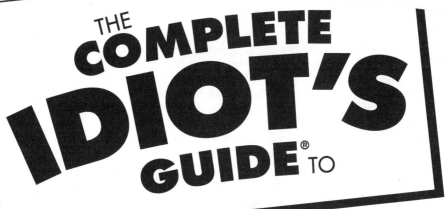

THE **COMPLETE IDIOT'S GUIDE**® TO

# Doing Your Taxes with TurboTax® Deluxe

*by Joe Kraynak*

201 W. 103rd Street, Indianapolis, IN 46290

## Trademarks

**Executive Editor**
*Angela Wethington*

**Acquisitions Editor**
*Jamie Milazzo*

**Development Editor**
*Nick Goetz*

**Technical Editor**
*Tony Boor*

**Managing Editor**
*Thomas F. Hayes*

**Project Editor**
*Karen A. Walsh*

**Copy Editor**
*Molly Warnes Schaller*

**Indexer**
*Lisa Stumpf*

**Proofreader**
*Tricia Sterling*

**Layout Technician**
*Brad Lenser*

**Cartoonist**
*Judd Winick*

# Contents at a Glance

# Table of Contents

## Part 3: Deductions, Credits, and Other Ways to Reduce Taxes 145

## 12 Income Reduction Through Deductions 147

## 13 Additional Deductions You May Have Overlooked 163

## About the Author

**Joe Kraynak** has been writing and editing computer books and other technical material for more than 10 years. His long list of computer books include *The Complete Idiot's Guide to PCs, The Big Basics Book of Windows 98, 10 Minute Guide to Excel, Easy Internet,* and *Windows 95 Cheat Sheet.* Joe graduated from Purdue University in 1984 with a Master's degree in English and a strong commitment to making computers and software easily accessible to the average user.

## Dedication

*To the IRS, for inspiring me to do my best work.*

## Acknowledgments

Special thanks to Jamie Milazzo for choosing me to write this book and for expertly dealing with contract details and all that other messy stuff; to Nick Goetz whose insightful comments and questions significantly enhanced this book; to Karen Walsh for shepherding this book through the production cycle.

Tony Boor deserves special kudos for not only painstakingly checking the step-by-step instructions, but also for adding some great tips that have made this book more than worth the manufacturer's suggested retail price. A special round of applause goes to the illustrators and page layout crew for transforming my loose stack of files, figures, and printouts into such an attractive, bound book.

# Tell Us What You Think!

As the reader of this book, *you* are our most important critic and commentator. We value your opinion and want to know what we're doing right, what we could do better, what areas you'd like to see us publish in, and any other words of wisdom you're willing to pass our way.

As the Executive Editor for the General Desktop Applications team at Macmillan Computer Publishing, I welcome your comments. You can fax, email, or write me directly to let me know what you did or didn't like about this book—as well as what we can do to make our books stronger.

*Please note that I cannot help you with technical problems related to the topic of this book, and that due to the high volume of mail I receive, I might not be able to reply to every message.*

When you write, please be sure to include this book's title and author as well as your name and phone or fax number. I will carefully review your comments and share them with the author and editors who worked on the book.

Fax:     317-817-7448

Email:   pcs@mcp.com

Mail:    Executive Editor
         General Desktop Applications
         Macmillan Computer Publishing
         201 West 103rd Street
         Indianapolis, IN 46290 USA

# Introduction: April Is the Cruelest Month

*April is the cruelest month, breeding*
*Lilacs out of the dead land…*

From T.S. Eliot's *The Waste Land*

Of course, T.S. Eliot wasn't writing about income tax deadlines, but the first two lines of *The Waste Land* express the feelings most of us have as the April 15th deadline approaches. Form 1040 is like some mysterious blanket of snow that hides the inevitable taxes and refunds that are sprouting beneath. Few of us have a clear idea of whether we'll receive a refund or have to pay additional taxes at year's end. And even those of us who are fairly certain that we'll receive a refund must take a wild guess as to how much that refund will be.

Face it, even with the 1997 Tax Reform Bill and the IRS gang's promise to be nice guys, taxes aren't fair and tax forms are so complicated that no two accountants can come up with the same numbers. If you take the easy way out (that's the 1040EZ way out) with the standard deduction, the IRS grabs more than your fair share of the taxes. If you try to save a little money and itemize deductions, you pay the price of time. And if you decide to hire a professional, the high fees take a big bite out of your tax refund. It seems like a lose-lose situation.

## Welcome to TurboTax, Your Personal Tax Guru

In this season of tax doubt and dread, TurboTax can help you center yourself and lead you step-by-step through the meandering trail of tax forms, schedules, and deductions. With TurboTax, you have a professional accountant right on your desktop, making sure you fill out the right forms and schedules, helping you take advantage of all the deductions and credits to which you're entitled, pointing out tax-saving tips and strategies, and even performing a mock audit to point out problems that could trigger a real audit.

In many respects, TurboTax is even better than a professional accountant. TurboTax interviews you in your own home or business without the intimidating countenance of an accountant, and provides feedback without delay. Are your records a mess? TurboTax will patiently wait as you get them in order. Need an extra form? No charge. Want to play with the numbers and see if you can save some money? Take your time.

As it says at the bottom of your tax return, you are solely responsible for the accuracy of your return, so take control. TurboTax gives you the power to determine your own tax destiny and to sign your return with complete confidence.

# But It's Not Always *That* Easy

Like every software program, TurboTax is an imperfect tool. It superimposes a linear approach on a three-dimensional tax return, making it nearly impossible to figure out where TurboTax is inserting your data and which forms are related. In addition, many of the questions that TurboTax asks are laden with the same technobabble and ambiguity that the IRS serves up in its publications.

Welcome to *The Complete Idiot's Guide to Doing Your Taxes with TurboTax Deluxe*. This book combines the technical aspects of navigating the TurboTax software with practical accounting advice and sound tax-saving tips to give you the highest possible tax refund allowed by law.

In this book, you'll learn how to deal with the TurboTax Interview, navigate the stack of forms it creates, unleash the TurboTax auditor, track down additional deductions, and even plan ahead to trim your taxes in 1999!

# Flipping Around in This Book

This book is a companion to the TurboTax software. As such, it follows the TurboTax Interview questions to keep you in step with the program. As you fill in the blanks during the Interview, refer to this book for answers and valuable tax-saving tips. If you decide to forego the Interview and fill out the forms yourself, use the Contents at a Glance (at the beginning of this book) and the following guide to skip around the book and find the answers you need:

- Part 1, "Ugh! Getting Started," deals with the preliminaries. Here, you learn how to install, run, and navigate TurboTax, use the TurboTax help system, gather the records and receipts you'll need, import data from last year's return and from your personal finance program (assuming you use a personal finance program), and enter personal information on your 1040.

- Part 2, "Inputting Your Income," provides comprehensive instructions on how to record income from various sources. In this part, you'll learn exactly what the IRS considers income and how the federal government taxes income from different sources.

- Part 3, "Deductions, Credits, and Other Ways to Reduce Taxes," shows you how to whittle down your income by claiming all the deductions and credits you can legally claim. Here's where you'll find out if you can deduct moving expenses, business expenses for the use of your home, or healthcare expenses for your dog.

- Part 4, "Reviewing and Filing Your Tax Return," introduces the TurboTax power tools. Here, you learn how to perform a pre-audit to catch any errors in your return and flag areas that could trigger an audit. This part also shows you how to scan your return for additional tax-saving entries and print your return or submit it electronically via modem.

- Part 5, "After the Fact: Amendments, Audits, and Future Plans," shows you how to handle errors on your return, file an amended return, reply to notices from the IRS, prepare for an audit, and plan for next year. In this part, you learn what the IRS can and cannot do and you learn your rights as a taxpaying citizen. This part also includes a list of common tax questions and answers.
- At the end of this book is an appendix of state tax agencies and contact information, just in case you didn't purchase the state version of TurboTax. You'll also find a glossary of IRS terms explained in plain English, just in case you want to start talking like an accountant.

## The Unconventional Conventions

To make this book a little easier to use, we took it upon ourselves to follow a few conventions. Anything you need to type appears in bold, like this:

Type **this entry**

If there's any variable information to be typed in, such as your own name or a filename, it appears in bold italic, like this:

Type ***this entry***

In addition, you'll find boxed information (like the examples below) scattered throughout the book to help you with terminology, boring technical background, shortcuts, and tax tips. You certainly don't have to read these little boxes, but if you skip the information, you'll miss out on some of the best stuff.

**TurboHelp!**

These boxes signal a bend in the road and point out some of the quirky steps inherent in TurboTax. Stop and think about what you're about to do *before* you make the wrong turn.

**CPA Tip**

Check out these professional tips from a genuine certified public accountant (CPA). Here, you'll find tricks of the trade, tips, shortcuts, and practical techniques for juggling numbers.

**IRS Speak**

When you're not sure what to make of a particular term on your tax form, this box transforms IRS lingo into clear definitions for us common folk.

## CPA Wannabe

When you're plugging in numbers, you might come to a place where the tax law just doesn't make sense. Here, you'll find in-depth explanations of the more ambiguous blanks on your tax forms along with additional information about new tax laws.

At the end of every chapter, you'll find a section called "Still on Track?" which makes sure you've crossed your t's, dotted your i's, and haven't done anything illegal (at least on your tax return).

# Part 1
# Ugh! Getting Started

*A journey of a thousand miles begins with a single step.*

   *—Confucius*

*Over the past year, you've been forking over your hard-earned cash to the government in the form of an interest-free loan—the IRS prefers to call it "withholding tax." Now it's time to get some of that money back or determine how much extra the government expects.*

*If the government owes you a refund, this could be one of the more pleasant seasons of the year, but getting started is still tough. You've stashed your forms, receipts, and records in envelopes and shoeboxes throughout your home or apartment, and the mere thought of organizing the mess and entering all that data is just too overwhelming.*

*To make the process more manageable, the chapters in this part show you how to gather essential records, get organized, fire up TurboTax, and start your return. After you take this first step, you'll have the momentum to carry through to the end and get your refund in time for summer vacation.*

AND IF YOU'LL STEP TO YOUR LEFT YOU'LL SEE OUR DESKTOP...

# Chapter 1

# TurboTax Nickel Tour

---

### In This Chapter

➤ Install TurboTax and fire it up

➤ Expertly navigate the new TurboTax screen

➤ Download and install TurboTax updates from Intuit's Web site

➤ Get help and information about the latest tax laws

➤ Consult with a tax expert in the TurboTax video library

---

You've been gathering forms, receipts, and records during the past year, stuffing them in envelopes, shoeboxes, filing cabinets, folders, and every other paper receptacle imaginable. You've accumulated a pile of papers just waiting for the day your copy of TurboTax arrives in the mail. Well, TurboTax is finally here, and it's time to get off your duff and start working.

This chapter explains how to get started with TurboTax, showing you how to install, run, and navigate TurboTax; update your copy of TurboTax with bug fixes and late-breaking changes; get help with the program; and tap the various tax resources on the TurboTax Deluxe CD.

# Installing TurboTax 1998

Although TurboTax can single-handedly slap together a tax return for you, it requires a little human intervention to get started. The first step is to install TurboTax from the TurboTax CD or installation disks.

### Activating AutoPlay

In Windows 95 or 98, AutoPlay starts playing a CD right when you insert it. To turn on AutoPlay, **Alt+**click **My Computer**, click the **Device Manager** tab, and click the plus sign (**+**) next to **CD-ROM**. Click the icon for your CD-ROM drive, click **Properties**, and click the **Settings** tab. Make sure there's a check mark next to **Auto Insert Notification**, and then save your changes and restart your computer. After your computer restarts, reinsert the TurboTax CD.

Installing from the CD is a no-brainer. If Windows AutoPlay is active, you simply pop in the TurboTax CD. A dialog box pops up on your screen, asking if you want to install TurboTax. Click **Yes** and then follow the onscreen instructions.

If AutoPlay is not on, or if you received TurboTax on disks, you must initiate the installation routine. Take the following steps:

1. Insert the CD or the first installation disk.
2. In My Computer or Windows Explorer, click or double-click the icon for the disk drive into which you inserted the CD or disk. (If you are installing from a CD, the setup routine might run automatically.)
3. If the setup routine does not start, click or double-click the **Setup** icon.
4. Follow the onscreen instructions to complete the installation.

*TurboTax leads you step-by-step through the installation.*

Follow the onscreen instructions.

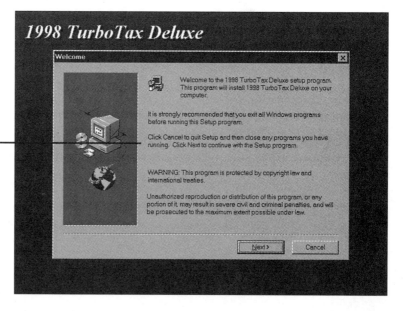

# Meeting TurboTax Face-to-Face

Every accountant, even an automated accountant like TurboTax, conducts an interview to gather the information required to complete a tax return. TurboTax requests your name, date of birth, social security number, and address; asks if you're married and, if you are, prompts you to enter information about your spouse and kids (or other dependents); and then leads you through the process of entering your income, deductions, and credits. To successfully respond, you need to know how to talk to TurboTax; but first, you have to get it up and running.

When you install TurboTax, the setup routine places an icon for running the program on the Windows desktop. To run TurboTax, simply click the icon (or double-click it if you have an older version of Windows). The TurboTax window pops up on your screen, as shown in the following figure. (If a registration dialog box pops up, click **No**. I'll show you how to register TurboTax later in this chapter.)

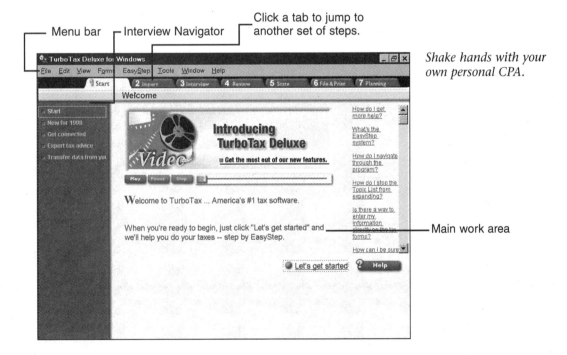

Menu bar — Interview Navigator — Click a tab to jump to another set of steps.

*Shake hands with your own personal CPA.*

Main work area

If you used TurboTax to file your return for a previous year, you might notice that Intuit has completely revamped the interface, making it easier to navigate and cutting down on the number of screens used for entering data. The following list describes the four general areas you'll be working with:

➤ Menu bar—At the top of the TurboTax window is a menu bar that contains the names of the available pull-down menus. To open a menu, click its name. These menus contain options and commands that enable you to wander off the interview path to work on other aspects of your return.

➤ Tabs—Just below the menu bar are seven tabs that lead you through the process of getting started, importing financial data, proceeding through the interview, reviewing your return, completing the State Return, printing and filing your return, and preparing for the next tax year.

➤ Interview Navigator—At the left of the screen is an outline that gives you a bird's eye view of the interview process. As you complete a step in the interview, the Interview Navigator places a check mark next to it. You can quickly jump around in the process by clicking on the desired step. To make the bar wider and view the entire description of each topic, click inside the bar. To return it to its original width, click in the main work area.

➤ Main work area—TurboTax devotes the largest chunk of its screen to the main work area. Here's where TurboTax displays its questions, the IRS forms and schedules, and links to other resources on the CD. (A *link* is a button, icon, or underlined word or phrase that calls up additional information.)

# I Just Bought TurboTax. Now I Have to Update It?

Before you do anything else, you should register your copy of TurboTax and download and install any updates from Intuit's Web site. Registering is important because it tells Intuit that you have a legal copy of the program. This gives you access to program fixes and updates, as well as special deals on the next version of TurboTax. More importantly, registering TurboTax makes Intuit responsible for any errors on your return caused by program bugs. Downloading and installing program updates is critical in ensuring that your copy of TurboTax covers late-breaking changes in the tax code and that any bugs in the program are eliminated.

## *Registering TurboTax*

You can register your copy of TurboTax the old-fashioned way—by completing and mailing the registration card—or (if your computer has a modem) you can register electronically. (If you purchased TurboTax directly from Intuit, you're already registered.) To register via modem, take the following steps:

1. Open the **Help** menu and click **Online Registration**. The Please Register Your Product dialog box appears.
2. Complete the registration form by entering settings just as you would in any dialog box.
3. Click the **Register** button. If you have an Internet account, TurboTax connects to your Internet service provider and sends the registration information you entered. Otherwise, a dialog box appears, informing you that you must have an Internet or AOL connection to proceed.
4. Click **OK**. The Internet Connection Setup dialog box appears.

5. Click the button to the left of one of the following options:

   ➤ I have an existing dial-up Internet connection—Click this if you use an Internet service provider to connect to the Internet via modem.

   ➤ I have a direct Internet connection—Click this if you have an Internet connection via a network connection (not using a modem).

   ➤ Use Intuit's complimentary dial-up Internet account—Click this if you don't have an Internet account. You can use this account only to register, download program updates, and file your return electronically. This sets up a Dial-Up Networking connection that dials a toll-free number.

6. Click **OK**. What happens next depends on the option you selected in Step 5. Follow the onscreen instructions to complete the setup.

## Download Program Updates with Update Assistant

The problem with any tax return software is that the software development runs parallel with the government's fine-tuning of the tax code. This makes it tough for the software manufacturer to release a bug-free, up-to-date program on a timely basis. To ensure that your copy of TurboTax is current with the latest tax code and includes the latest bug fixes, you must download and install TurboTax updates from Intuit's Web site. Take the following steps:

1. Click the **Start** tab, if it's not already up front.

2. In the Interview Navigator, click **Get connected**.

3. In the main work area, click the **One-click Updates** link.

4. If prompted to save your file, click **Yes**, type a name for the file, and click **Save**. The Internet Connection Setup dialog box appears. (If you registered online previously, you need not complete the steps required to set up an Internet connection; skip to step 7.)

5. Click **Next**. You are now prompted to specify how you connect to the Internet.

6. Click the appropriate button to the left of one of the following options:

   ➤ I have an existing dial-up Internet connection—Click this if you use an Internet service provider to connect to the Internet via modem.

   ➤ I have a direct Internet connection—Click this if you have an Internet connection via a network connection (not using a modem).

   ➤ Tell me how to sign up for an Internet account—Click this if you don't have an Internet account. The TurboTax CD contains several programs for connecting to the Internet. The Connection Wizard will lead you through the process of setting up an account and connecting to the Internet. (Have your credit card handy.)

7. Click **Next** and follow the onscreen instructions to set up your Internet connection (if necessary) and connect to the Internet. When you connect, TurboTax automatically downloads the required program updates and installs them. If no product updates are available, the Product Updates dialog box tells you so; click **Cancel**.

If TurboTax informs you that there are no updates, but you want to check for yourself, open the **Help** menu and choose **Online Support Solutions**. This connects you to the TurboTax solutions Web page, which contains links for program updates, alerts, and additional online help from Intuit.

*Go to the TurboTax support site to download the latest changes and fixes.*

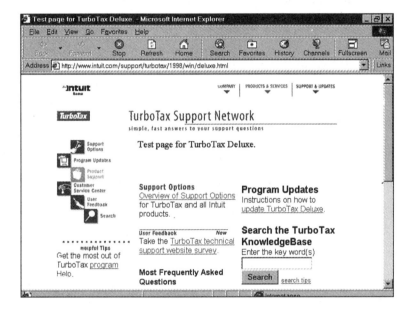

## Help Is Just a Click Away

TurboTax Deluxe isn't just some fancy automated tax form. The CD version also comes packed with a complete tax reference library, including IRS publications, *Money* magazine's *Income Tax Handbook*, a library of video clips, and a list of the most common tax questions and answers. TurboTax also includes standard program help to answer questions about how to use TurboTax.

To access any of this additional information, open the **Help** menu and choose the desired type of help. For help with using TurboTax, open the **Help** menu and choose **Program Help**. This displays the Program Help window, as shown in the following figure. The Help system is divided into three areas:

➤ Finding answers to your tax questions—This area provides a list of links for searching through the electronic library for tax-related issues.

➤ Learning more about using TurboTax—This area provides links for instructions on how to use TurboTax to complete and file your tax return. It also includes links for information on navigating TurboTax, setting software preferences, planning for next year's taxes, and uninstalling TurboTax.

➤ Getting help from Intuit—This area provides links for accessing online help and for contacting Intuit's technical support and customer service departments.

Click a link to view specific information and instructions.

The Bookmarks menu lets you flag a page.

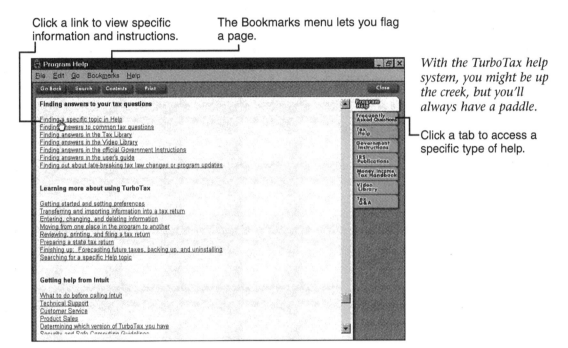

*With the TurboTax help system, you might be up the creek, but you'll always have a paddle.*

Click a tab to access a specific type of help.

The help window provides its own navigational tools. On the right side of the window are tabs that enable you to quickly skip from one type of help to another. For example, you can display a list of available IRS publications by clicking the **IRS Publications** tab. Each tab displays a list of links that point to specific publications or instructions. Simply click the desired link.

Just above the main help area are several buttons that enable you to bypass the menu system:

➤ Go Back—This takes you back to the previous screen.

➤ Search—This displays a searchable index of help topics. Click **Search** and type one or two words to describe the topic. This scrolls the list of help topics to display topics that match your entry. When you see the desired topic, double-click its name.

➤ Contents—This takes you back to the list of help topics that are displayed when you choose **Help**, **Program Help**.

➤ Print—This prints the currently displayed information and instructions, providing you with a paper copy for quick reference.

➤ Close—This closes the Program Help window so you can continue working on your return.

You'll find one of the most useful navigation tools for the help system via the Bookmarks menu. When you finally track down the answer to your question, you can flag the "page" with a bookmark to quickly refer to it later. Simply open the **Bookmarks** menu and click **Add Bookmark**. This places the name of the page at the bottom of the Bookmarks menu. To return to the page, open the **Bookmarks** menu and click the name of the page. (You can delete a bookmark by choosing **Bookmarks**, **Delete Bookmark**.)

# Checking Out the Latest Tax Laws

Knowledge is power. If you don't know the latest tax laws, you can't take advantage of them. With that in mind, Intuit places a list of the latest tax laws right at your fingertips. Most of these new tax laws are a result of the Taxpayer Relief Act of 1997, but many of the changes have become active in the current tax year, 1998. To view the list of changes, open the **Help** menu and click **What's New This Year**. Scroll down the page to read about the Taxpayer Relief Act and learn about the new tax breaks.

Don't try to memorize the list. To help you take advantage of these new laws and understand how they apply to your tax return, we have highlighted the changes throughout this book whenever they apply to a particular form you're filling out.

### Why Does Tax Code Keep Changing?

Although taxes are primarily a way for the government to generate revenue, they are also used to control the actions of its citizens and help one party or the other win elections. The latest changes to the tax code strongly encourage people to invest more money and become more educated by offering tax breaks for retirement investments, college tuition, and continuing education. In addition, to promote family values, the government chose to provide additional tax credits for married couples with children.

# Picking Tax Brains Via the Video Library

Publications, whether on paper or online, are still the primary source of help in TurboTax. For a detailed explanation of your tax questions, be prepared to do some heavy reading. However, for a more human touch, TurboTax provides a library of video clips, which let you watch and listen to professional accountants and tax consultants explain some of the more tricky tax issues.

To play these video clips, your computer must have a sound card installed and video card and monitor that are capable of handling video. The best way to find out if your computer is up to the task is to try to play a clip. To do this, perform the following:

1. Open the **Help** menu and click **Video Library** or click the **Video Library** tab in the Help window. A list of categories appears.
2. Click the category of the desired topic (for example, Business or Family).
3. Click the link for the desired video clip. A dialog box appears, providing controls for playing the clip.
4. Click the **Play** button. The video starts to play.
5. When the video clip is over, click the **Close** button to continue working.

Click Play to start the clip.

**Using the Kiddie Tax to Your Advantage**

Click Close when you're done.

*The video library lets you consult with a tax pro.*

If your PC has trouble playing the audio or video portion of the clip, and you know that you have the required hardware (sound card, video card, and monitor), check the following:

➤ Crank up the volume on your speakers.
➤ Right-click the speaker icon in the lower-right corner of your screen and choose **Open Volume Controls**. Make sure none of the controls is set to Mute, and drag each control to the top.
➤ Check the display settings. Right-click a blank area of the Windows desktop, click **Properties,** and click the **Settings** tab. Make sure **Colors** is set to at least 256 and **Desktop Area** is set to 640-by-480 or higher.

➤ Try closing any other programs that are currently running. Video clips consume a great deal of memory and might have trouble running if other programs are fighting for the same resources.

# Getting More Help and Information on the Web

Although Intuit crams more information than you probably need on the TurboTax CD, the answers might not address an obscure tax question and can be slightly out of date. To obtain the latest information, you might need to hit the Internet, specifically the Web. The TurboTax help system provides access to Intuit's Web site, where you can find links to several additional help sources on the Web. To tap these resources, open the **Help** menu and choose one of the following options:

➤ TurboTax Web Site—This connects to the TurboTax home page, where you'll find links to product information and updates, tax law changes, a list of U.S. averages for deductions, additional online tax guides and tips, and much more.

➤ Online Support Solutions—This loads the TurboTax help page, which provides links for accessing program help and updates and dealing with more immediate concerns and specific issues on your current return.

If you have an insatiable thirst for tax knowledge, check out these other Web sites for additional information:

➤ Internal Revenue Service (www.irs.ustreas.gov)—Look here for the most current changes in tax laws and information about what's going on at the IRS.

➤ *Money* Magazine (jcgi.pathfinder.com/money/plus/index.oft)—For general tips on personal finances, investments, and tax-saving strategies, *Money* magazine's Web site can't be beat, especially during the tax season.

➤ H&R Block (www.handrblock.com/tax)—If you want tax help from the country's largest tax return firm and you don't want to pay for it, check out the H&R Block Web site. At this site, you'll also find a useful refund calculator to give you a general idea of the refund you can expect.

➤ TaxHelp Online (www.taxhelponline.com)—TaxHelp Online offers free help and suggestions for lowering your personal income tax and protecting your small business. This site also contains a link for submitting a question to an expert tax consultant.

➤ Inform America (www.informamerica.com)—Are you required by law to pay income taxes? Inform America says, "No!" Check out its rationale at this Web site, but be careful about following its advice—the IRS can make your life miserable, even if Inform America is right.

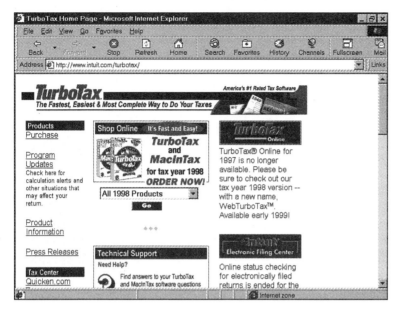

*For sticky tax issues, visit Intuit's tax page.*

## Still on Track?

Before you move on to the next chapter, make sure TurboTax is set up and ready to roll and that you've mastered the basics:

➤ Did you install TurboTax? See "Installing TurboTax 1998," on page 8.

➤ Is TurboTax running? See "Meeting TurboTax Face-to-Face," on page 9.

➤ Did you register TurboTax and download the latest updates? See "I Just Bought TurboTax. Now I Have to Update It?," on page 10.

➤ Can you find answers to your TurboTax and tax questions using the TurboTax help system? See "Help Is Just a Click Away," on page 12.

➤ Can you locate the IRS Web site? See "Getting More Help and Information on the Web," on page 16.

# Chapter 2

# The Paper Chase: Gathering Your Records

## In This Chapter

➤ Make sure you have all the records and receipts you need to get started

➤ Track down missing W-2s and other documents

➤ Strategic filing procedures for the bored and compulsive

➤ Practical advice for the organizationally deprived

➤ Other paperwork that might come in handy

The Paperwork Reduction Act might have trimmed the amount of paperwork in Washington and streamlined some federal procedures, but it sure hasn't trickled down to the average citizen. My files are packed with old tax returns, donation receipts, W-2s and 1099s, and boxes of other records from years I don't want to remember. I have so many boxes full of useless papers that I've started using the boxes as furniture.

The tax system places the burden of proof on the taxpayer. In the eyes of the IRS, you are guilty until proven innocent, and the only way to prove yourself innocent of tax evasion is to have records of all your income, expenses, and deductions. Without such records, the IRS can simply deny your claims or take the liberty of overestimating your income and underestimating your deductions.

This chapter provides a checklist of all the records you need to gather and hold on to along with some useful advice on how to organize your paperwork.

# W-2s, 1099s, and Other Records the Feds Already Have

At the end of the year, your employer(s) and anyone else who paid you money (a contractor, your bank, your mutual fund, and so on) are required to issue you a W-2 or 1099 form. The information on these forms is sent directly to the IRS, which can use the information to make sure you've reported the correct income. If there's a discrepancy between the amount you reported receiving and the amount you're reported to have been paid, you become audit bait. To avoid problems, make sure you have the following forms:

➤ W-2s for you and your spouse (if you're married).

➤ 1099-MISC for any miscellaneous income you received. This includes income you received from working on contract or as a freelancer or independent contractor, from royalties or rental properties, and from prizes.

➤ 1099-INT for any interest you received from bank accounts or loan payments you've received over $10 and from bonds or T-bills.

➤ 1099-DIV for any dividends or capital gains you received from your investments, not including dividends or capital gains that were reinvested in a tax-deferred account, such as an IRA or SEP. 1099-DIV is also issued for dividends paid in S corporation distributions.

➤ 1099-G for any payments you received from the government. This includes unemployment compensation and any tax refund you received from your state tax return.

➤ 1099-R for distributions from your pension, profit-sharing, IRAs, or other retirement plans. If you're not retired, your fund probably automatically rolls any dividends or capital gains back into the account—you don't claim this gain for tax purposes.

➤ Additional 1099 forms for income from the sale of stocks and barter transactions (1099-B), cancelled debts (1099-C), real estate transactions (1099-S), discounts on time deposits and certificates (1099-OID), security interest for trade or business debt (1099-A), and cooperatives (1099-PATR).

If you have any additional income for which you have not received a W-2 or 1099, you should have some record of that income. For example, if your mutual fund did not issue a 1099-DIV for the dividends it paid during the year, use the end-of-year statement from the mutual fund as your record.

**No W-2?!**

If you haven't received a W-2 form by the end of February, contact your employer. If your employer fails to dig up your W-2, call the IRS at 1-800-829-1040. If you lost your copy of your W-2, have your employer make you a copy. It's perfectly all right to send a photocopy of your W-2 instead of the original.

# Income That the Feds Might Not Know About

Whether you make extra money from tips, by charging people to park on your lawn during the local festival, or by doing side jobs for your neighbors, the IRS wants its cut of the proceeds. There's no "Don't ask, don't tell" policy when it comes to taxes. With that in mind, here's a list of types of underground income you are obligated to report:

➤ Tips—If your employer does not withhold taxes from your tip income, keep detailed records of your tips and consider submitting estimated quarterly tax payments to avoid a large tax bill and penalties at the end of the year. See "Calculating and Paying Estimated Taxes," in Chapter 22, "Tax Planning for 1999," for details on paying estimated taxes.

➤ Alimony—If you receive alimony from your ex, it's taxable unless you have a clause in your separation agreement in which your ex agrees not to claim alimony as a deduction on his tax return. (Child support does not qualify as alimony and cannot be deducted.)

➤ Bartering—If you trade materials or services, the IRS expects you to report the fair market value of those services. Skilled laborers often trade services to avoid paying taxes for those services; for example, a mechanic might fix a carpenter's car in exchange for a new set of cabinets. The IRS hates it when this happens.

➤ Employee fringe benefits—Generally, any fringe benefits you receive from your employer are tax-free, assuming the benefits are business-related. For example, you are not expected to pay taxes for a company car when used for business purposes, but you are expected to pay taxes on the personal use of the vehicle. If you receive any fringe benefits that are not business-related, you must keep a record of the personal gain from that benefit.

➤ Gambling winnings—If you win anything—money, a TV set, a two-week vacation—you must pay taxes on the fair market value of your winnings. In some cases, the gambling establishment will issue you a W-2G. In other cases, the IRS relies on the honor system (or on prosecuting the less honorable, if the IRS hears about it).

➤ Hobby income—Yep, the feds want a cut of any proceeds you make from collecting stamps, coins, or dolls, as well as buying and selling antiques, or any other hobby that brings in a profit. However, you might be able to reduce the amount of income reported by keeping track of your expenses.

**Roll the Dice**

The IRS can't lose. If you win any money gambling, you must pay taxes on your winnings. If you lose money, you can deduct the amount you lost from your winnings, but you cannot deduct your losses beyond the amount of your winnings. In short, if you didn't win anything, you can't deduct gambling losses.

➤ Illegal income—Make any money selling pot? Embezzling money? Smuggling diamonds? Well, at least be honest about it and include it on your income tax return. (Sounds like a violation of the 5th Ammendment to me.)

Although there's no direct penalty for not having the right records to support your claim, if the IRS learns of income you have not reported, it can overestimate your income and require you to pay back taxes and penalties. For example, if you're a waiter and fail to keep detailed records of your tips, the IRS can overestimate your tip income based on average tip income for your place of employment. If you have records to back up your claims, you'll generally win if your case goes to court.

# Reaping the Rewards of Your Donations

At tax time, it's better to give than to receive. You can significantly beef up your itemized deductions by claiming cash and non-cash contributions to charitable organizations. Just make sure that you have the required documentation:

**Maximize Your Contributions**

To qualify for a full deduction, give only to organizations that the IRS has listed as bona fide charitable organizations. If you're not sure, ask the organization to provide written proof. Also, check your state income tax return to determine if your state provides special deductions for donations to a state college or university. Some states provide a fifty-cent tax credit for every dollar you contribute to a state college or university. You can fully deduct your contribution on your federal income tax return and take the credit on your state income tax return, as well.

➤ For any cash contribution over $250, you must have a written receipt from the non-profit organization.

➤ For cash contributions of less than $250, obtain a copy of the cancelled check or a receipt from the organization, or at least write down the date and amount of your contribution and contact information for the organization.

➤ If you do any volunteer work, you can't claim a deduction for the time or expertise you donated. However, you can claim a deduction for anything you purchased for the organization and for mileage (14 cents per mile). Keep your receipts and log the number of miles you drive as a volunteer.

➤ For non-cash contributions, you must have a receipt listing the items you gave to the organization along with the fair market value of each item you donated. When you drop off your old junk at Goodwill, get a receipt.

➤ If you purchased products from an organization for a fund drive, find out the amount of the purchase that goes to the organization. You can then deduct that amount. For example, if you purchase a box of Girl Scout cookies, find out how much money actually goes to the Girl Scouts. (If you purchased tickets for a carnival, fish fry, or other entertainment or meal, your purchase is not deductible.)

If you donated money to an organization and received a "free gift" in return, you must deduct the fair market value of the gift from your contribution. For example, if you donated $100 to PBS and received a copy of the *Riverdance* video, you must deduct $19.95 for the video, even if you never watch it.

# The Tax Benefits of Owning a Home

Although your home might seem like a money pit throughout the year, it can provide you with some tax relief in April. If you itemize your deductions, you can deduct the interest portion of your mortgage payments along with any points and property taxes you paid in 1998. In addition, if you use a portion of your home exclusively for business purposes, you can deduct a portion of your utilities and other expenses you incurred. To take advantage of your homeowner's deductions, gather the following records:

➤ Form 1098, from your mortgage company, specifies the amount of interest you paid on your mortgage loan in 1998. You might also receive form 1098 if you took out a home equity loan. You can deduct mortgage interest you paid on up to two homes, so if you have a vacation home or other second residence, make sure you have a 1098 for each home.

➤ If you purchased a home and paid points (to borrow the money at a lower interest rate), dig out the papers you received at closing, and find out how much you paid in points. Add this to your mortgage interest.

➤ Property taxes are deductible. You should have received a statement showing the amount of property taxes you paid. If your mortgage company pays your property taxes out of an escrow account, this amount should be shown on your year-end statement from the mortgage company.

### An Important Point About Points

You must deduct points paid for a home equity loan or for refinancing your mortgage over the life of the loan. For example, if you pay $1,500 in points to refinance your 30-year mortgage, you can deduct only 1/30 of $1,500 each year, or $50 each year for 30 years. However, if you used the home equity loan for a home improvement on your main home, you can fully deduct the points.

# Did You Pay Interest on Other Loans?

If you racked $50,000 on your Visa card or hit up your local credit union for a $20,000 auto loan, don't expect any sympathy from the IRS. Any interest you paid on these loans is NOT deductible; the feds phased out interest deductions for personal loans several years ago. However, the feds have provided a couple ways to deduct interest:

➤ Interest on mortgage and home equity loans is deductible. If you take out a home equity loan and use it to pay off those high-interest credit card bills, you get a tax break.

➤ Up to $1,000 interest on personal loans for education is deductible. The deduction applies only to the first 60 months on which interest payments are required, and you can't be claimed as a dependent on someone else's return.

➤ Interest on money you borrowed for investments is deductible. For example, if you buy stocks on margin (betting that the stock will go down in value), you can deduct the interest on that loan. However, the investment must earn taxable income, so you can't deduct interest if you borrowed money for a tax-deferred account, such as an IRA or if your high-risk venture lost money.

### Buying Stocks on Margin

Although it's risky, you can actually make money when a stock loses value by buying the stock *on margin* and then selling it *short*. To buy on margin, you borrow shares of stock, immediately sell the shares, stick the money in your margin account, and wait for the stock to take a dive. You then buy the shares back (the shares you borrowed and sold) and return them to the lender.

# Medical and Dental Bills

Every year my wife hands me a file stuffed with receipts from the doctor, dentist, and pharmacy along with the amount she paid in health insurance, thinking that all those receipts will result in a big fat tax refund. I dutifully add up the amounts and then subtract the total from 7.5% of our adjusted gross income to prove that we don't even come close to qualifying for the medical/dental deduction.

Unfortunately, to see any tax savings from these bills, the total expense must exceed 7.5% of your adjusted gross income. For instance, if you made $60,000 last year, you would need to have spent at least $4,500 in health insurance and medical and dental bills before you can claim a deduction. In short, most people don't qualify for this deduction, but it's worth a try. If you have your medical and dental receipts lying around, enter them in TurboTax. TurboTax will then perform the required calculations and enter any deduction you're qualified to take.

## Child Care Bills and Other Kids' Stuff

Kids are expensive, but at tax time, your kids can actually *save* you some money. You get to claim each child as an exemption, deduct a percentage of the money you pay for child care, and chop four hundred bucks off your tax bill for each kid. Unfortunately, you might have to deal with additional tax issues if your kids have investments or other sources of income.

We'll deal with all these issues as they crop up in TurboTax. However, you should make sure you have the required paperwork before you get started:

**Cafeteria Plans**

Ask your company's personnel manager if your company sponsors a *cafeteria plan* (or FSA, *flexible spending account*). With a cafeteria plan, you place pre-taxed dollars into a separate account and then use the money to pay your medical and dental bills and any other qualifying dependent care expenses. At the end of the year, you forfeit any extra money that's left in the account—the closer your estimate, the more you save.

➤ Your child's full name, birthday, and social security number.

➤ The amount of money you paid in child care, along with the address and taxpayer identification number of the child care institution or the person who cares for your children.

➤ Your children's bank statements and year-end investment reports. If your child is under 14 and has investment income of more than $1,300, you qualify for the Kiddie Tax, which you'll learn about in Chapter 16, "More Taxes (As If You Weren't Paying Enough)."

## Employee Business Deductions: If You Don't Own a Business

Many jobs require you to shell out some of your own hard-earned cash for union dues, continuing education, journals, tools, special supplies, and uniforms. When the amount you pay exceeds 2% of your adjusted gross income, you can claim losses over your 2% AGI as a deduction. Following is a list of the types of employee business expenses you can claim, assuming you have the documentation to back it up:

**Auto Expenses**

If you use your car for both personal and business use, keep a journal of the total number of miles you drive and the number of miles related to business activities. Also keep track of every penny you spend on gas, oil, maintenance, repairs, insurance, license fees, toll charges, and parking fees. You might find that by deducting a percentage of the total expenses, your deduction exceeds the standard mileage deduction.

➤ Union dues and membership fees for professional organizations.

➤ Business use of your personal vehicle. Commuting to and from your job doesn't count, but if you had to run errands or visit clients, you can deduct mileage or a percentage of your gas, vehicle maintenance, and insurance.

➤ Trade publications, books, and magazines that relate to your current job.

➤ Work clothes or uniforms that are required for your job and not suitable for general use. That Armani suit doesn't count.

➤ Job hunting costs for a job in the same field in which you are currently working. If you're changing careers and looking for a job in a different field, your job hunting costs are not deductible.

➤ Safety equipment and small tools that you must purchase to perform your job.

➤ License fees.

➤ Depreciation for your home computer, cellular phone, or other equipment required for your job and not for personal use.

# Home Office Deductions

Whether your employer gave you the "opportunity" to work at home or you voluntarily chose to join the ranks of the self-employed, and you use a portion of your home exclusively for business-related activities, you can deduct a portion of your mortgage interest, utilities, qualifying home improvements, and maintenance costs. The deduction is limited to the percentage of the area of your home you use for business purposes. For instance, if you have a 2,000 square foot home and use a 12-by-12 room (144 square feet) as your office, you can deduct only 7.2% of your expenses (144 divided by 2,000). Fish out the following receipts to take advantage of your deduction:

➤ Your 1098, showing the amount of mortgage interest you paid in 1998.

➤ Utility receipts, including gas, electricity, water, sewer, and trash. You can deduct long-distance charges directly related to your job, but you cannot deduct your standard phone charges. (If your job requires you to have a second phone line, you can deduct the entire phone bill for that line.)

➤ Receipts for home repairs and improvements that apply specifically to your home office or to the entire house. If you knock the wall out between your kitchen and living room, that doesn't count. However, if you build shelves in your office or put a new roof on the house, you can claim the improvement or repair as a home office deduction.

➤ Insurance statements. You can deduct a portion of your homeowner's insurance, plus any extra insurance related specifically to your business.

➤ Real estate tax statements. If your mortgage company pays your real estate taxes out of an escrow account, the numbers you need should be on form 1098.

# Tracking Your Assets

When you run your own business, you use equipment, machines, furniture, and other stuff, called *assets*, to generate income. In some cases, you can deduct the entire cost of an asset in the year in which you purchased it. In other cases, you deduct the cost over several years or *depreciate* the asset. This enables you to spread your tax savings over several years.

You'll learn more about depreciation in Chapter 8, "Depreciating Your Old Stuff." For now, just make sure you have receipts for all your depreciable assets, including the following:

➤ The vehicle you use for your business.

➤ Breeding hogs, race horses, and other livestock that loses value over time.

➤ Your computer.

➤ Furniture, appliances, and office equipment, not including computers.

➤ Carpeting used in your business or home office.

➤ The cost of your office building (or home, in the case of a home office).

➤ Anything else you own that helps you generate income and that loses its value over more than one year.

# IRAs, 401(k)s, and Other Tax Deferred Tricks

Every financial manager on the planet will give you the same advice on cutting your tax bill: contribute to a tax-deferred retirement account, such as an IRA, 401(k), or SEP (self-employed pension) plan. The trouble is that a large chunk of the middle class can't afford to contribute enough to take full advantage of this savvy tip. Sure, if you're in a 28% tax bracket, you save two hundred eighty bucks on every thousand dollars you invest, but who has a thousand bucks lying around?

Be that as it may, if you have the financial discipline, foresight, and free cash to invest in a tax-deferred retirement account, make sure you have a year-end statement showing how much you contributed to the account in 1998. (If you contributed to an employer-sponsored retirement play, such as a 401(k), this information should be on your W-2 form.) In Chapter 14, "Getting a Tax Break with Retirement Investments," I'll show you how to enter the numbers in TurboTax to make the most of your retirement investments.

### Contribute Up to April 15

You can contribute to a tax-deferred retirement account up to April 15, 1999, and claim the deduction on your 1998 tax return. If you plan on sending in your tax return before April 15, you can claim the deduction even if you haven't yet contributed the money. Just make sure the money you claim makes it into your tax-deferred account by April 15.

## Get Organized

You can run out and purchase a special tax folder from any office supply store, but these specialized folders rarely suit the needs of the average taxpayer. Here are some better (or at least more realistic) methods of organizing your records:

➤ Use Quicken—With Quicken (and other personal finance programs), you can easily track every penny of income and expenses and import the data into your TurboTax return, as explained in the next chapter, "Grabbing Financial Data You've Already Entered."

➤ Use 10-by-13-inch envelopes—Label each envelope with a description of its contents: Income, Interest, Home Deductions, Contributions, Job-Related Expenses, Medical Expenses, Child Care, and so on. You can even jot a running total on the front of each envelope.

➤ Use an accordian file—Label each pocket with a description of its contents, as explained for the 10-by-13-inch envelope method. This keeps the records all in one place, so you don't risk misplacing an envelope.

➤ Go hi-tech—If you have a scanner, you can scan in your receipts and records and store them in related folders on your hard drive. When you need a form or receipt, just pull it up onscreen.

➤ The "hide the evidence" technique—After you're done filing your tax return, place your return and all receipts, forms, and records in a grocery sack and shake it up. Just hope the IRS never audits you.

## Still on Track?

This is the easiest chapter to read, but the most difficult to work through. You'll find yourself digging through files in your home or apartment, running out to your car to write down your mileage and check your vehicle registration, and placing calls to track down the documents you can't find. When you're done, make sure you have at least the following records:

➤ W-2s for any job-related income.

➤ 1099s for investment, self-employment, dividend, and interest income, and for any other income that's not job related.

➤ A log of any tips, alimony, gambling winnings (and losses), and other miscellaneous income not reported on a W-2 or 1099.

➤ A list of your cash and non-cash contributions to tax-exempt and not-for-profit organizations, along with receipts.

➤ Form 1098 showing the amount of mortgage interest you paid in 1998. If you purchased your home in 1998, have your closing statement handy.

➤ A statement showing the amount of property taxes you paid in 1998.

➤ Bills and receipts from hospitals, doctors, dentists, and pharmacies, along with the amount you paid in health insurance.

➤ If you have children, their birth dates and social security numbers and any child care expenses for children under the age of 13.

➤ Receipts for any job-related expenses for which you were not reimbursed by your employer.

➤ If you run your own business, receipts for all supplies and equipment you purchased for the business.

➤ A statement showing the amount of money you contributed throughout the year to a tax-deferred retirement account.

# Chapter 3

STUFF
STUFF

# Grabbing Financial Data You've Already Entered

You're sophisticated, intelligent, savvy. You own a computer and use it to manage your personal finances and do your taxes. And you know that the big advantage of computers is that they make your financial activities less redundant. Well, then, it just doesn't make sense to retype entries you've carefully entered on last year's return and in your personal finance program. Not only is retyping a waste of time, but it also makes your tax return vulnerable to data entry errors...just ask the IRS.

To save time and reduce errors, yank your data from last year's return and from your personal finance program. TurboTax has several tools to streamline the process and make your job a whole lot easier. This chapter shows you how to unleash these powerful tools.

# Pilfering Data from Last Year's TurboTax Return

If you used TurboTax last year, your 1997 tax return has a good chunk of information that you can carry over to this year, including your name, address, social security number, information for your dependents, information about depreciable assets and year-end inventory, and passive-loss and capital-loss carryovers.

Before you transfer this data from last year's tax return, you should be aware of some important transfer issues:

➤ If you used tax software other than Intuit's TurboTax, TurboTax cannot transfer data from last year's return. You'll have to manually enter the data. That'll teach you!

➤ If you transfer data and have second thoughts, you can edit the data or start a new return.

➤ If you and your spouse filed separately last year, you can import data from only one of your tax returns. Pick the more complicated return and go for it.

➤ If you find an error in the imported data, consider filing an amended return for 1997. See "Filing an Amended Return," in Chapter 21, "Oops, I Made Some Honest Mistakes." After correcting last year's return and saving it, transfer data from the amended return.

With these standard cautions in mind, take the following steps to transfer data from last year's return:

### Oops, I Deleted the Wrong Form

You can create forms at any time, although the new forms will be blank. Open the **Forms** menu and click **Go to Forms**. Click the **Open a Form** button (just below the menu bar), choose the desired form, and click **Open**. To get the completed form back, you can retransfer the data from your 1997 return to a new return, but you cannot retransfer data to the current return.

1. Make sure you have a virgin tax return. If you just started TurboTax, you're set. Otherwise, open the **File** menu and choose **New Tax Return** or press **Ctrl+N**. (You can choose to save the current return or to dump it.)

2. Click the **Start** tab if it is not already in front.

3. In the Interview Navigator, click **Transfer Data from Your 1997 Tax Return**.

4. Click the **Transfer from Last Year** link.

5. Change to the drive and folder in which you stored last year's TurboTax return, typically C:\Tax97. If your return is on a disk, insert the disk into your computer's floppy drive and change to drive A or B.

6. Click the icon for last year's tax return and click the **Open** button. A small window appears, indicating that TurboTax is transferring the data. When the transfer is complete, the Transfer Report appears, as shown.

7. If you don't need one of the forms that TurboTax imported, click the name of the form and click the **Remove Selected Form** button.

When you're done, you can proceed to the next section to import data from your personal finance program, skip to the next chapter to start the interview, or continue filling out forms manually.

Click Transfer data from your 1997 tax return.

Click the Start tab.

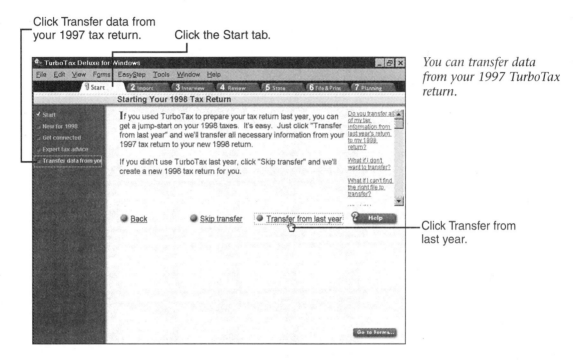

*You can transfer data from your 1997 TurboTax return.*

Click Transfer from last year.

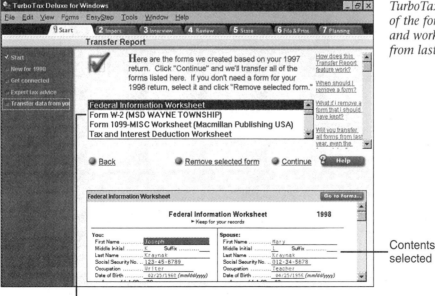

*TurboTax displays a list of the forms, schedules, and worksheets it grabbed from last year's return.*

Contents of the selected item.

List of forms, schedules, and worksheets.

33

# Importing Data from Quicken

### Transfer Data from Your 1997 Return First!

If you haven't transferred data from your 1997 TurboTax return, transfer that data now. When TurboTax imports data from a financial program, it adds the values to the values currently in your return.

### Print a Tax Report

Before you import data, run Quicken and print a tax report to help you verify that TurboTax properly retrieved the correct data and inserted entries in the proper blanks.

If you use Quicken to keep track of your personal finances, you know that it's a real time-saver, helping you reconcile your checking account, manage your budget, and make smart investment decisions. Quicken can also cut down on the time it takes to complete a tax return by supplying totals for your income, personal and business deductions, mortgage interest payments, contributions, child care, and any other cash that's flowing in or gushing out.

To take advantage of Quicken at tax time, you should first make sure your accounts are in order and that you have properly assigned categories to every tax-related transaction. Refer to your Quicken documentation for details. This is the most important and time-consuming step in the process. Without this prep work, TurboTax will have no idea where to stick the numbers, and might end up listing personal deductions as business deductions, omitting mortgage interest, and even overstating your income.

After you've completed the drudge work of assigning your transactions to categories, you can start thinking about importing your financial data. TurboTax gives you two options, which are covered in the following sections:

➤ If you have Quicken 6, Quicken 98, Quicken 99, or QuickBooks 4 or later, you can use TaxLink to import data. However, TaxLink allows you to import data from only one file. If you have more than one file to import, use TaxLink for one file and then save the other file in TXF (Tax eXchange Format) and import it.

➤ If you have an older version of Quicken or a different financial program, use the program to save your financial file in TXF, and then import it. You can import as many TXF files as you like. (QuickBooks cannot save files in TXF.)

# Doing a Mind Meld with TaxLink

Spock would love TaxLink. With TaxLink, TurboTax establishes a live connection with Quicken, enabling you to change category assignments on-the-fly to make your categories conform to your tax forms. To use TaxLink, take the following steps:

### Man, I Don't Have Time for This!

If you did some overly creative work with Quicken categories, don't fight what you already have. Print a report in Quicken and then manually enter the numbers.

1. In TurboTax, click the **Import** tab and click the **Quicken** link.

2. Click **Import Now**.

3. If the Quicken file from which you want to import data is not listed, click the **Browse** button, change to the drive and directory where the file is stored, click the file's name, and click **Open**.

4. Click the **Continue** button. TurboTax runs Quicken and displays the Tax Link Instructions dialog box. (Don't close Quicken while TaxLink is running.)

5. Click **OK**. TurboTax displays a list of Quicken categories and classes that are linked to your tax forms.

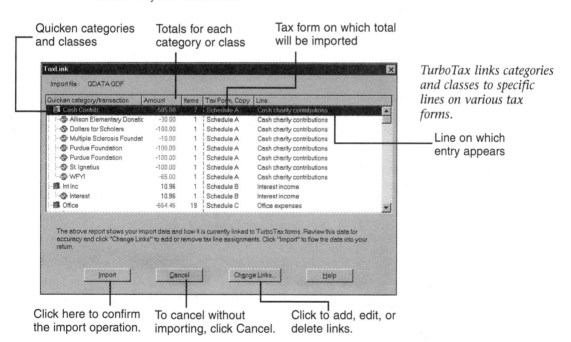

Quicken categories and classes | Totals for each category or class | Tax form on which total will be imported

*TurboTax links categories and classes to specific lines on various tax forms.*

Line on which entry appears

Click here to confirm the import operation. | To cancel without importing, click Cancel. | Click to add, edit, or delete links.

6. To link a transaction to a different line on your tax return, click **Change Links**. The TaxLink dialog box appears, listing your transactions and the lines to which they apply on your tax forms. This dialog box has three tabs—All Transactions, Linked, and Unlinked—to help you focus on only those transactions you want to change.

**35**

*You can specify the categories and classes you want to link to lines on your tax forms.*

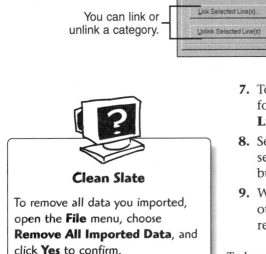

Click the desired category or class.

You can link or unlink a category.

7. To link a transaction to a specific line on a tax form, click the transaction, click **Link Selected Line(s)**, and click **OK**.

8. Select the form and line to which you want the selected transaction linked, and click the **Link** button.

9. When all the links are correct, click **Import**. If other data was linked to this line, TurboTax replaces that data with the newly imported data.

To break the link between a transaction and a particular line on a tax form, repeat steps 1-6. In step 7, click **Unlink Selected Line(s)**.

**Clean Slate**

To remove all data you imported, open the **File** menu, choose **Remove All Imported Data**, and click **Yes** to confirm.

## *Doing the Standard TXF Transfer Tango*

Older versions of Quicken (Quicken 5 and earlier) don't support TaxLink. Fortunately, you can import the data by saving your Quicken file as a TXF file and then importing the file into TurboTax. If you decide to take this approach, make absolutely sure that you have your house in order in Quicken. Check your categories and classes, and flag them as tax-related. To do this in Quicken 5, open the **Lists** menu and choose **Category & Transfer**. At the top of the Category & Transfer list, click the **Tax Link** button. This displays a list of categories and the tax forms and lines to which they are linked. Make any adjustments, as desired.

When your Quicken file is in order, take the following steps to save it as a TXF file and import it in TurboTax:

1. In Quicken, open the **Reports** menu, point to **Home**, and click **Tax Schedule**.
2. Make any changes to the report, as desired, and click the **Create** button.
3. At the top of the Tax Schedule Report, click the **Export** button.

Type a name for the file.    Click the Export button.

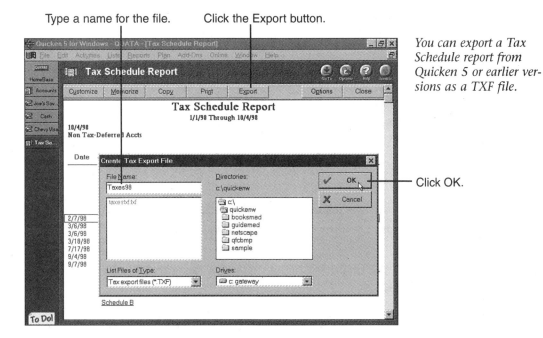

*You can export a Tax Schedule report from Quicken 5 or earlier versions as a TXF file.*

Click OK.

4. Name and save the file as a TXF file.
5. In TurboTax, open the **File** menu and click **TXF Import**.
6. Change to the drive and folder in which you saved the TXF file.
7. Click the TXF file and click the **Open** button. The Importing dialog box appears and then another dialog box appears indicating that the process is complete.
8. Click **OK**.

### Importing Capital Gains

To import data on capital gains or losses, create a capital gains report in Quicken. Open the **Reports**, **Investment** submenu and click **Capital Gains**. Then, follow the same steps in TurboTax to import the data.

# Importing Data from QuickBooks

Do you own your own business? Do you have more than one employee? Do you use QuickBooks to manage your business finances? If so, and you use QuickBooks version 4 or later, you can import tax data into TurboTax using the TaxLink feature. If you have an older version of QuickBooks, you're out of luck. Your only option is to print a tax schedule and then type the numbers in TurboTax.

Before you take the plunge, you should be aware of the following issues:

➤ QuickBooks cannot save files as TXF files, so you must use TaxLink to import data.

➤ If you have a 1997 TurboTax return, transfer that return to TurboTax *before* you import data from QuickBooks.

➤ Don't close QuickBooks during the TaxLink operation.

➤ You can import QuickBooks data to only one copy of each tax form. If you have two Schedule Cs, you can import data only to one of them.

Are you ready to rumba? Then take the following steps to import data from your QuickBooks file:

1. Save your tax return, as explained later in this chapter, and then exit TurboTax.

2. Run QuickBooks and open the file whose data you want to import.

3. Run TurboTax.

4. In TurboTax, click the **Import** tab and then click the **QuickBooks** link.

5. Click **Import Now**.

### Cash or Accrual?

The cash method of accounting requires you to claim income when you receive it and expenses when you pay them. With the accrual method, you log income when you perform a service or sell a product, even if you don't immediately receive payment. You log expenses when you incur the expense, even if you pay it later.

6. Enter the beginning and ending dates for your tax year. In most cases, these dates will correspond to the first and last dates of the calendar year, unless your fiscal year differs.

7. Choose the desired accounting method for your business: **Cash** or **Accrual**.

8. Click **Continue**. TurboTax displays a list of QuickBooks accounts that are linked to your tax forms.

9. To link an account to a different line on your tax return, click **Change Links**. The TaxLink dialog box appears. This dialog box has four tabs—Setup, All Accounts, Linked, and Unlinked—to help you focus on only those accounts you want to change.

10. Click the **All Accounts** tab.

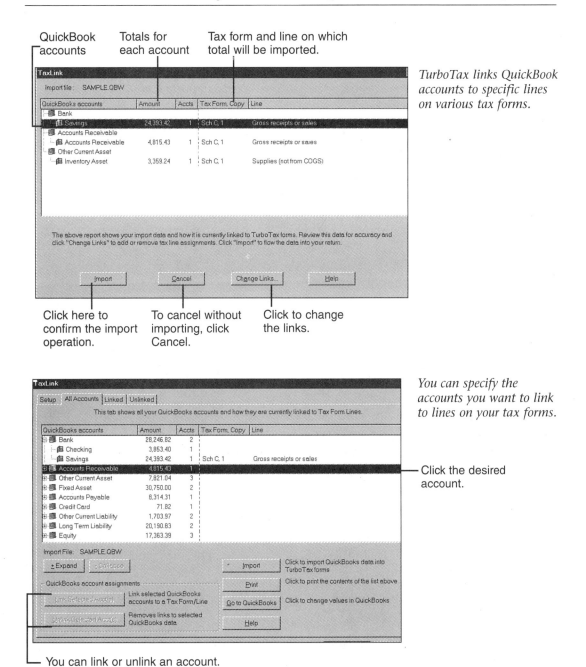

QuickBook accounts

Totals for each account

Tax form and line on which total will be imported.

*TurboTax links QuickBook accounts to specific lines on various tax forms.*

Click here to confirm the import operation.

To cancel without importing, click Cancel.

Click to change the links.

*You can specify the accounts you want to link to lines on your tax forms.*

Click the desired account.

You can link or unlink an account.

**11.** To link an account to a specific line on a tax form, click the account, click **Link Selected Acct(s)**, and click **OK**. (You might need to click the plus sign next to the name of the account type to display a list of specific accounts.)

**39**

12. Select the form and line to which you want the selected account linked, and click the **Link** button.

13. When all the links are correct, click **Import**. If other data was linked to this line, TurboTax replaces that data with the newly imported data.

To break the link between an account and a particular line on a tax form, repeat steps 1-10. In step 11, click **Unlink Selected Acct(s)**.

# Importing Data from Other Personal Finance Programs

You took the cheap way out and decided to go with some second-rate personal finance program, such as Microsoft Money or Kiplinger's Simply Money. Now, you're worried that the few bucks you saved might not have been worth the bargain.

Fortunately, most personal finance programs allow you to save or export your data file as a TXF file. Unfortunately, because I don't know which personal finance program you're using, I can't give you step-by-step instructions telling you how to pull it off. Check the documentation or online help system in your personal finance program to figure it out. After you have the TXF file, you can import it into TurboTax:

1. In TurboTax, open the **File** menu and click **TXF Import**.

2. Change to the drive and folder in which you saved the TXF file.

3. Click the TXF file and click the **Open** button. The Importing dialog box appears and then another dialog box appears indicating that the process is complete.

4. Click **OK**.

# What Exactly Was Imported?

Automation has its price. When TurboTax imports data, it automatically carries over numbers to various tax forms, which can make you a little uneasy. Did TurboTax get the right numbers? Did it put those numbers on the right lines? Should I have entered the numbers myself?

Stop worrying so much. TurboTax can help you track down the information it imported and double-check your return. To determine which entries TurboTax imported, where TurboTax lifted those entries, and where TurboTax inserted the entries, open the **Tools** menu and click **My Tax Data**.

TurboTax displays the My Tax Data dialog box listing the imported data, as shown in the following figure. On the left is the list of the forms and the lines on each form where TurboTax inserted imported data. The center column displays the actual entries TurboTax inserted. The right column displays the source from which TurboTax obtained the data:

➤ Transfer—This indicates that the data was lifted from your 1997 tax return.

➤ Import—This indicates that the data was lifted from Quicken, QuickBooks, or another personal finance program.

➤ Blank—This indicates that you manually entered the data.

Form and line on which
the entry appears      The exact entry

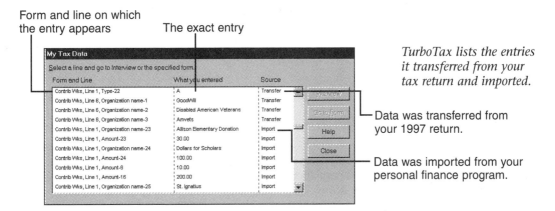

*TurboTax lists the entries it transferred from your tax return and imported.*

Data was transferred from your 1997 return.

Data was imported from your personal finance program.

To edit an entry, click it and then click the **Go to Form** button. TurboTax fetches the form and highlights the imported entry so you can edit it. (You'll learn more about editing entries in the next chapter.) You can also click an entry and click the **Interview** button to edit the entry on the EasyStep Interview screen.

# Still on Track?

If you log every penny of your income and expenses using a personal finance program and you successfully imported all relevant tax data into TurboTax, you should be well on your way to having completed your 1998 tax return. Before moving on to the next chapter, make sure you're still on track:

➤ If you filed your 1997 tax return with TurboTax, that data should be transferred to your 1998 return. See "Pilfering Data from Last Year's TurboTax Return," on page 32.

➤ Every tax-related income and expense transaction in Quicken should be assigned to a category and class and be flagged as tax-related. See "Importing Data from Quicken," on page 34.

➤ If you have Quicken 6 or later, you should have used TaxLink to import tax-related data to your tax forms. See "Doing a Mind Meld with TaxLink," on page 35.

➤ If you use Quicken 5 or earlier, you should have exported your financial file as a TXF file and then imported it into TurboTax. See "Doing the Standard TXF Transfer Tango," on page 36.

➤ If you use QuickBooks version 4 or later, you should have used the TaxLink feature to import your data into TurboTax. See "Importing Data from QuickBooks," on page 38.

➤ If you use any other financial program that can save or export files in the TXF format, you should have imported data from the TXF file into TurboTax. See "Importing Data from Other Personal Finance Programs," on page 40.

➤ If you transferred data from your 1997 tax return or imported data from a personal finance program, check the data to make sure everything is correct up to this point.

ON YER MARK!!

# Chapter 4

# Okay, Let's Get Started

---

### In This Chapter

➤ Start your tax return with a brief Interview

➤ Do your tax return the old fashioned way—by filling out forms

➤ Jump from one form to another without tripping

➤ Enter your name, rank, and social security number

➤ Determine and specify your filing status

➤ Save your return so you won't lose anything when you quit

---

You've done your legwork. You've collected all the required records and receipts, transferred entries from your 1997 return, and grabbed any useful data from your personal finance program. Now it's time to start filling out the necessary forms, schedules, worksheets, and other paperwork required by the IRS.

This chapter gets you started by showing you how to proceed through TurboTax's EasyStep Interview, skip around from one form to another, and enter personal information on form 1040. Here, you also learn how to determine your filing status, claim the right number of personal exemptions for you and your kids, and save your return so you can open it and work on it later.

### Already Done?

If you transferred data from your 1997 TurboTax return, you might be able to skip some sections in this chapter. However, you should read through the chapter to learn how to navigate the EasyStep Interview and enter information directly on forms.

### Switch from Forms to Interview, and Back

You can quickly switch back and forth between the Interview and forms methods. In the Interview, just above the form that's displayed near the bottom of the screen, click the **Go to Forms** button. When working in Forms view, click the **Back to Interview** button to the upper right of the form.

# Interview or Forms Method? You Decide.

The programmers at Intuit know that no two people are the same. Some taxpayers can't get started on their tax returns without a little prodding from an accountant. Others prefer to pull up a form and start filling in the blanks. To accommodate everyone, TurboTax gives you a choice: You can follow the EasyStep Interview, fill out the forms manually, or use both methods.

The EasyStep Interview is definitely the best way to start your return. You simply answer questions, type entries, and complete *worksheets* during the interview. (A worksheet is an unofficial form that TurboTax uses to gather information.) TurboTax takes care of the rest, figuring out which forms you need to fill out and then transferring your entries from the worksheets to the proper lines on each form.

After you're done with the Interview, you can go back and fill in any gaps and make the required adjustments. This ensures that you provide all the information for which the IRS is looking and that you have reviewed your tax return and made the necessary corrections. The following sections show you how to proceed using both methods.

## Being Grilled in the EasyStep Interview

If you lug your records and receipts into H&R Block, one of its accountants will lead you through an interview, asking you to hand over your W-2s, 1099s, receipts for deductions, and any other tax-related material. The EasyStep Interview leads you through a similar interview process. You simply select options and type the entries that TurboTax requests.

To start the EasyStep Interview, click the **Interview** tab (or choose **EasyStep, Interview**). The Interview Navigator appears on the left side of the window, showing a step-by-step outline of the Interview process. On the right side of the screen is the area in which the Interview will proceed. To get started, click **Let's start my return**.

Interview Navigator

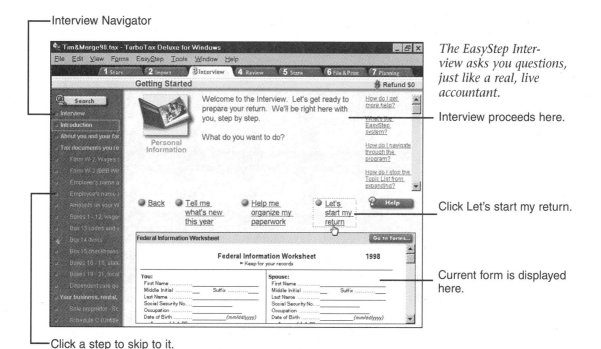

*The EasyStep Interview asks you questions, just like a real, live accountant.*

Interview proceeds here.

Click Let's start my return.

Current form is displayed here.

Click a step to skip to it.

As you proceed through the Interview, the Interview Navigator keeps track of your progress and displays the current step in yellow. Whenever you check out an Interview topic or question, the Interview Navigator places a yellow check mark next to it. This does not indicate that you have completed the step by entering all the required information; it indicates only that you have visited this step.

Although the EasyStep Interview is linear, you can skip around to different questions to make the Interview process more self-directed. Just click the desired question or topic in the Interview Navigator. However, don't jump around too much—some questions depend on the answers to other questions.

**Streamlining with the Smart Interview**

To bypass steps for tax questions that don't apply to you, TurboTax offers the Smart Interview System. During the Interview, when you indicate that you don't have or need a specific form, TurboTax avoids questions that deal with that form.

### Get Help

On the right side of the interview area is a list of links to help topics that deal with the current question or topic. Click the link for the desired topic to access the TurboTax help system.

## Plodding Through the Federal Tax Forms

You didn't purchase TurboTax to manually fill out forms. You could do that with a stack of printed forms from the IRS. However, the forms can give you the "big picture," and they enable you to edit individual entries without having to go through the interview middleman. TurboTax offers a couple ways to switch from the EasyStep Interview to forms view:

➤ Open the **Forms** menu and click **Go to Forms**. If you haven't yet filled out the Federal Information Worksheet, TurboTax displays it, so you can enter the required information to get started. If you're somewhere else in the Interview process, TurboTax displays the form that corresponds to the current Interview topic.

➤ Open the **Forms** menu and click **Open a Form,** or press **Ctrl+A**. The Open Form dialog box appears, displaying a list of all available IRS forms and additional worksheets used by TurboTax. Double-click the name of the desired form. If you haven't yet created the selected form, a dialog box appears, prompting you to name the new form. For example, you might name a new W-2 form Linda's W-2. Isn't that convenient?

➤ Open the **Forms** menu and click **Show My Return**. The Open Form dialog box appears, displaying a list of only those forms that are currently included in your tax return.

*The Open Form dialog box lists all IRS forms TurboTax worksheets.*

Double-click the desired form.

Open Form

Options
○ Show My Return    ● Open a Form

Form 1040 Individual Tax Return
Federal Information Worksheet
Form W-2:Wage & Tax Statement
Form W-2G:Certain Gambling Winnings
Form 1099-MISC Worksheet
Form 1099-G:Certain Government Payments
Form 1099-R:Pension Distributions
Form 1099-MSA:Medical Savings Account Distributions
Wages & Salaries Worksheet
Earned Income Worksheet
State Tax Refund Worksheet
IRA Contribution & Information Worksheet
Keogh/SEP/SIMPLE Contribution Worksheet
Social Security Income Worksheet
Other Income Statement

Open    Remove    Done

Navigating a form is as easy as navigating a standard dialog box. To place an X in a check box, simply click in the box. To type an entry, click in the desired box or on the line and type your entry. For additional information and options for an item on a form, right-click the line or box.

Be careful about replacing entries on any form. Some entries are carried over from another form or worksheet. If you replace the entry, your tax return will contain conflicting data that could trigger an audit. Fortunately, TurboTax warns you whenever you try to replace an entry that has been carried over.

TurboTax also flags any entries that are carried over from other forms and worksheets. If you click a box and notice that one of the following QuickZoom buttons appears next to your entry, it's a good sign that you need to leave the entry alone or edit it on the supporting worksheet or form:

**Start with the Federal Information Worksheet**

If you choose to bypass the Interview process, fill out the Federal Information Worksheet before you do anything else. The entries on this worksheet ensure that your return has the most basic entries required by the IRS.

See the source for this line item—This indicates that the entry is carried over from another worksheet or form. Don't edit the entry here. Click the button to go to the source and edit the source. The change will appear on all forms that use this entry.

List supporting details—This indicates that this entry is a summation or total of entries on another worksheet. Don't change the entry here. Click the button to view the list of supporting details and enter your adjustments on that list.

**Supporting Details and Statements**

A *supporting details* list is an informal record that shows you how you arrived at a total for a particular entry on a form. A supporting statement is a formal record that shows the IRS how you arrived at a total.

## Do-It-Yourself: Creating a New Form

As you learned in the previous section, if you try to view a form that doesn't exist, TurboTax displays a dialog box prompting you to create a new form. However, if you need additional copies of a form (say one for you and one for your spouse), you must create a copy of the form. Fortunately, you don't need to run out to the copy shop to run off copies. You can create a copy directly in TurboTax. Take one of the following steps:

➤ Open the **Forms** menu and select **Open a Form**. Double-click the form you want to create. In some cases, TurboTax automatically creates the form. In other cases, TurboTax displays a dialog box asking if you want to create a new copy of the form. Click the **Create New Copy** option button and type a descriptive name for the form. Click the **Create** button.

➤ To create a copy of the currently displayed form, open the **Forms** menu and click **New Copy**. Click the **Create New Copy** option button and type a descriptive name for the form. Click the **Create** or **Finish** button.

## Nuking a Form or Supporting Details List

As you create forms and complete your tax return, you might find that a particular form isn't required or that you'd like to take the 5th ammendment on that list of supporting details. Whatever the case, TurboTax enables you to quickly purge any form or supporting details list from your return:

1. Open the **Forms** menu and click **Show My Return**.
2. Click the form or list of supporting details you want to remove and click the **Remove** button.
3. When prompted to confirm the deletion, click **Yes**.

# Getting Personal with Your Interviewer

If you followed my advice, you chose to answer the Interviewer's questions rather than plod through a stack of forms. This is generally a smart move. However, when it comes to entering personal information, you might be able to save some time by typing entries directly on the Federal Information Worksheet. If you want to give it a go, check out "Completing the Federal Information Worksheet," following this section. You can then return to the Interview for the more obscure entries.

Did you decide to stick with the EasyStep Interview? Before you can enter any financial data, the EasyStep Interview needs you to answer a few personal questions. It automatically transfers your entries to the Federal Information Worksheet. Take the following steps to work through the first stage of the Interview:

1. Click the **Interview** tab to bring it front and center.
2. Click **Let's start my return**, and then click **Continue**. Funny, but TurboTax's first question isn't "What's your name?" It wants to know if you are married and have kids. Do you feel like you're sitting in a pick-up joint?
3. Click the option that best represents your marital status: **Married**, **Single or divorced**, **Separated**, or **Widowed**.
4. If you have children click **Children** to place a check mark next to the option. (If you're not sure if the kids are yours, leave this unchecked.)
5. If you have any other dependents (not including Fido), click **Other People I Support**.
6. Click **Continue**. Now TurboTax wants your name.

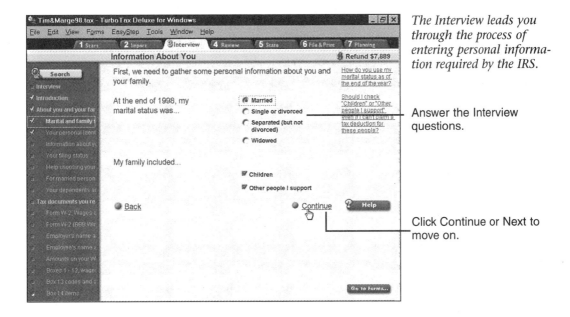

*The Interview leads you through the process of entering personal information required by the IRS.*

Answer the Interview questions.

Click Continue or Next to move on.

**7.** Enter the requested information: your first and last name and your social security number. If you checked the Married option in step 3, enter similar information for your spouse. Note that TurboTax enters this information on the Federal Information worksheet displayed at the bottom of the screen.

**8.** Click **Continue**. TurboTax now asks you to enter your primary occupation and birth date.

**9.** Type a brief description of your primary occupation, enter your birth date (in the form mm/dd/yy), and click **Continue**. If you have two jobs, the IRS wants to know which one brings in more money. TurboTax now asks you to enter your contact information.

**10.** Type your mailing address, home phone number, and work phone number(s). Click **Continue**.

**11.** If you want to kick three bucks into the presidential election campaign fund so candidates will ask for less from Chinese businesses, click ___ **designates $3 for the Campaign Fund**. This doesn't affect the amount of your refund. Click **Continue**.

**12.** Click the check boxes next to each option that describes a special filing situation that applies to you (for example, blind or disabled). Click **Continue**.

**13.** Specify your state of residence, and enter any information you want to include on your state income tax return. Click **Continue**.

**14.** Specify your filing status, as explained later in this chapter under "Married, Single, or Single Wannabe?" Click **Next**.

**15.** Proceed through the Interview, making selections and entering the requested information until you have reached the end of the personal information stage of the Interview.

That gets you through the personal part. The following section shows those who don't like interviews how to enter the same information using the forms method.

# Completing the Federal Information Worksheet

The Interview is a pretty cool way to enter all that preliminary information about who you are, where you live, and what you do, but boy is it long and drawn out. For an easier fill-in-the-blanks approach, display the Federal Information Worksheet and fill it out yourself. You can always return to the Interview later.

To type entries directly on the Federal Information Worksheet, take the following steps:

1. Open the **Forms** menu and click **Open a Form**. (If the Federal Information Worksheet is already displayed at the bottom of the screen in the EasyStep Interview, click the **Go to Forms** button just above and to the right of the Worksheet.)

2. Double-click **Federal Information Worksheet**.

3. Complete the worksheet by typing entries in the various blanks and clicking any check boxes to place an X inside the box. To quickly move from one line to the next, press the **Tab** key. Press **Shift+Tab** to move back a line.

4. When you're done, you can return to the Interview by clicking the **Back to Interview** button that's to the upper right of the form.

Go back to the Interview.

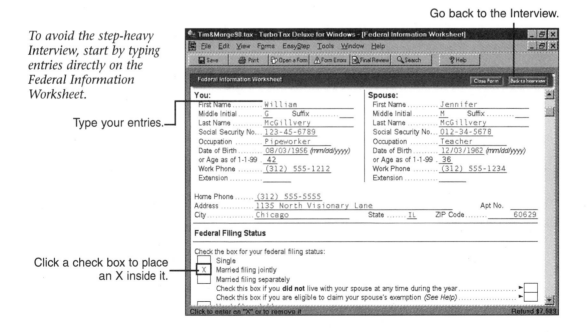

*To avoid the step-heavy Interview, start by typing entries directly on the Federal Information Worksheet.*

Type your entries.

Click a check box to place an X inside it.

# Married, Single, or Single Wannabe?

"Are you married?" seems like a simple question until tax time rolls around. Then, everything gets a little more complicated and the questions become a little more pointed: Are you married filing jointly? Are you married filing separately? Are you the head of the household? (Now that's a loaded question.) Your filing status is one of the most important items on your tax return, so give it some careful thought, and read through the following sections to determine the most lucrative filing status for your situation.

## *Single and Paying for It*

If you're not married and have no kids, there is no choice—in the eyes of the IRS, you're single. Look at the bright side—you won't suffer from the marriage penalty.

### The Marriage Penalty

If you're married, have no children, and you and your spouse make nearly the same amount of money, the tax code might penalize you for being married. The problem is that the tax rates are graduated—the higher your income, the higher percentage you pay in taxes. When you and your spouse combine your incomes, you boost yourself into a higher tax bracket and pay a higher percentage than you would by filing separately. No, don't run out and get divorced, but after you've created your joint tax return, create separate returns to see if you can save any money by filing separately.

## *Conubial Bliss: Married Filing Jointly*

If you're married, Married Filing Jointly is usually the best option for cutting your tax bill. You and your husband/wife combine your income and deductions on a single form and typically qualify for lower tax rates. In addition, if you have kids together, Married Filing Jointly entitles you to additional tax credits, such as the child tax credit.

If you were married at any time during the year, even on December 31, 1998, the IRS considers you married for the entire year.

## *Marriage on the Rocks: Married Filing Separately*

This option is typically used by couples who are separated but not divorced and choose to keep their finances separate. This might also be a smart option if you don't trust your spouse to prepare your taxes. Both you and your spouse are legally responsible for a tax return you file jointly, so if your spouse is cheating on taxes and you don't want to be involved, file your own tax return. Just make sure that your spouse doesn't file as Married Filing Jointly, or you'll both end up in trouble.

If you and your spouse are happily married, you might save money by filing separately. If you're a victim of the marriage penalty, as explained earlier, filing separately can help reduce the penalty by taxing each income at a lower rate.

In addition, if you and your spouse have widely differing income and deduction levels, filing separately might be beneficial. For instance, say you had an adjusted gross income of $70,000 and your spouse had an adjusted gross income of $30,000 and medical bills of $5,000. Before you could claim a medical deduction filing jointly, your combined medical bills would have to exceed $7,500, giving you a deduction of $0. The reason is that you can't deduct medical bills unless they exceed 7.5 percent of your adjusted gross income: .075 x ($70,000 + $30,000) = $7,500. If your spouse filed separately, he could deduct bills in excess of $2,250 (.075 x $30,000) and would see a deduction of $2,750.

## *Head of Household*

If you're not married and have a child or other dependent living with you, choose the Head of Household filing status. This typically results in a lower tax rate. To qualify for this filing status, you must meet the following conditions:

➤ You didn't remarry in 1998.

➤ You and your spouse (sorry, your ex) have not lived together for the last six months of 1998.

➤ You and your spouse file separate tax returns.

➤ Your child (or at least one of your children) lived with you for more than half of 1998.

➤ You claim the child as a dependent on your tax return. If your spouse claims the child as a dependent because of some legal agreement you worked out, you still qualify to file as Head of Household if you meet all the other conditions.

➤ You paid at least half the cost of maintaining your residence.

## *Widow or Widower with Child*

If your spouse passed away within the last two years, you did not remarry in 1998, and you have one or more dependent children, choose the Qualifying Widower filing status. This status provides lower tax rates than both Single and Head of Household.

# Claiming Kids and Other Dependents

You've been taking care of your children, live-in mother-in-law, and a host of other dependents for the past year (or at least six months). Now it's time for them to do their part and help you reduce your taxable income. For each dependent you claim (including yourself), you get an income reduction of $2,700. That's $2,700 the government won't tax. So if you're taxed at a 28% rate, you see a savings of $756!

In most cases, determining if you can claim a dependent is fairly easy. You're a dependent as long as someone else, such as a parent, doesn't claim you as a dependent. If you're married, your spouse is a dependent. If you have kids living with you who do not claim themselves as dependents, they're your dependents. If you invited a street person to live with you, or if you have some other complicated issues, figuring out if someone qualifies as a dependent can be a little tricky. If you can answer "Yes" to all of the following questions, you can claim the person as a dependent:

➤ Did the person live with you for the better part of 1998?

➤ Did you pay for the person's living expenses?—This includes housing, food, medical bills, clothes, cable TV, and so on.

➤ Did the person earn less than $2,700 in 1998?—If the person is your child, you can pretty much ignore this question. As long as the person is under the age of 19 or is a full-time student under the age of 24, you can claim your child as dependent. If your kid insists on filing a separate return and claiming the exemption, tell your kid to take a hike. As long as your child qualifies as your dependent, you have the right to claim the exemption.

➤ Is the person directly related to you?—Direct relations include your children, stepchildren, grandchildren, parents, uncles, aunts, siblings, half-siblings, neices, nephews, and in-laws. (The exception to this rule is that you can claim *anyone* as a dependent as long as you supported the person and the person lived with you for an entire year. Direct relations must live with you for only six months.)

➤ Is the person a citizen, national, or resident of the U.S., a resident of Canada or Mexico, or a child you adopted and who lived with you for the entire year?

One more thing: If the person files a joint return for 1998, you cannot claim the person as a dependent. In other words, if your uncle Louie moves in with you and then files a joint return with your ex-aunt Francine, you can't claim Louie as your dependent. Kick him out and tell him to move back with his wife where he belongs.

## *Back to the Interview to Answer More Questions*

When you answered all those personal questions earlier in this chapter, you were asked to specify if you have children. Assuming you clicked the little check box next to **Children**, the Interview ask you to enter additional information about your kids, including their names, social security numbers, and the years they were born. Enter the requested information, as shown below.

*The feds want details about your kids and other dependents.*

Enter each child's social security number.

Enter each child's birth year.

Enter the name of each child.

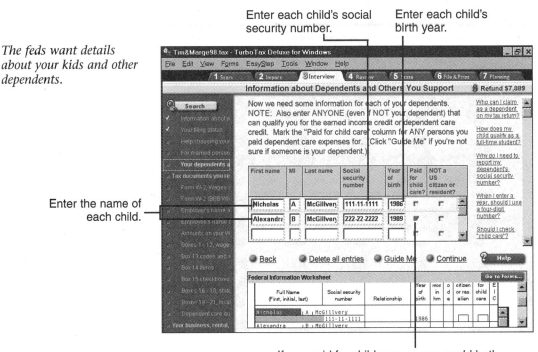

If you paid for child care so you could both work or seek employment, check this box.

After you enter the requested information and click **Continue**, the Interview displays another form requesting you to specify the type of dependent you are claiming, the number of months each dependent lived in your home, and the dependent's relationship to you. Use the drop-down lists to enter the information and click **Continue**.

TurboTax lets you know that any children you claim under the age of 17 may qualify you for a generous tax credit (the new Child tax credit). Click **Continue**. See Chapter 17, "Making the Most of the IRS Tax Credits," for details.

## *Daycare, Babysitters, and Summer Camp*

If you clicked the check box indicating that you paid for child care, you might qualify for the child or dependent care credit. If you paid for daycare for a child under the age of 13 or for any dependent who is incapable of self-care so you and your spouse could work, attend school, or seek employment, click **Enter my dependent care expenses**.

The Interview leads you through the process of entering information about the person you paid to provide care and the amount you paid for care for each of your dependents. Work through the Interview and enter the requested information.

### What Qualifies as Child Care?

Child care expenses include any expenses you pay others to help raise your children (under the age of 13) while you work, study, or seek employment. This includes daycare; a cook, maid, or babysitter; nursery school; summer camp; day camp; or private kindergarten. When you hire a babysitter so you and your spouse can go dancing, that doesn't count.

When entering information about dependent care expenses, don't overlook dependent care medical expenses. Of course, every kid goes to the doctor for check-ups, shots, and the occasional unexplained rash, but those expenses aren't included here. To qualify as a dependent care medical expense, the expense must meet the following criteria:

➤ The dependent for which the care was provided must be physically or mentally handicapped.

AND

➤ You hired a professional healthcare worker to care for the dependent so you could work, attend school, or seek employment.

You can enter dependent care medical expenses as dependent care expenses in this section of the Interview or list the total expenses as an itemized deduction later in the Interview.

## Save It or Lose It

Before you do much more work on your tax return, you should save it to prevent losing what you have so far. To save your tax return, take the following steps:

1. Open the **File** menu and click **Save**.
2. Type a descriptive name for the file (for example, **Jenny1998**).
3. Choose the drive and folder in which you want the file saved.
4. Click the **Save** button.

### Play What If?

If you want to play around with your tax return to see if a different set of numbers gives you a higher refund, choose **File**, **Save As** and give the file a different name. You can then edit entries without affecting your original return. This is useful to determine if you and your spouse would be better off filing a joint return or filing separately.

# Still on Track?

In the next chapter, you will begin to enter your financial data by listing your sources of income. Before you move on, make sure you have done the following:

➤ Started your tax return using either the EasyStep Interview or the forms method. See "Interview or Forms Method? You Decide.," on page 44.

➤ Completed the personal information section of the interview. See "Getting Personal with Your Interviewer," on page 48.

OR

➤ Completed the Federal Information Worksheet. See "Completing the Federal Information Worksheet," on page 50.

➤ Verified your filing status. See "Married, Single, or Single Wannabe?" on page 51.

➤ Claimed yourself, your spouse (if you are married filing jointly), your kids, and any other qualifying human beings as dependents. See "Claiming Kids and Other Dependents," on page 53.

➤ Saved and named your tax return. See "Save It or Lose It," on page 55.

# Part 2
# Inputting Your Income

*If you drive a car, I'll tax the street,*
*If you try to sit, I'll tax your seat.*
*If you get too cold I'll tax the heat,*
*If you take a walk, I'll tax your feet.*

> —From Taxman *by George Harrison*

*The government (we the people) wants its cut of every dollar that passes through your greedy little fingers, as well as some dollars you never touch. It wants to know how much you've earned from your day job and tips, how much extra you've pocketed from that little business you're running on the side, and how much you've raked in from investments.*

*And that's only the obvious stuff. You're also responsible for reporting less apparent sources of income, such as income from selling your sports coupe, interest from a savings account, dividends you reinvested in your mutual funds, income from gambling, benefits you received from your employer, and even that three hundred bucks you made on your last garage sale!*

*The chapters in this part list the types of income the government requires you to report and shows you how to enter your various sources of income in TurboTax.*

# Chapter 5

# W-2s for Salaried Employees

---

### In This Chapter

➤ Determine the significance of all those boxes on your W-2

➤ Transfer the numbers from your W-2(s) to your TurboTax return

➤ Create additional W-2s in TurboTax

➤ What to do when you win the lottery

➤ Peek behind the scenes to find out where TurboTax puts all the numbers

---

Your employer has been sending a good chunk of your salary to the government for the past year. You'd think the government would know how much it pinched from your pocketbook, but at the end of the year, the government still demands that you attach a copy of your W-2 forms to your tax return.

However, that's not such a bad thing. Your W-2 gives *you* the opportunity to see how much you've earned over the year and how much you've paid in taxes, and it provides you with a way to double-check your company's accounting department (accountants have been known to make mistakes). It also provides you with the most important numbers requested on your income tax return.

This chapter shows you how to make sense of your W-2 form, find the essential numbers, and enter them on your return in TurboTax. I've also thrown in a few tax-saving tips along the way to keep you from dozing off.

## Making Sense of Your W-2

The W-2 form looks a little like an overcomplicated credit card receipt. You peel off one copy for your records, submit one copy with your federal income tax return, and attach the third copy to your state income tax return. You might have a fourth copy for local taxes.

A quick glance at a W-2 reveals that it's just a collection of boxes with numbers. Each box contains a number showing the amount of money you've earned and the amount deducted for various items, such as federal, state, and local income taxes; social security; Medicare; medical insurance; and tax-deferred retirement plans.

Even if you're not curious as to what each item on the W-2 represents, read through the following list and verify the numbers on your W-2. If your company's accounting department made an error, now's the time to get it fixed. Later in this chapter, you'll learn how to answer the questions posed by the EasyStep Interview and transfer the numbers, one box at a time, to a TurboTax W-2 form.

### Is This Entrapment?

The IRS already has a copy of your W-2, compliments of your employer. When your return arrives, the IRS compares the W-2 forms it already has to the amounts you listed on your tax return. If there's a discrepancy, the IRS will let you know about it.

*Although it looks innocent enough, your W-2 is packed with potentially incriminating evidence.*

| a Control number | 22222 | Void ☐ | For Official Use Only ▶ OMB No. 1545-0008 | | |
|---|---|---|---|---|---|
| b Employer identification number | | | 1 Wages, tips, other compensation | 2 Federal income tax withheld | |
| c Employer's name, address, and ZIP code | | | 3 Social security wages | 4 Social security tax withheld | |
| | | | 5 Medicare wages and tips | 6 Medicare tax withheld | |
| | | | 7 Social security tips | 8 Allocated tips | |
| d Employee's social security number | | | 9 Advance EIC payment | 10 Dependent care benefits | |
| e Employee's name (first, middle initial, last) | | | 11 Nonqualified plans | 12 Benefits included in box 1 | |
| | | | 13 See instrs. for box 13 | 14 Other | |
| f Employee's address and ZIP code | | | 15 Statutory employee ☐ | Deceased ☐ | Pension plan ☐ | Legal rep. ☐ | Deferred compensation ☐ |
| 16 State | Employer's state I.D. no. | 17 State wages, tips, etc. | 18 State income tax | 19 Locality name | 20 Local wages, tips, etc. | 21 Local income tax |

**Form W-2** Wage and Tax Statement **1998**

Copy A For Social Security Administration— Send this entire page with Form W-3 to the Social Security Administration; photocopies are **Not** acceptable.

Cat. No. 10134D

Department of the Treasury–Internal Revenue Service
**For Privacy Act and Paperwork Reduction Act Notice, see separate instructions.**

**Do NOT Cut, Staple, or Separate Forms on This Page    Do NOT Cut, Staple, or Separate Forms on This Page**

➤ **a** Control number—You must enter this number on the W-2 form in TurboTax, but otherwise you can ignore it. This number is for bean counters and IRS employees.

➤ **b** Employer identification number—This number helps the feds keep track of your employer and make sure your company is filing the proper paperwork for you.

➤ **c** Employer's name, address, and ZIP code—This information tells the IRS where your company is located. It doesn't end up on your income tax return, but you have to enter it anyway.

➤ **d** Employee's social security number—Yeah, they want your social security number again. This ensures that the W-2 form you submit matches at least one of the social security numbers on your tax return. Double-check your social security number. If it's wrong on your W-2, contact your employer immediately. Your employer must void the erroneous W-2 form and issue you a corrected form. You can't just cross out the wrong number and write in your correction.

➤ **e** Employee's name—You know what goes here.

➤ **f** Employee's address and ZIP code—This information helps the IRS verify that you are who you say you are. Make sure you haven't received someone else's W-2 by mistake. If the address is incorrect, you can submit the W-2, but inform your employer, so the address can be corrected for next year.

➤ **1** Wages, tips, other compensation—This number represents the total amount of money (and anything else of value you earned by working for this employer) that is subject to income tax. Wages are pretty clear; it's the "tips and other compensation" that can be a little tricky. See the following sections—"More About Tips" and "What Qualifies as 'Other Compensation'" for details.

➤ **2** Federal income tax withheld—This is the amount that your employer withheld from your paychecks as income tax. If the number looks questionable, get out your old paycheck stubs and start adding.

➤ **3** Social security wages—This number represents the total amount of money you earned that is subject to social security tax. If you invested part of your income in a tax-deferred retirement account, this number will be larger than the number in box 1, because social security tax is levied on your tax-deferred investments. Social security tax is levied only on the first $68,400 of earned income. Any amount you earn over that is not subject to social security tax.

➤ **4** Social security tax withheld—This box reports the amount of money that your employer withheld for social security.

➤ **5** Medicare wages and tips—This number is typically the same as the number in box 3. You pay Medicare tax on everything you earn, even if you contributed a portion of your earnings to a tax-deferred retirement account. Unlike social security tax, which applies to only the first $68,400 of earned income, Medicare tax is applied to all earned income—there is no limit.

➤ **6** Medicare tax withheld—Yeah, Medicare is great, but someone has to pay for it. This box shows your contribution to the general health and well-being of the nation.

➤ **7** Social security tips—This box shows the amount of tip income that you reported to your employer. See the following section, "More About Tips," for details.

➤ **8** Allocated tips—Allocated tips represent the difference between the tip income you reported to your employer and the theoretical amount you made in tips as calculated by your employer. See "More About Tips," for details.

➤ **9** Advanced EIC payment—If you made at least one dollar but not more than $1,030 (without a dependent child), $26,473 (with one child), or $30,095 (with two or more children), then you qualify for an Earned Income Credit, and can actually make money by filing a return. In addition, you can submit a W-5 form for an advance on your EIC for 1999. If you submitted a W-5 and received an advance (on your regular paycheck), the amount you received appears in box 9.

➤ **10** Dependent care benefits—If you work for a family-oriented company that provides child care for your kids, the value of that care appears in this box, and any amount over $5,000 is included in the total of box 1. TurboTax will lead you through the process of filling out the applicable portion of Form 2441, Child and Dependent Care Expenses, to determine if you must pay taxes on the portion over $5,000.

➤ **11** Nonqualified plans—This number is the amount that you contributed to retirement plans that does not qualify as tax-deferred. For example, if your employer's plan allows you to contribute up to 10 percent of your pre-tax income to a 401(k) and your contributions exceed this amount, the excess is subject to taxes and is included in this box. This amount is automatically included in the amount in box 1.

➤ **12** Benefits included in box 1—If you received any benefits from your employer in addition to your salary, the value of these benefits appears in this box and is included in the amount in box 1. See "What Qualifies as 'Other Compensation'," later in this chapter.

➤ **13** See instrs. for box 13—This box typically is blank or includes a number with a secret code next to it. The number represents 401(k) contributions, uncollected social security or Medicare tax on tips, the cost of group life insurance in excess of $50,000, sick pay that wasn't included as income, employer contributions to your medical savings account, and a host of other miscellaneous sources of income or benefits. Check the flip side of your W-2 for a complete set of codes.

➤ **14** Other—To cover anything not listed in the other boxes, the IRS included this box for miscellaneous items of interest. This box is for your employer to describe compensation it provided that doesn't fit any of the other categories.

For example, if your employer helped you pay job-related education expenses, the amount is listed here and is included in the amount in box 1. By breaking out this amount, your employer enables you to claim the amount as a deduction, assuming it qualifies as a deduction.

➤ **15**—Box 15 contains a collection of check boxes that indicate various tax situations:

> ➤ Statutory employee means that although you are officially an employee, you work on your own. Insurance salespeople, agents, travelling salespeople, and some home office workers might qualify. If Statutory employee is checked, you can report your income on Schedule C or C-EZ and claim your business-related expenses as expenses rather than business deductions. Because business deductions are reduced by 2% of your adjusted gross income, claiming your expenses against your overall profit can save you some money.

> ➤ Deceased is checked only if you received a W-2 from the employer of a relative, friend, or close relation who passed away in 1998 (or your employer's accountant made a serious boo-boo).

> ➤ Pension plan indicates that you participated in a tax-deferred pension plan offered by your company. This tells the IRS that you are ineligible to contribute to an IRA or that your contributions are limited.

> ➤ Legal rep. tells the IRS that the employer sent the W-2 to your legal representative rather than directly to you. This is common on W-2s issued to minors.

> ➤ Deferred compensation indicates that you and your employer have some shady deal going in which your employer agrees to pay you at some future date so you won't have to pay taxes on the money this year. This can save you some money, but for most people, it's a risky venture—if the company folds or tax rates jump, you could lose money.

➤ **16-21** State and local stuff—At the very bottom of the W-2 is a row of boxes that include numbers for your state income tax return. Even if you don't use TurboTax to do your state income tax return, you should enter these numbers in TurboTax. If you itemize your deductions, you can deduct the state and local income taxes you paid.

## More About Tips

If you receive tips, you're required to report the amount you receive to your employer, so your employer can withhold the correct amount of income and social security tax from your pay.

**CPA Tip for Tips**

Keep detailed records of all the tips you earn and tips you share with coworkers so you won't be over-taxed. If your actual tips are less than the allocated tips reported by your employer and you have records to back it up, report only the amount you actually made in tips and inform your employer.

When someone leaves you a cash tip, it's tempting to slip that sawbuck in your pocket and hit the grocery store on your way home. That's okay, as long as you received less than $20 in cash tips during the current month and you eventually report that tip income on your tax return. If you make any more than that, your life gets a little more complicated—you must report the cash tips you received to your employer using form 4070. Don't include tip income that your employer already knows about, such as tips charged to a credit card.

The IRS knows just how tempting it can be to keep your tip income secret, so it has a way to keep you honest. If you earn tip income, the IRS figures that each waiter or waitress makes a share of at least 8 percent of the restaurant's gross receipts. For instance, if the restaurant has 16 waiters and waitresses all working the same number of hours, the feds assume you each make .5 percent of the restaurant's gross receipts. If you report less than that amount to your employer, the difference appears in this box, and you must report it as income or have proof that you made less in tips (it is not included as part of the amount in box 1).

In addition to reporting your tip income on your income tax return, you must also report it on form 4137 to determine additional social security and Medicare taxes you owe. By using the EasyStep Interview and answering all pertinent questions, you can have TurboTax handle the details for you.

## What Qualifies as "Other Compensation"

Box 1 (Wages, tips, other compensation) casts a wide net over what the IRS considers income. This box includes tip income you reported to your employer, the taxable portion of fringe benefits (such as your personal use of a company car), bonuses, the cash value of prizes you win for being so successful, vacation pay, severance pay, and pay for jury duty.

If you contributed to a tax-deferred retirement plan (such as a 401(k)), the pretax amount you are entitled to contribute to the plan is not included in the amount in box 1.

If the number in box 1 is higher than the amount you actually received as your salary, your employer has added in the value of additional compensation you received. If you discover a discrepancy between your records and the amount in box 1, ask your employer for a detailed list of "other compensation" you have supposedly received.

### Maximize Your Tax Cut

If you contribute to a tax-deferred retirement plan, add the amount in box 13 that's flagged with an E to the amount in box 1 and you should get the amount in box 3 (representing your total income). If the number comes up short, you might have exceeded the limit on pretax dollars you can contribute to your retirement plan. Anything you contribute over the limit is subject to income tax. You might have intended to do this to build your retirement savings through the tax-deferred growth in your account. However, if you're married, and your spouse is contributing less than the allowable limit, you might save money by decreasing your contribution and having your spouse increase his contribution.

# Data Entry 101

Whew! At this point, you should have a correct copy of your W-2 from each of your employers and, if you're married, a W-2 from your spouse's employers.

After you have verified the numbers on your W-2(s), enter those numbers in TurboTax. You can enter the numbers by following the EasyStep Interview or by typing the numbers directly on a W-2 form in TurboTax. The following sections show how to proceed using either method.

## Entering Your Income, Interview Style

After you have entered personal information and answered the standard questions about your kids and dependents (assuming you have some), the EasyStep Interview displays a list of income-related tax documents that you might have received, including W-2s, 1099s, and schedule K-1s (for partnerships, S corporations, and trusts). Check all those that apply and click **Continue**.

The Interview then leads you through the process of transferring the numbers from your paper W-2s to the TurboTax W-2s. There's nothing tricky here. Just follow the interview and enter the numbers into the corresponding boxes in TurboTax. (We'll deal with those other income-related forms in later chapters. Just focus on your W-2s for now.)

*The EasyStep Interview matches your W-2s box for box.*

Enter the requested numbers from your W-2.

Click Continue. ─

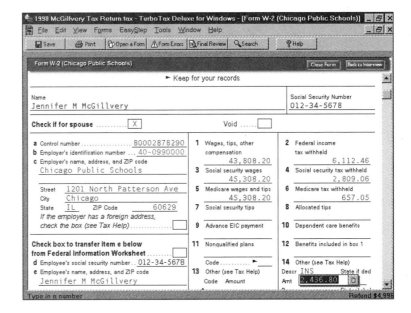

## Doing Your TurboTax W-2s by Hand

If you prefer a more standard approach to filling out your W-2s, choose **Forms**, **Go to Forms** to display a standard W-2 form, like the one shown below. This displays a standard W-2 form that looks more like the paper version and may make a little more sense to you. Type your entries in the matching boxes, pressing **Tab** to move from one box to the next. When you're done, you can quickly return to the Interview by choosing **EasyStep**, **Back to Interview** or pressing **Ctrl+R**.

*Use the forms method to work with a W-2 that looks a little familiar.*

## *Multiple W-2s for Moonlighters and Couples*

Moonlighters and married couples are likely to have more than one W-2. If you're one of the lucky few who has chosen to work his life away, TurboTax can supply you with an unlimited stack of W-2s. Just take one of the following steps to pull up a blank W-2:

**Excess Social Security Withheld**

If you work two or more jobs and your total income is more than $68,400, your employers might have withheld too much social security tax (there is a limit). Fortunately, TurboTax will make this determination for you, list the excess on your tax return, and include it as taxes you've paid. This will reduce your tax bill or result in a higher refund.

➤ If you are married filing jointly, the Interview will prompt you to fill out a W-2 for your spouse after you've entered the information from your own W-2.

➤ If you or your spouse has a second job, after you've entered the information for one W-2, the Interview will ask if you have another W-2 lying around. Click **Yes**, and TurboTax will serve up another form.

➤ Are you using the forms method? If so, choose **Forms**, **Open a Form**, choose **Form: W-2, Wage & Tax Statement**, and click **Open**. Click the **Create New Copy** option button, type a descriptive name for your next W-2, and click **Create**.

To change from one W-2 to another, choose **Forms**, **Show My Return**, and double-click the W-2 you want to view.

# Reporting Your Gambling Income with W-2G

Did you win the lottery? Hit the jackpot at the local casino? Win a Lamborghini at the Knights of Columbus raffle? Take your brother-in-law to the cleaners during your Friday night poker games? Then the IRS wants to share in your good fortune.

If you won big by playing the lottery, or you received a large chunk of cash or a valuable prize from an organization, the organization typically issues a form W-2G to you at the end of the year. You can expect to receive a W-2G under the following conditions:

➤ The organization that issued the prize withheld taxes from it.

➤ You won more than $5,000 (or merchandise of equivalent value) in the lottery, a sweepstakes, or a betting pool.

➤ You won $600 or more and your winnings are more than 300 times the amount you wagered. For example, if you purchased a raffle ticket for a buck and won a $500 television, you might receive a W-2G.

If you received a W-2G, and you checked the box telling TurboTax that you have one, the Interview leads you through the process of entering the required information and claiming any gambling losses against your gross winnings.

*If you received form W-2G, the feds already know you're a winner.*

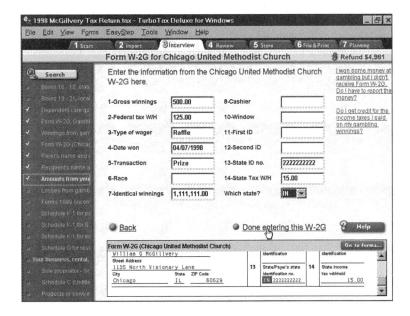

## Where Does TurboTax Put All These Numbers?

As you fill in the blanks, TurboTax juggles the numbers for you, generates the required forms and schedules, and shifts the numbers to the proper lines on your forms and schedules. This can be a little disconcerting when you're trying to understand what's going on and why you have to answer all of these questions.

The following list gives you a clearer understanding of what TurboTax has done behind the scenes up to this point. To check things out for yourself, choose **Forms**, **Show My Return**, and double-click **Form 1040: Individual Tax Return**. You can then scroll down and see what TurboTax has already accomplished:

### Loser!

If you lost more than you won in 1998, you can't claim your net losses. In other words, you don't get a tax break for being a loser. However, if you won a thousand bucks and lost $500 in the process, you can deduct your losses against your winnings. In this example, you would end up with net winnings of $500. And another thing—your travel expenses to Vegas are not deductible as losses.

➤ Transferred your name, address, and social security number to the top of form 1040.

➤ Logged your filing status on form 1040.

➤ Totaled your exemptions, inserted the total on form 1040, line 6d, multiplied the total by $2,700, and subtracted the result from your gross income.

➤ Totaled your wages, tips, and other compensation from your W-2 forms and inserted the total on form 1040, line 7.

➤ Totaled any child care expenses you've entered, listed them on a new form 2441, calculated your credit for child and dependent care, and listed the amount on form 1040, line 41.

➤ Subtracted the standard deduction from your gross income to determine your taxable income. (You might be able to cut this down later by itemizing deductions.)

➤ Calculated the amount of tax due on your taxable income and inserted the result on form 1040, line 40.

➤ Subtracted any tax credits to which you are entitled, including child and dependent care credit and the child tax credit from the amount of tax due, and inserted your total tax liability (up to this point) on form 1040, line 56.

➤ Totaled the amount of income tax withheld from the various W-2 forms you've completed to determine the amount of income tax you have already paid and inserted the total on line 64.

➤ Determined the amount of income tax you have overpaid (which the IRS will refund to you) or the amount you have underpaid (which you owe to the IRS).

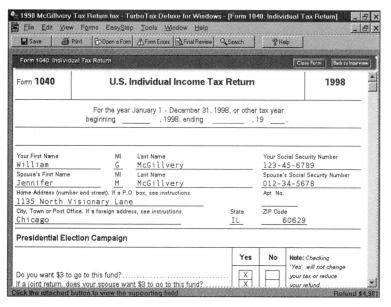

*You have a long way to go, but TurboTax has already roughed-out your income tax return.*

### What About Those K-1s?

If you clicked any of the K-1 check boxes, skip to Chapter 11, "What Else Constitutes Income?" under the section titled "Schedule K-1 for Parterships, S Corporations, and Estates."

# Still on Track?

Don't write that check to the IRS just yet—the Interview is long from over, and you probably want to whittle down that number on the "Taxable income" line. Before you move on to the next chapter, make sure you've done the following:

➤ Verified the information on all the W-2 forms that you have. See "Making Sense of Your W-2," on page 60.

➤ Accounted for any tip income you received. See "More About Tips," on page 63.

➤ Transferred the numbers from the paper copy of your W-2 to TurboTax. See "Entering Your Income, Interview Style" on page 65 or "Doing Your TurboTax W-2s by Hand," on page 66.

➤ Entered numbers from any additional W-2s (for your spouse or a second job) on TurboTax W-2s. See "Multiple W-2s for Moonlighters and Couples," on page 67.

➤ Checked out your progress. See "Where Does TurboTax Put All These Numbers?" on page 68.

# Chapter 6

# 1099s for Interest, Investments, and Capital Gains

## In This Chapter

➤ Report that ten bucks of interest you earned from your savings account

➤ Report income from dividends paid on your investments

➤ Take advantage of the 20% tax limit on capital gains

➤ Report your profit or loss from the sale of stocks and bonds

➤ Report tax refunds, unemployment payments, and other income you received from the government

➤ Save taxes with a medical savings account (MSA)

➤ Reap your retirement rewards (and pay taxes on them)

Making a buck usually requires you to sell a portion of your life. You put in your 40 hours a week and come home with a paycheck. For the more fortunate and financially disciplined, making money doesn't require much time. Savvy investors set aside a portion of their hard-earned cash (or easily obtained inheritance) and use it to make more money.

But the government doesn't really care how you make your money. Money is income, and sooner or later the government will tax it. In this chapter, you learn about the various sources of investment, retirement, and interest income the government taxes and how to enter these types of income in TurboTax. Be sure to check out the CPA tips along the way to learn how to take advantage of some of the more lucrative loopholes in the current tax code that apply to investment income.

# Got Any 1099s?

1099s are the catch-all form for any income that doesn't make it on a W-2. These forms come in an assortment of flavors and cover everything from interest on savings accounts to income from royalties. For a list of the various 1099s you might encounter, skip back to Chapter 2, "The Paper Chase: Gathering Your Records," in the section "W-2s, 1099s, and Other Records the Feds Already Have."

When you're done typing the entries for your W-2(s), the Interview displays a list of available 1099 forms. If you have any of the forms on the list, click the check box next to the name of each form you have. For details about the form, click the form's name and read through this chapter for additional information, tips, and cautions. (Chapter 7, "1099-MISCs and Schedule C (for the Self-Employed)," goes into excruciating detail about the 1099-MISC and its sister form, Schedule C.)

After you have specified which forms you have, click **Continue** and follow the Interview to enter the requested information.

*TurboTax takes inventory of the 1099s you have in your possession.*

Click the check box to indicate that you have the form.

Click Continue.

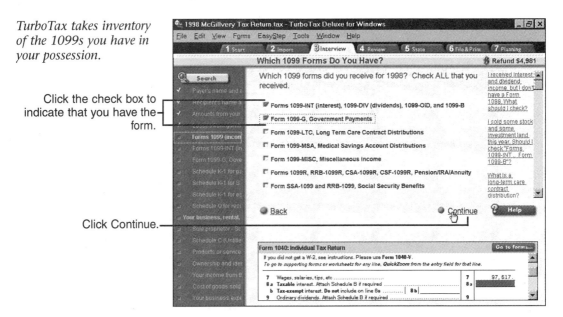

# 1099–INT: Grab Your Bank Statements

One of the easiest sources of income to overlook is interest on a savings account. Because interest on a savings account doesn't keep up with inflation, I think you should be able to claim it as a loss. Unfortunately, the government doesn't see it that way. Any interest you earn is taxable, and you're required to report it on your tax return.

If you earned more than $10, your bank should issue you a 1099-INT. If you didn't receive a 1099-INT, get out your year-end bank statement and look for the line that starts with "Interest paid to date." If you received less than $10 in interest, you can enter the amount directly on form 1040, line 8a. If you received a form 1099-INT, click the **Interest income** link and follow the Interview to enter the requested information.

Type your entries.

*Enter the amount of interest you received.*

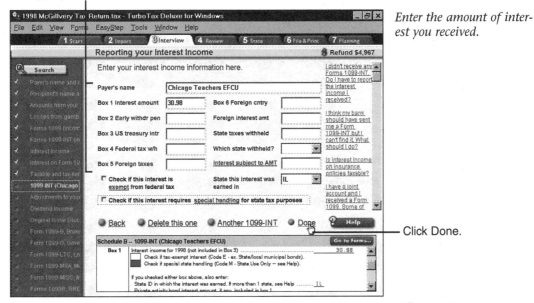

Click Done.

Although the 1099-INT typically is used to report interest you received from savings accounts and loans, it might also report the following penalties and withholdings:

➤ Early withdrawal penalties.

➤ Interest you received from the sale of treasury bonds. (TurboTax will determine later if any of the interest is deductible.)

➤ Federal, foreign, and state taxes withheld from your interest.

➤ Your tax-exempt status.

TurboTax transfers your entries to Schedule B, calculates the total, and inserts the total interest on form 1040, line 8a.

**Loan Shark**

If you loan someone money informally and charge interest on it, the person probably won't issue you a 1099-INT at the end of the year, but you are still required to report that interest income on form 1040, line 8a. This rule also applies if you sell your home on contract and the buyer makes mortgage payments to you. Don't report the entire payment as interest income; report only the interest portion of the payment.

### Tax-exempt Interest

The interest on state or municipal bonds is exempt from federal income tax, but not from social security tax, so you must report tax-exempt interest. The IRS also uses this amount to determine if you qualify for IRA deductions and to calculate your alternative minimum tax (AMT), if necessary. See Chapter 16, "More Taxes (As If You Weren't Paying Enough)," for details about the alternative minimum tax.

### Tax-Deferred Investments

Reinvested dividends and capital gains in a tax-deferred retirement account are not subject to tax until you start withdrawing money from the fund. Don't report this as income.

# 1099s for Dividends, Capital Gains, and Other Investments

Whether you're a high-roller on Wall Street or a little guy riding the rising and falling tide of the stock market with a mutual fund portfolio, you must report your gains and losses on your tax return. At the end of the year, you should receive a form 1099-DIV, 1099-OID, or 1099-B indicating the amount of money you have gained or lost.

The following sections explain the various ways you can earn money through investments and how to report your earnings (and losses) in TurboTax.

## 1099-DIV for Dividends and Capital Gains

In the eyes of the IRS, your investments earn income in two ways: through dividends and through capital gains. A *dividend* is any cash that your holdings have earned, whether they are paid directly to you or reinvested. A *capital gain* is the increase in value of your holdings. For example, if you purchase 100 shares of a stock at $2/share and it increased to $3/share by the end of the year, the capital gain is $100. Even if you don't touch the money, the IRS considers it income.

If you indicated that you have a 1099-DIV, the Interview displays the boxes you need to complete. Type the numbers from the boxes on the paper copies of your 1099-DIV into the boxes displayed in the Interview. TurboTax automatically transfers the numbers to Schedule B. If you reported capital gains, TurboTax also completes Schedule D and inserts the total on Schedule B.

## 1099-OID for Discounted Notes and Bonds

The human race has concocted all sorts of ways to make money without working for it. One of the more popular techniques is to purchase notes or bonds at a discount and then redeem them when they mature. For example, you might purchase a $1,000 note or bond from a company at $900 and then cash it in for $1,000 when it matures to make a $100 profit. The OID (original issue discount) is $100. As the bond matures, the company should issue you a 1099-OID to inform you of the amount of interest the bond earned so far. Even though you don't receive the interest until you redeem the bond, you must claim the interest as income.

## Capital Gains Cap

The top tax rate on long-term capital gains (for assets held over 18 months) is 20%, or 10% if your top tax bracket is 15%. By filling out Schedule D, TurboTax takes advantage of this limit. If your long-term capital gains were not recorded on Schedule D, they would be taxed as normal income. If you were in a 36% tax bracket, your capital gains would be taxed at 36% rather than 20%.

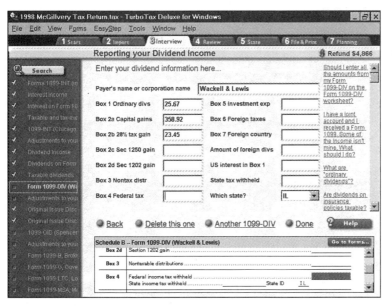

*The Interview collects information about income from dividends and capital gains.*

Assuming you clicked the check box to indicate that you have a 1099-OID, the Interview leads you through the process of entering the required information, including the name of the company that issued the note or bond, the OID income amount (interest you earned in 1998), and whether or not the interest is exempt from federal income tax.

### Shared Accounts and Income

If you have a joint account with someone other than your spouse, enter the total interest you received from the account. After you enter the details from your 1099, the Interview asks if you have any adjustments. Follow the instructions to specify the adjustment amount. You must then inform the other person and the IRS the amount of interest or dividends the account earned that does not belong to you. Contact the IRS for the required forms.

*TurboTax prompts you to enter numbers for a 1099-OID.*

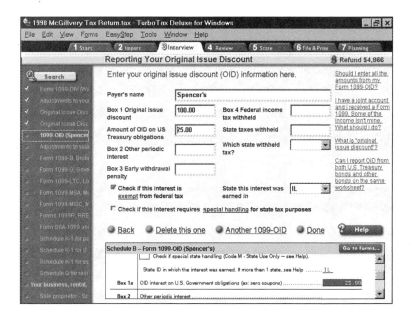

## 1099-B: Sales of Stocks

If you sold stocks or bonds through a broker, the broker will send a copy of form 1099-B to you and to the IRS. The form lists the purchase price and the net sales price (the price minus the broker's commission).

Again, the EasyStep Interview displays the boxes you need to fill out. Enter the details from each 1099-B you have, being sure to add a detailed description of each transaction.

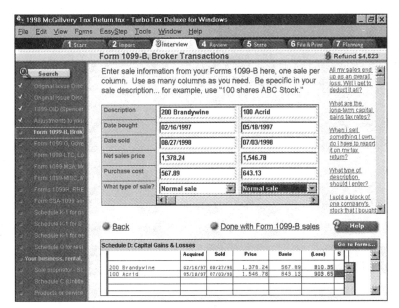

*If you sold stocks or bonds through a broker, you must enter the purchase and net sales price of each stock or bond.*

# 1099-G: When the Government Pays *You*

At tax time, it's tempting to think that our government is nothing more than a bunch of pickpockets. As George Bush used to say, "Watch your wallet!" But the government is also pretty good at shelling out money; otherwise, we wouldn't have a 6-trillion-dollar national debt.

Occasionally, the government gives a little money back to its citizens in the form of unemployment compensation, tax refunds, and checks for earned income credit. If you received any of these generous donations from the government, you should also receive a form 1099-G. This is the government's subtle way of telling you that it wants some of that money back. Yes, the government even taxes the money it gives you.

**Your Basis**

Whenever you sell anything at a profit or loss, you need to specify *your basis*—the purchase price of an investment (or the purchase price plus cost of improvements on a property). For example, if you buy a home for $500,000 and build a $150,000 wing onto it, the tax basis is $650,000. If you sell the home for $700,000, only your net profit of $50,000 is subject to tax.

If you told the EasyStep Interview that you received a form 1099-G, it obediently displays the form you need to fill out. Type the requested entries and follow the onscreen instructions.

*The government giveth
and the government
taketh away.*

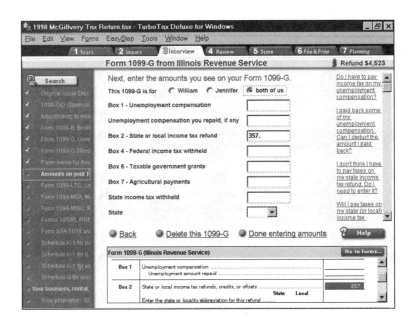

# 1099-MSA: Medical Savings Account

You can tell that medical expenses are getting a little out of hand when you have to set up a special savings account to pay your bills. A medical savings account (MSA for short) is a cross between an IRA and a flexible spending account (FSA). MSAs are offered by insurance companies for health insurance plans that carry a high deductible. An MSA enables you to contribute money to an investment account and pay your deductible and any qualifying medical expenses out of the account with untaxed dollars.

**Reporting Tax Refunds**

Report your 1997 state and local income tax refund *only* if you itemized your deductions and claimed a deduction for the state and local taxes on your 1997 federal income tax return.

The main benefit of an MSA is that you don't forfeit any money that's left over in your account at the end of the year. You leave the money in the account and it earns interest, just as if it were invested in an IRA.

If you received taxable distributions from an MSA in 1998, you will receive a 1099-MSA. The Interview will lead you through the process of determining whether the distributions are taxable and help you complete the distributions section of form 8853, Medical Savings Accounts and Long-Term Care Insurance Contracts. Later, the EasyStep Interview will help you complete the form by entering your contributions to the MSA. See the section called "Medical Assistance Via MSA," in Chapter 14, "Getting a Tax Break with Retirement Investments," for details.

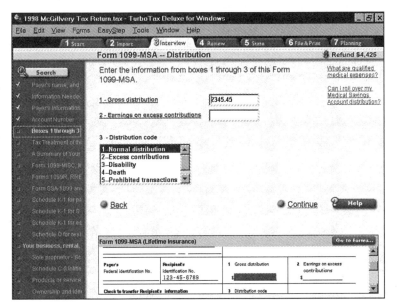

*If you received taxable distributions from an MSA, you might be required to pay taxes and penalties.*

# 1099s for Retirement and Social Security Income

You've worked for more than half your life, contributing to social security and stashing money away in an IRA or other tax-deferred retirement account. Now that your knees are wobbly and your back's giving out, it's time to start enjoying your life and making the most of your golden years.

When you start receiving social security benefits and receiving distributions from your tax-deferred accounts, you should also receive special 1099 forms that report this income:

➤ 1099-R reports income from tax-deferred retirement accounts, including IRAs, SEPs, 401(k)s, KEOGH, and SIMPLE accounts.

➤ SSA-1099 reports income from social security benefits.

➤ RRB-1099 reports income from railroad retirement benefits that are treated as social security benefits for tax purposes.

**Flexible Spending Account**

An FSA is a special account offered by some employers that enables you to set aside a portion of your salary before taxes are taken out and pay your medical and dental bills out of that account. You can also pay qualifying childcare and dependent care expenses using your FSA account. The main drawback of an FSA is that you forfeit any money that's left over in your account at the end of the year.

## MSA Early Withdrawal Penalties

Withdrawals from an MSA for non-medical expenses are taxed as income and sub-ject to a 15% penalty. At age 65, you can cash out your account without facing a penalty, but the money will still be taxed.

*TurboTax collects infor-mation about income from your retirement accounts.*

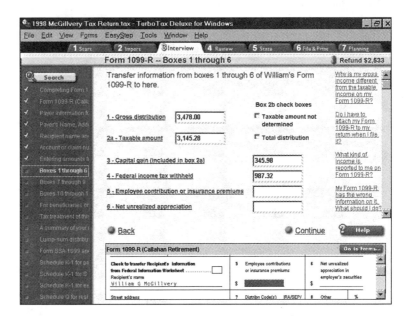

Of course, the EasyStep Interview leads you through the process of entering the required numbers, as shown below. However, as you receive these benefits and distri-butions, you should be aware of some of the techniques for withdrawing funds, determining the portion that's subject to tax, and avoiding penalties. The following sections provide additional information.

## Withdrawing from Your Tax-Deferred Accounts

It's tempting to think of a tax-deferred retirement account as tax-free. However, the government eventually gets around to taxing your money—when you withdraw it. The benefit is that by the time you withdraw the money, your house and any other big-ticket items should be paid for, so you need only living expenses. You need less income and you earn less income, so your income falls in a lower tax bracket (theo-retically at least).

The trick to minimizing the tax on your tax-deferred accounts is to follow the rules for withdrawing from your accounts:

➤ Don't touch the money till you're 59 1/2—Early withdrawals face stiff penalties. You pay income tax on the money you withdraw plus a 10% penalty. If you're in a 28% tax bracket, that's a 38% loss!

➤ Don't touch the money when you transfer it—If you withdraw money from one account to place it in another, do a direct rollover from one account to the other. If your mutual fund company or other investment firm pays you the money first, it automatically deducts 20% for taxes and sends it to the IRS. If you don't put the money back in, the IRS whacks you with an additional 10% penalty at the end of the year.

➤ 60 days same as cash—If you must borrow money from your tax-deferred account, make sure you pay back the money within 60 days. This isn't the best way to borrow money. 20% is automatically deducted and you must pay back not only the money you borrowed, but also the 20% withheld. As long as you pay back the money within 60 days, the IRS credits your tax bill for the 20% it withheld when you file your return. Some employer-sponsored plans allow you to borrow money against the account for extended periods (more than 60 days) without penalty.

➤ Don't opt for the lump-sum distribution—With a lump-sum distribution, you withdraw all funds at once. If you have a load of money in your account, this places it in a higher tax bracket. Subtract your current age from your life expectancy and divide the total number of years into the amount in your account to determine the minimum amount you can withdraw each year. The goal is to die broke.

➤ Stretch it out by using the joint life expectancy—To make your retirement money last longer, calculate your distributions based on the joint life expectancy of you and your beneficiary. This enables you to withdraw less each year and keep your money in the tax-deferred account for a longer time.

➤ When you're 70 1/2 you must start withdrawing—On April 1 of the year after you turn 70 1/2, the government requires you to start withdrawing from your tax-deferred accounts.

**Exceptions**

Early withdrawals from a tax-deferred account are not subject to penalties if used for the purchase of a home (first-time home buyers only), to pay medical expenses that exceed 7.5% of your adjusted gross income, or to pay the cost of higher education. In these cases, the money is still taxed, but you face no 10% penalty.

## Withdrawing Nondeductible Contributions

Although the tax code limits the amount of tax-deductible money you can invest in a tax-deferred account each year, you can contribute additional, taxed money. Be sure you keep track of your taxed contributions. When you withdraw this money, it is taxed at a lower rate, because you have already paid taxes on it. Be sure to hang onto your records for the rest of your life.

A better solution is to set up a Roth IRA for any additional money you want to invest. Contributions to a Roth IRA are taxed, but as long as you keep the money in the Roth IRA for more than five years, you can withdraw the money tax-free. This makes your record-keeping much easier and makes your investment money more accessible.

## Taxed Again: Social Security Benefits

You might think that social security benefits are tax-free, but it's a little more complicated than that. To determine the taxable portion of your social security benefits, the tax code adds the benefits to a portion of your other income and performs a few fancy calculations.

Fortunately, TurboTax handles all these calculations for you. Just enter the amounts from your SSA-1099 form and from any other income-related forms.

# Sales of Your Home and Other Capital Assets

Because this chapter deals with income from dividends, capital gains, and other investments, you might be wondering about the income you receive from selling your home or other valuable assets. These are investments, after all, and you might have received additional 1099 forms reporting your gains or losses.

Set these forms aside for now. The Interview will lead you through the process of calculating your gains and losses on these sales and help you determine whether to list the assets as business-related or personal.

# Still on Track?

Up to this point, you should have entered all the income from your W-2s and most of your 1099s. Nine out of ten taxpayers can now skip ahead to Part 3, "Deductions, Credits, and Other Ways to Reduce Taxes," to start claiming deductions, and the self-employed can move on to the next chapter to take care of business. Before you move on, make sure you've done the following:

➤ Placed a check mark next to each type of 1099 form you received. See "Got Any 1099s?," on page 72.

➤ Recorded your interest income from any savings accounts or loan payments you received, even if you didn't receive a 1099-INT. See "1099-INT: Grab Your Bank Statements," on page 72.

➤ Reported any income you received from dividends and capital gains on investments. See "1099-DIV for Dividends and Capital Gains," on page 74.

➤ Completed form 1099-OID for interest you earned on discounted notes or bonds. See "1099-OID for Discounted Notes and Bonds," on page 74.

➤ Reported earnings or losses from the sale of stocks as reported to you by your broker. See "1099-B: Sales of Stocks," on page 76.

➤ Reported any income you received from the government in unemployment, state tax refunds, and other payments. See "1099-G: When the Government Pays *You*," on page 77.

➤ Entered any taxable distributions you received from a medical savings account. See "1099-MSA: Medical Savings Account," on page 78.

➤ Entered income from social security benefits and distributions from your tax-deferred retirement accounts. See "1099s for Retirement and Social Security Income," on page 79.

# Chapter 7

# 1099-MISCs and Schedule C (for the Self-Employed)

---

## In This Chapter

➤ Report miscellaneous income, even if it's your sole income

➤ Transfer numbers from your 1099-MISC to TurboTax

➤ Trim your business profit by logging expenses on Schedule C

➤ Claim your home office deduction without audit jitters

➤ Miscellaneous deductions to offset your miscellaneous income

---

When you strike out on your own and start your own business or work as an independent contractor, the IRS no longer considers you an employee. You're a business owner. A good sign that you're no longer any employee is that you no longer receive a W-2 form at the end of the year. You now receive a 1099-MISC from anyone who uses your services (and pays you for them), or you just have a stack of receipts (if you're in the business of selling products).

This relationship between you and your "employer" (a.k.a. customer) has advantages and disadvantages. I'll give you the bad news first: Your employer no longer pays half of your social security and Medicare tax (also known as FICA, or Federal Insurance Contributions Act) and unemployment contributions (also known as FUTA, or Federal Unemployment Tax Act). The good news is that you can deduct any business expenses from your income (by filling out Schedule C) and pay taxes only on your net profit. This chapter shows you what to do.

# What's This About "Nonemployee Compensation?"

If you received non-salary payments of $600 or more from a person or company who used your services in 1998, the person or company should have sent you a 1099-MISC with the total amount it paid entered in box 7, Nonemployee Compensation. If you did not receive a 1099-MISC, refer to your records and enter your income directly on Schedule C, in the Income section.

To qualify as a "nonemployee," you must be self-employed or work as an independent contractor. You may not work as an employee for the person or company who uses your services. This might seem obvious, but some companies have been known to categorize their employees as independent contractors to avoid paying their share of FICA and FUTA.

If you consider yourself an employee of the company that issued you the 1099-MISC, but you're not quite sure, the following list can help you decide. You're probably an employee, if…

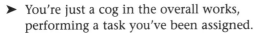

**W-2 Statutory Employees, Too**

If "Statutory Employee" is checked on your W-2 form, you can complete Schedule C to deduct any unreimbursed business expenses related to your job that couldn't be reimbursed.

➤ You're just a cog in the overall works, performing a task you've been assigned.

➤ Your boss controls the process you use to perform the task. This is the biggie. If a person or company contracts you to perform a job or create a product and leaves the rest up to you, the IRS generally considers you an independent contractor. If you're just following orders, you're an employee.

➤ You are not allowed to subcontract the work.

➤ The company sets your hours.

➤ You work at the company most of the time.

➤ You receive regular payments, even if you sit around all day playing FreeCell.

➤ Your company reimburses you for travel and business expenses.

➤ The company supplies your tools and other work-related supplies.

➤ The company pays for your continuing education and training.

➤ It's nearly impossible for you to personally experience a financial loss if the business experiences a loss.

This list merely scratches the surface. The IRS has a 160-page training manual called "Independent Contractor or Employee?" designed to help its field workers determine whether a person is an employee or independent contractor. 160 pages!

# Rents, Royalties, and Other Business Profits

Although 1099-MISC's most popular use is as a tool for evading taxes, it's also used for a wide variety of other types of income and withholdings, including the following:

➤ Rents—This category consists of income from property, machinery, or other business assets that you lease to other businesses. This includes office space and farm land. See Chapter 10, "Rentals and Royalties for Landlords, Authors, and Inventors," for details.

➤ Royalties—This category consists of money you receive from your creations, such as articles you've written, original artwork, and songs. Royalties also include income you receive from other depletable resources, such as oil and gas. When you receive royalty payments, you're not giving up your right to the work or resource. You retain ownership and "rent" the work to someone else or, in the case of resources, you allow some-one to tap those resources for a percent-age of the profit.

**Inform Your Employer**

When you realize that you're not the self-employed entrepreneur you thought you were, let your employ-er hear about it. Otherwise, you'll be paying the FICA and FUTA your-self, and your employer could face some stiff penalties.

➤ Other income— This category may include anything from your winnings on *The Price Is Right* to punitive damages paid to you as the result of a lawsuit.

➤ Income tax withheld—This category reports any income tax that the payer with-held from your payment. Few companies withhold taxes from income reported on a 1099-MISC, placing the responsibility to pay estimated taxes on you.

➤ Fishing boat proceeds—This category consists of any money you've made by hauling in a catch, not including the five bucks you won in the bass contest. (Only fishermen need apply.)

➤ Crop insurance proceeds—This category includes insurance or disaster payments that farmers receive when a crop fails or is wiped out by Mother Nature. See Chapter 9, "Living Off the Land (Farming Can Be Taxing)," for details.

➤ Golden parachute payments—These payments are essentially severance payments for big-wigs at large corporations.

➤ Attorney fees—Items in this category consist of payments over $600 to an attor-ney for a business related activity. If you're an attorney and you receive a 1099-MISC for the total amount of the lawsuit you won, report only your cut. Your client is responsible for reporting the rest of the income.

# Completing Form 1099-MISC

The previous chapter skipped the 1099-MISC form so we could deal with all the self-employment issues in a single chapter. To skip back to the 1099-MISC in the Interview, click in the Interview Navigator and click **Form 1099-MISC, Miscellaneous Income**.

If you filled out 1099-MISC forms last year in TurboTax, and you transferred data from last year's TurboTax return, TurboTax displays a list of 1099-MISCs, enabling you to edit the forms instead of start from scratch. Simply click the form you want to edit, click **Work on the selected 1099-MISC**, and edit the entries, as necessary. To create a new 1099-MISC, click **Start a new 1099-MISC.**

*You can edit any 1099-MISC forms transferred from your 1997 TurboTax return instead of starting over.*

Click form 1099-MISC, Miscellaneous Income.

Click the 1099-MISC you want to edit.

To add a 1099 to your return, click here.

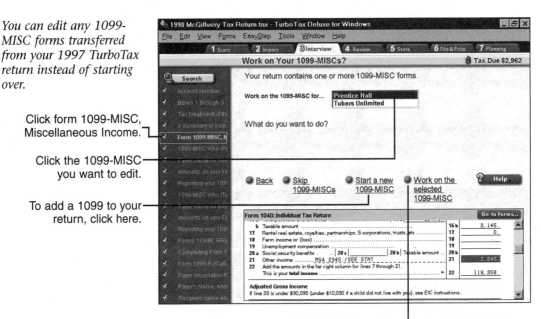

Click Work on the selected 1099-MISC.

If you did not transfer data from last year's return or you chose to create a new 1099-MISC, take the following steps to type the required entries in TurboTax:

1. At the opening 1099-MISC screen, click **Continue** and then click **Yes** when asked if you or your spouse received a 1099-MISC form this year.

2. Type the name of the person or company that issued the 1099-MISC and click **Continue**.

3. If you are married filing a joint return, click the name of the person (you or your spouse) to whom the 1099-MISC is issued.

4. Enter the numbers from boxes 1-13 of your paper copy of 1099-MISC into the matching text boxes in TurboTax. (For more information about the entry in a particular box, click the name of the box.)

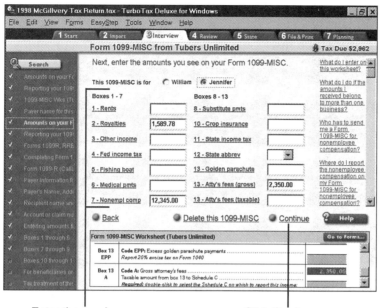

*Enter the numbers from the paper copy of your 1099-MISC into the matching text boxes in TurboTax.*

Enter the numbers.          Click Continue.

5. Click **Continue**. The Interview asks you to pick the schedule on which you want this income reported.

6. To report the income as self-employment income, click **Schedule C** and move on to step 7. If you received the income from property or assets you leased to someone, click **Schedule E** and skip to Chapter 10 for more information.

7. Type a brief name for your business, such as **Bill's Printing**, and click **Done with this 1099-MISC**.

8. Click one of the following options:

   ➤ No, I'm done with 1099-MISCs— Click this option if you have no other income from 1099-MISCs to report.

   ➤ Yes, update an existing 1099-MISC—Click this option to check or edit information you already entered for one of your 1099-MISCs.

### Schedule C or E?

If you earn royalty income from a creation related to your primary work activity, report your royalty income on Schedule C as business income. If you worked on the project on the side, report your royalty income on Schedule E. Income reported on Schedule C is subject to self-employment tax, so if you make the wrong choice, it'll cost you.

   ➤ Yes, enter a new 1099-MISC—Click this option to enter information for another 1099-MISC you received.

When you complete a 1099-MISC form, TurboTax automatically inserts the number in the Income section of Schedule C, calculates your total self-employment income reported to you on 1099-MISCs, and inserts the total in the Income section of form 1040.

# Paring Down Your Business Profit with Schedule C

At this point, TurboTax is calculating taxes on all your self-employment income as well as any other income you entered on 1099-MISC forms. It's time to roll up your sleeves and start chopping away at that number by deducting your expenses on Schedule C. Schedule C is sort of like a 1040 for businesses. It lists your self-employment income or business income, deducts your expenses, and calculates your net profit—the amount subject to taxes.

When you indicate that you're done working with your 1099-MISCs, the Interview leads you through a series of questions to gather information about your business expenses. Take the following steps to enter the requested information:

1. In the Interview Navigator, click **Sole Proprietor—Schedule C**, if it is not already selected.

2. Type a brief description of the business and click **Continue**. If you already created a Schedule C, click the Schedule C on which you want to work and click **Work on the selected Schedule C**.

3. In the **Business code** text box, type the code that best describes your business. (Click **Business code** for a list of codes from the IRS.)

*Enter the name and address of your business.*

Click for a list of IRS business codes.

Enter the name of your business or click the check box to insert your name.

Enter the address of your business or click the check box to use your home address.

Click Continue.

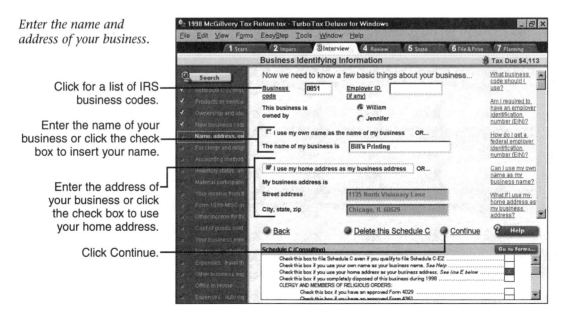

4. If you have employees, click in the **Employer ID** text box and type your code. (To apply for an employer identification number, obtain a copy of form SS-4 from the IRS.)

5. Type the name of your business and its address in the appropriate text boxes. To use your name and home address as your business name and address, click the appropriate check boxes—TurboTax will obtain the information from the Federal Information Worksheet. Click **Continue**.

6. Choose the accounting method you use for your business:

   ➤ Cash—Click this option if you report income in the year in which you receive it and report expenses in the year in which you pay them.

   ➤ Accrual—Click this option if you report your income in the year in which you earn it (rather than the year you actually receive the money) and report expenses in the year in which you incur them (rather than the year in which you actually pay them).

   ➤ Other—Click this option if you use some weird combination of cash and accrual.

### Materially Participated

If you are your only employee, you materially participated in the business. If you have additional employees and you put in more hours than anyone else did, or you put in at least 500 hours, you materially participated. If you just stood by, watched, and counted the money, you didn't materially participate. For a list of conditions that qualify you as materially participating, follow the Interview. If you're married, you can count the number of hours your spouse contributed to the operation of the business.

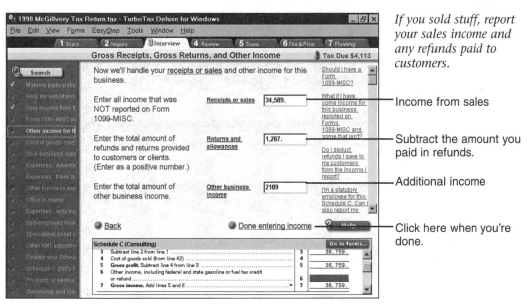

*If you sold stuff, report your sales income and any refunds paid to customers.*

Income from sales

Subtract the amount you paid in refunds.

Additional income

Click here when you're done.

**91**

7. Click any of the check boxes that apply to your business to indicate if your business carries an inventory, if you started or closed the business this year, and whether you materially participated in the operation of the business.

8. Click **Continue**. If you are asked if you want to enter any more information from forms 1099-MISC, click **No, don't enter any Forms 1099-MISC**.

9. Enter any additional income and expenses that were not reported to you on a form 1099-MISC, including income from items you sold and refunds to customers. Click **Done entering income**.

10. If you sold any products, enter the costs for producing those products and click **Continue**. If you didn't sell anything, just click **Continue**. See the following section, "Taking Inventory: Cost of Goods Sold," for details.

11. Now for the fun part. Enter any other expenses related to this business, including advertising, office supplies, travel expenses, mortgage interest (for property other than your home), and legal and professional fees. When you're done with one screen of deductions, click **Continue** to move on to the next screen.

*Enter your business expenses in the appropriate text boxes.*

Click a link to view an explanation of the expense.

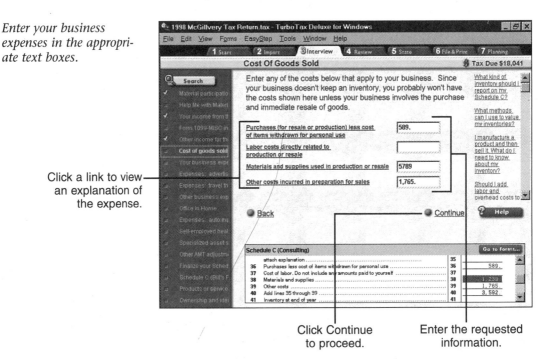

Click Continue to proceed.

Enter the requested information.

12. Continue with the Interview until you reach the question about vehicles and assets. Then, click the desired check boxes to specify if you own assets or sold assets related to this business, if you use a portion of your home as your office, and if you incurred auto expenses. The following sections deal with these trickier issues.

# Taking Inventory: Cost of Goods Sold

If you manufacture and sell products or resell products you purchase, the government taxes only your net profit on those products. To determine your net profit, you subtract the cost of goods you sold from your gross sales. Because the IRS is interested in only the cost of those products you actually sold in 1998, you must take inventory. When taking inventory, record the actual amount you paid for each product, subtracting any discounts, returns, and refunds you received from the supplier. Use one of the following three methods to determine the value of your inventory:

➤ Actual cost—This is the easiest method. You calculate what you actually paid for everything that's sitting in your warehouse or garage.

➤ Lower of cost or market value—This method is a little more complicated than the actual cost method. Compare the actual cost of the products and other materials in your inventory to their current market value. Use the lower number.

➤ Retail—This method, which is only for retailers, consists of determining the retail value of your inventory and then subtracting the markup percentage from that value.

### Multiple Schedule Cs

If you have more than one business, you can create additional Schedule Cs for reporting your income. When prompted to assign your miscellaneous income to a Schedule C, click **Begin a new Schedule C**, and follow the onscreen instructions. TurboTax enables you to complete up to 10 copies of Schedule C.

To determine the entire cost of materials or products you sold, you must also account for any labor costs you incurred for manufacturing, packaging, and shipping your products. By following the TurboTax Interview, you can be sure that you enter all the right numbers.

# Dealing with Business Assets

Business assets consist of desks, computers, software, machines, automobiles, and anything else that belongs to your business. Reporting business assets on your tax return is fairly complicated. It's not just a matter of reporting how much you paid for the asset or how much you made when you sold it. You must also consider *depreciation*—the sinking value of the asset over time.

Because depreciation is such a complex issue, this book devotes an entire chapter to it: Chapter 8, "Depreciating Your Old Stuff." If you have any questions as you report your business assets on Schedule C, skip ahead to Chapter 8 to find the answer and to gain a better understanding of why the IRS requires you to depreciate business assets and how different types of assets are depreciated.

# Your Car Could Save You Some Cash

Remember back when you were a teenager? You would see a car on the used car lot for $500 and think, "Man, I could afford that!" Then your parents would sit you down and give you your first lesson in personal finance: $500 is only the start-up cost. You must then add on the license and registration fees, costs for repairs and maintenance, and that whopping auto insurance bill. And the total didn't even include the trip or two to the gas station each week.

Now that you know that a car guzzles not only gas, it's time to learn how to offset the costs by claiming an automobile deduction on Schedule C. Keep in mind that you can deduct only the percentage of the expenses that relate to the business use of your vehicle and that commuting doesn't count. With that in mind, proceed through the Interview to enter the following information about the vehicle you used for your business:

➤ Make and model—For example, Chevy Geo.

➤ Date it was placed in service—This is the date you started using the vehicle for business purposes. (The person may have owned the car for several years and just started using it for a new business, so the purchase date and the date the person placed the vehicle in service may differ.)

➤ Type of vehicle—For example, car, truck, or van.

➤ Total mileage, business mileage, and commuting mileage— TurboTax uses these numbers to determine the percentage that the vehicle was driven for business and personal use.

➤ Standard mileage rate— If this is the first year the vehicle has been used for your business or if you used the standard mileage rate last year, you can click this option and avoid entering the actual cost and expenses for the vehicle. The IRS allows you to claim 32.5 cents per mile. You cannot use the standard mileage rate if you leased the vehicle.

➤ Actual expenses—Actual expenses include depreciation (or a portion of the cost of leasing the vehicle) and the cost of license and registration, gas, oil, tires, maintenance, repairs, and insurance. You must have a record of these expenses to back up your claims. Leases are a little complicated; just enter the numbers from your lease agreement, and TurboTax handles the rest. Later in the Interview, TurboTax will prompt you to enter information for additional deductions, including interest on the car loan and personal property taxes.

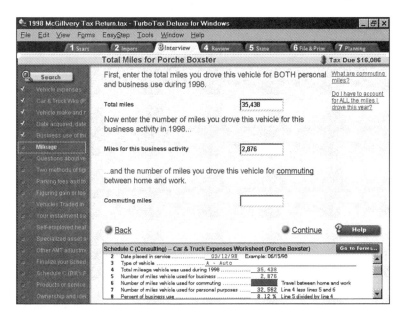

*TurboTax gathers all pertinent information about the vehicle you use for business.*

# SOHO Deductions for the Home Office

Working at home comes with a host of benefits. You get to talk to your pets during lunch, clean the house, do laundry, get the kids ready for school, pick them up, cook dinner, and still hold down a full-time job. In addition, the government lets you fill out the overly complicated form 8829 to deduct the tiny percentage of your home you use as an office from the gross profit of your business.

But, hey, every little bit counts.

The following sections provide details about the home office deduction, help you determine if you're qualified to claim it, and get you started on the time-consuming process of entering the required information.

### Are You an Employee?

If you're an employee and you're claiming your vehicle expenses as a deduction, you must do so on form 2106, Employee Business Expenses, not on Schedule C. You cannot claim the miles you use to commute, but you can claim mileage you rack up by visiting clients, going on sales calls, travelling to a work site, or driving from one job to the next. The IRS rules that govern this deduction are fairly complicated, but TurboTax leads you through the process of claiming a deduction on form 2106 later in the Interview.

## *Does Your Office Qualify?*

Taxpayers who submit form 8829, Expenses for Business Use of Your Home, slightly increase their chances of receiving a call from the IRS, because some taxpayers have abused the home office deduction. To determine if your work area qualifies for the home office deduction, you must answer "Yes" to all three of the following questions:

➤ Do you use the room exclusively for business, and not as a den, bedroom, or storage area for personal items? If the IRS field worker finds a Barbie's Playhouse under your desk, you might be in trouble.

➤ Is your work area a distinct area that is not open to other living areas? A room with a door is best.

➤ Is this the only place available for carrying out your business? If you have another office outside of your home, you can't take the home office deduction.

**Selling Your Home?**

When you take the home office deduction, selling your home can be a little more complicated. Your office space is treated as a business asset rather than as a part of your home, and it is taxed as such.

## *Direct and Indirect Expenses*

With a home office, you have two types of expenses: direct and indirect. A *direct expense* is any expense that applies only to your office space. For example, the cost of a phone line used exclusively in your office is a direct expense. If you put up walls to give yourself some privacy or have bookshelves built in, that's a direct expense. An *indirect expense* is one that applies to the entire house. Utility bills, overall home repairs (such as plumbing or a new roof), property taxes, insurance, and mortgage interest are indirect expenses. You can deduct the entire cost of a direct expense, but you can deduct only the portion of your indirect expenses that is equal to the percentage of your home you use as office space.

The first three entries on form 8829 calculate the percentage of your home you actually use for business. This is typically the smallest room in the house—the 10-by-10-foot corner room that can barely hold a double bed. After you

**New Law**

Currently, if you conduct your business on the road or at the homes or businesses of your clients, you cannot take the home office deduction. However, in 1999, the rules will change slightly to allow you to claim the deduction if you perform management or administrative activities in your home office and have nowhere else to perform these tasks.

divide the square footage of your office by the total square footage of your house, you're usually lucky to see anything over 7%. You then multiply this percentage by the total of your *indirect* expenses and add it to your total *direct* expenses to determine your deduction.

Don't expect too much, but because this deduction reduces your overall business income, it reduces not only your income tax but also your self-employment tax. In other words, it's worth the added work.

## *Entering the Numbers*

To claim the home office deduction, click **Office in Home** in the Interview Navigator and click the **Continue** button. Click the check box next to **I have expenses pertaining to an office in my home**, and click **Continue**. When asked if you want to claim a home office deduction for this business, click **Yes**. Follow the Interview to answer the pertinent questions and enter the required information.

This section of the Interview will test your record-management skills. You'll need to track down your utility bills, cleaning bills, bills for home improvements, mortgage interest statement, property tax statement, and any other receipts for direct and indirect expenses. You should also have a tape measure handy to determine the square footage of your office space and a calculator to add up the totals. (Choose **Tools**, **Calculator** to use the TurboTax calculator.)

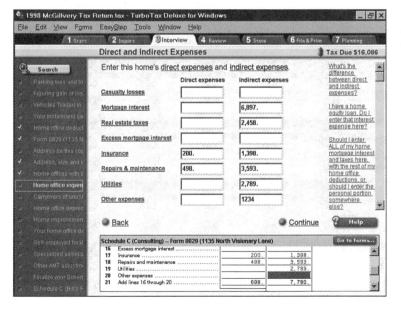

*The TurboTax Interview leads you through form 8829 step-by-step.*

# Other Business Deductions

Don't look to Schedule C for reminders on which deductions you can take. There's no box for shipping costs, journals, publications, and the other minor expenses that can add up to major deductions.

After you have entered the numbers for the big-ticket items, the Interview asks if you have any other expenses, and then displays a collection of text boxes for entering other expenses. Type a category for each additional business expense, along with the total expenses in each category. Use the following list for inspiration:

➤ Postage and shipping costs.

➤ Magazines and professional journals required for your business. *People* magazine doesn't count unless you have a waiting room.

➤ Credit card and bank fees for accounts you use strictly for your business.

➤ Collection fees.

➤ Dues to professional organizations.

➤ Photocopy fees.

➤ Fees to outside services.

➤ Sample products.

➤ Small tools, such as a calculator or adding machine.

➤ Gifts to customers not exceeding $25 per person.

**Business Insurance**

Some homeowner's insurance policies do not cover business-related property, such as computers. Check with your insurance company to determine if you need additional insurance. Claim this portion of your insurance as a direct expense.

*If you have leftover receipts, here's where you enter the numbers.*

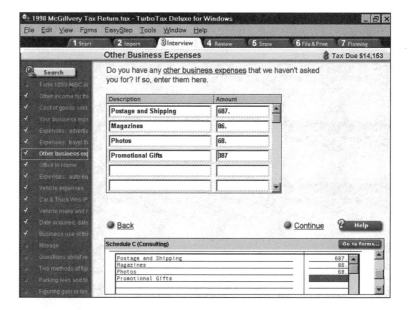

# Still on Track?

Running your own business or working as a freelancer has its share of rewards and headaches, especially at tax time. By working through the TurboTax Interview, you're assured that you're taking advantage of all the tax breaks to which you're entitled. Just make sure you have done the following:

➤ Entered your income from every 1099-MISC you have received. See "Completing Form 1099-MISC," on page 88.

➤ Subtracted your business expenses from your business income to determine the net profit for your business. See "Paring Down Your Business Profit with Schedule C," on page 90.

➤ If you sold any products, subtracted the cost of the products you sold from your gross sales. See "Taking Inventory: Cost of Goods Sold," on page 93.

➤ Accounted for the cost of the vehicle you use for your business. See "Your Car Could Save You Some Cash," on page 94.

➤ Deducted business expenses for use of your home, assuming you qualify for the home office deduction. See "SOHO Deductions for the Home Office," on page 95.

➤ Accounted for any other expenses related to running your business. See "Other Business Deductions," on page 98.

# Chapter 8

# Depreciating Your Old Stuff

---

## In This Chapter

➤ Why it's in your best interest to depreciate assets

➤ Assets that depreciate and assets that don't

➤ The two methods used to depreciate assets

➤ How to list your depreciable assets in TurboTax

➤ How to avoid the depreciation issue with a Section 179 deduction

---

Unlike a fine wine that gets better with age, most stuff just gets old. As your belongings age, their value sinks until they're actually worth nothing (at least for accounting purposes). To account for an asset's loss of value and claim the loss as an expense, you *depreciate* the asset over time. For instance, you can depreciate your computer over five years, so you can claim a business deduction for it every year you use it to generate income. This makes your tax bill a little more consistent from year to year and helps you save for new equipment.

This chapter provides some background information about depreciation, shows you a couple methods for calculating depreciation, and provides instructions on how to list your depreciable assets on your tax return. If, after reading this, you think depreciation is just a lot of busy work, this chapter shows you how to avoid the issue altogether.

## Two, Four, Six, Eight, Why Do We Depreciate?

When you're running a business or buying and selling big-ticket items, such as rental property or a car for your business, you must consider the fact that these assets lose value over time. By depreciating your business assets, you can string out your expenses over several years. For example, if you purchase a $2,000 computer, you can claim it as a $400 expense for five years.

If you were to claim the entire cost of the asset in the first year you purchased it, you would see a big deduction the first year, but you'd pay for it in the future. It could boost you into a higher tax bracket or make you eligible for the evil alternative minimum tax.

Depreciation does have a downside when you sell the asset. By depreciating big-ticket items, such as cars and rental property, you claim a reduction in their value. When you sell the asset and report a profit from the sale, you calculate your profit by subtracting the asset's depreciated value (not the price you paid for it, or even its market value) from the sale price. This typically results in a larger taxable gain than you would see if you had not depreciated the item. And, as you already know, higher gains mean higher taxes.

**Spending Sprees**

Don't go on a spending spree thinking that the government is going to *reimburse* you for your expenses. When you claim an expense, you only lower your taxable income. For instance, if you're in a 28% tax bracket, you save only 28 cents on every dollar's worth of business expenses—you don't get a dollar back for every dollar you spend. The goal of your business is to turn a healthy profit, not just pay zero taxes (although that would be nice, too).

**Reducing Your Basis**

The *basis* of an asset is the amount you have invested in the asset. When determining net profit from a sale, you subtract the asset's basis from the sale price. By depreciating an asset, you reduce the asset's basis, which increases your net profit (the profit that's subject to tax).

# Ten Things That Depreciate (and a Few Things That Don't)

When you first encounter the depreciation issue, it's tempting to depreciate everything in your office: your computer, calculator, paperclips, day planner, and anything else you have a receipt for. But not everything is a depreciable asset. Some items, including pens and paper, are *supplies*, whose entire value you claim as an expense.

An asset is depreciable only if it's not a supply and it has a useful life of more than one year. The following table lists common depreciable assets and their average life span as specified by the IRS.

## Table 8.1 Common Depreciable Assets

| Category | Asset Type |
|---|---|
| 3-year property | Computer software; special handling devices for the manufacture of foods and beverages; racehorses over two years old and other horses over 12 years old when placed in service; and special tools used in the manufacture of plastic products, fabricated metal products, and automobiles. |
| 5-year property | Automobiles, light trucks and vans, computers, calculators, copiers, research equipment, and other office equipment. |
| 7-year property | Desks, chairs, tools, cellular phones, fax machines, refrigerators, carpeting, and other furniture and equipment that doesn't fit in the five-year category. |
| 10-year property | Trees and vines that bear fruit or nuts, water transportation vessels, and assets used in oil refining or the manufacture of tobacco products and some food products. |
| 15- and 20-year property | Land improvements, fences, roads, bridges, sewage treatment plants, telephone distribution plants, and other infrastructure-related items. |
| 27.5-year property | Residential rental property. |
| 31.5- and 39-year property | Commercial real estate property. |

**Rent to Own**

If you rent equipment with the intent to purchase it when the lease expires, treat it as a depreciable asset. If you plan on returning the equipment when the lease expires, treat it as a rental. The IRS has fairly extensive rules related to expenses for leasing capital assets. Consult with a qualified accountant before you decide to lease.

There are a couple exceptions for computer software. First, software that has a useful life of less than one year (such as TurboTax) is fully deductible as a standard business expense; don't depreciate it. If the software came bundled with the computer, include it in the cost of the computer (unless the cost of the software was broken down on the bill) and depreciate the cost of the computer over five years.

# There's More Than One Way to Depreciate

Depreciation could be very easy, but with the government involved, can you really expect it to be simple? The IRS allows you to use any of several methods to calculate depreciation. In most cases, you select the easiest or most lucrative method for your business. In a few cases, the tax code dictates the method you must use. Here's a list of the most common ways to depreciate:

➤ Straight line—This method gives you the same deduction each year over the life of the asset. For example, if you depreciate a $3,000 computer using the straight-line method, you deduct $600 per year for five years.

➤ MACRS (Modified Accelerated Cost Recovery System)—This method provides a higher deduction for the first year and lower deductions for following years. If you choose this method, TurboTax refers to the IRS MACRS depreciation tables for you and plugs in the appropriate numbers.

➤ ACRS (Accelerated Cost Recovery System)—This method is used only for assets placed in service before 1987.

When you enter information about your depreciable assets in TurboTax, TurboTax chooses the best method for you and performs the required calculations.

# Don't Want to Depreciate? See Section 179

You just lost your job, blew your severance pay on a new computer, took out a second mortgage, and now you have to listen to some clown tell you to depreciate your equipment to spread out your expenses over *five years*! You want your deduction, and you want it now!

Never fear. The IRS has something called Section 179 that lets you list more than $18,000 of business assets placed in service in 1998 as direct expenses rather than depreciating them. The only catch is that that the business use of the asset must exceed 50%. For instance, if you use your computer 40% of the time for business and 60% of the time for personal use, you can't claim it as a Section 179 deduction. You can claim a portion of the cost of each asset as a Section 179 deduction; for example, you can deduct half of the cost this year and half of the cost next year.

As you work through the Interview, TurboTax will ask if you want to claim your asset as a Section 179 business expense. Just give your confirmation, and TurboTax fills out the proper forms.

# Special Considerations for Depreciating Your Car

When it comes to cars, my advice is to take the 32.5-cent-per-mile deduction and forget all this nonsense about saving your receipts and depreciating your vehicle. However, if you chose to calculate your automobile deduction based on the actual costs of running and maintaining your car, then you should also figure in depreciation for that vehicle.

Unfortunately, the IRS imposes some limits. You can't purchase a new Porsche Boxster for your business and write it off as a Section 179 business expense or depreciate it as a standard business asset. The most you can deduct for depreciation in the first year is $3,160. The amount increases to $5,000 in the second year and then drops off to $3,050 for the third year, and $1,775 for the fourth and all remaining years. In short, for cars over $15,800, the deduction for depreciation is limited.

Also keep in mind that if you don't use the car solely for business activity, you must reduce the depreciation expense by the percentage you drive your car for personal use. See Chapter 7, "1099-MISCs and Schedule C (for the Self-Employed)," for details about automobile deductions.

**When to Shun Section 179**

If your business is operating at a loss, it doesn't make much sense to use Section 179. Section 179 deductions are limited to the net profit of your business. You can carry the expenses over to next year, but you'll see no benefit this year.

**What About Section 179?**

Like any other business expenses, you can claim the total cost of your car (or the percentage of its cost based on business use) as a Section 179 deduction, up to $3,160. However, if claiming your car pushes you over the Section 179 limit of $18,500 or if you're already receiving a $3,160 deduction through depreciation, stick with depreciating the car.

# Entering Descriptions of Depreciable Assets

As you complete Schedule C in the Interview, TurboTax eventually pops the question of whether you have any depreciable assets you need to record. If you skipped the question or haven't yet reached that point, take the following steps to enter information about your depreciable assets:

1. In the Interview Navigator, under Sole proprietor—Schedule C, click **Depreciation** and click **Yes**.

2. Type a brief description of the asset and click **Continued**. If you transferred data from last year's TurboTax return, some depreciable assets might already be listed. To record a new asset, click **Create a new asset**.

*Name your assets so you can easily identify them later.*

Type a description of the asset.

Click Depreciation.

Click Continue.

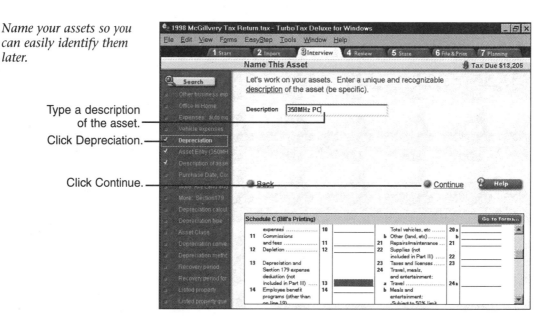

3. Enter the date you placed the asset in service and the amount you paid for it.

4. Open the **Asset Type** drop-down list, choose the category that best describes this asset, and click **Continue**. (If the asset doesn't fit any category on the list, choose **Other**, click **Next**, and enter the requested information.)

5. If you are asked whether the asset was used exclusively for this business (and not for personal use), click **Yes** or **No**.

6. Enter the percentage of business use for this asset and click **Continue**. Based on your answers up to this point, TurboTax determines if the asset qualifies as a Section 179 deduction.

Enter the date you placed
the asset in service.

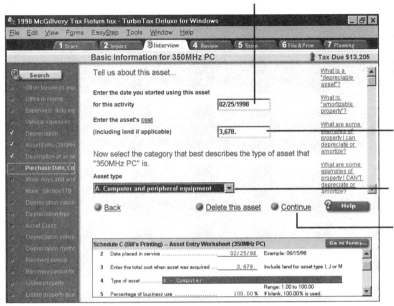

*TurboTax needs to know
when you placed the asset
in service and how much
you paid for it.*

Enter the purchase price or
fair market value of the
asset.

Choose the category that
best fits the asset.

Click Continue.

7. If the asset qualifies as a Section 179 deduction, and you want to list it as such, click **Continue**. If you know that the asset doesn't qualify, click the check box next to **This asset isn't eligible for section 179** and click **Continue**. (If the asset does qualify as a Section 179 deduction, but you don't want to list it as such, click **Continue** and enter **0** in step 8.)

8. If you chose to list the cost of the asset as a Section 179 deduction, you can enter the amount you want to deduct. TurboTax assumes you want to deduct the entire cost of the asset. If you don't want to claim the cost of the asset as a Section 179 deduction, enter **0**, or enter the amount you want to claim. Click **Continue**.

9. Click **Done with this asset**.

10. To enter information for another asset, click **Yes, enter a new asset**. (You can edit information about an asset that you already recorded by clicking **Yes, update an existing asset**.)

11. When you are done entering information for all your assets, click **No, done with assets**.

**Transfers from Your 1997 Return**

The best part about using TurboTax every year is that when you transfer information from last year's tax return, TurboTax picks up where it left off on depreciating your business assets. You don't have to go back and check last year's tax return and the current depreciation tables from the IRS.

**107**

# Still on Track?

As your business expands and your profits grow, you will begin to realize how important depreciation is to keeping your tax bill at a reasonable level. At this point, you should have the final figure on how profitable your business was in 1998, and you can move on to the remaining chapters in this part to record any other income you received, or skip to Part 3 to whittle down your taxable income. Before you move on, make sure you have done the following:

➤ Determined whether or not it's in your best interest to calculate depreciation for your assets. See "Two, Four, Six, Eight, Why Do We Depreciate?" on page 102.

➤ Figured out what you have that's depreciable and what's not. See "Ten Things That Depreciate (and a Few Things That Don't)," on page 103.

➤ Picked the best depreciation method for your situation. See "There's More Than One Way to Depreciate," on page 104.

➤ Learned how to avoid the complexities of depreciation by taking the Section 179 deduction. See "Don't Want to Depreciate? See Section 179," on page 104.

➤ Entered information for every one of your depreciable assets in TurboTax. See "Entering Descriptions of Depreciable Assets," on page 106.

# Chapter 9

# Living Off the Land (Farming Can Be Taxing)

---

**In This Chapter**

➤ Harvest your profits and tally them

➤ Pick the right accounting method for your farm

➤ Down on the farm with Schedule F

➤ Special deductions just for farmers

➤ Account for crop insurance and government payments

---

As a farmer, you really take a beating. An early frost can wipe out your crop, disease can destroy your herd, and a windstorm can blow away a good chunk of your profits. Then, after you've survived all that Mother Nature could throw at you and turned a profit, the IRS comes a knockin', asking for its share of the proceeds.

Although this chapter doesn't teach you how to protect your crop or increase your harvest, it can help you survive your annual encounter with the IRS. This chapter introduces you to some of the unique tax issues that deal with farming and how to take advantage of special deductions. It also shows you how to survive Schedule F, enter farm income and expenses in TurboTax, and save taxes by averaging your income over several years.

# March 1st Filing Deadline

To reward you for your hard work and lighten your load during your spring planting, the IRS requires you to submit your tax return *early*. You do have a choice, however:

➤ File by March 1st and avoid estimated taxes—By filing your tax return by March 1, 1999 and paying your tax bill in full, the government does not require you to pay estimated taxes for 1998.

➤ File by April 15, 1999 and pay estimated taxes by January 15, 1999—If you choose to wait, you must pay your estimated taxes for 1998 by January 15, 1999. You make only one payment equal to the total income taxes you paid in 1997 or two thirds of the taxes due in 1998.

➤ Pay quarterly estimated taxes and file by April 15, 1999—If your income from farming is less than two thirds of your total income in 1998 and was not two thirds of your income in 1997, you must pay quarterly estimated taxes and file your return by April 15, 1999. For example, if you make more than one third of your income selling insurance or fireplace inserts, and you make less than two thirds from of your income by farming, you must pay estimated taxes each quarter. (If you're married, you must account for your spouse's gross income when determining if two thirds of your gross income is from farming.)

# It's All a Matter of Income and Expenses

Just like any other business, an agricultural business has income and expenses. Your farm might have several sources of income, including income from a harvest, the sale of livestock, payments from government programs and insurance, and even the sale of old farm machinery. Expenses might include everything from seed and fertilizer to livestock purchases, and from farm machinery to wages paid to hired hands. In addition, as your income-producing farm assets age, you can claim deductions for depreciable assets, as explained in the previous chapter.

There's nothing tricky about the calculations for income and expenses on your farm. To calculate your overall profit, you simply deduct your expenses from your income. However, there are special asset categories that apply only to farm assets, and the IRS performs some fancy calculations for taxing government and insurance payments. Fortunately, with TurboTax, you simply fill in the appropriate blanks and TurboTax handles all the details.

# Income Averaging Is Back!

Back in 1986, the government did away with income averaging for farmers, penalizing farmers when they made a good profit after several years of reporting losses. If your farm reported a loss for three years and then made a huge profit in the fourth year, you would have to pay taxes on that huge profit. In 1998, income averaging is back.

Income averaging helps you take advantage of the lean years by counting your previous losses against your current profit. If your farm reported a profit in 1998 but losses in previous years, income averaging distributes the profit from the current year over the past three years, determines the taxes you would have paid in those years, and adds the total to your 1998 return. This lowers your 1998 tax bill.

As you proceed through the Interview, TurboTax asks if you want to use income averaging and then leads you through the process of entering the required details, as explained later in this chapter.

# Pick Your Accounting Method: Accrual or Cash?

One of the first questions TurboTax asks you is what type of accounting method you use for your farm: cash or accrual? You've probably heard this song about cash and accrual earlier in this book, so feel free to sing along. Using the cash method, you report payments you receive for the year in which you received them and report expenses for the year in which you paid them. With the accrual method, you report payments for the year in which you sent the bill or invoice and expenses for the year in which you incurred the expense (whether you paid the bill in that year or the next).

Because the cash method is so easy and logical, most farmers use the cash method. Although you still need to keep track of who owes you money and to whom you owe money, you report income and expenses when you actually see the money coming in or going out. The cash method also gives you additional flexibility on your income and expenses for tax purposes. For instance, if you just sold a record harvest, you could pay next year's crop-dusting bill by December 31st and reduce your taxable profit for 1998. You also don't need to fiddle with inventory.

If you choose the cash method, you should be aware of the following quirks:

➤ If you purchased livestock or equipment for resale, you must keep track of what didn't sell. You can't deduct the expense until you've actually sold the item.

➤ You cannot deduct the full cost of equipment, buildings, race horses, livestock used for breeding, and other depreciable assets in the year you purchased the item. You must depreciate these assets over their useful lives.

# Plowing Through the Income Section on Schedule F

Gather up your receipts, and let's get started. The TurboTax Interview will lead you through the process of entering the required numbers on Schedule F, determining if income averaging will help reduce your tax bill, and calculating your net profit or loss from farming. To complete Schedule F, take the following steps:

1. In the Interview Navigator, click **Farm—Schedule F**.

2. If TurboTax asks if you have income from farming, click **Yes**. The first screen introduces income averaging. To view a video about income averaging, click the **Play** button.

3. Click **Continue**.

4. Type a brief description of your farm (for example, Apple Orchard) and click **Continue**. Click **Continue** again when the Farm Income Averaging screen appears.

5. Type a description of the main crop or other item your farm produces.

6. Open the **Principle agriculture activity code** drop-down list and click the code that best describes your farm's activity.

7. If you pay wages to workers, click in the **Employer ID no.** text box and type your employer ID number.

8. Click the accounting method you use for tracking income and expenses: **Cash** or **Accrual**. Click **Continue**. TurboTax asks if you materially participated in this farm.

*TurboTax needs to know some general information up front.*

Describe what your farm produces.

Enter the IRS code for your farm.

Enter your employer ID number, if applicable.

Specify the accounting method you use.

Click Continue.

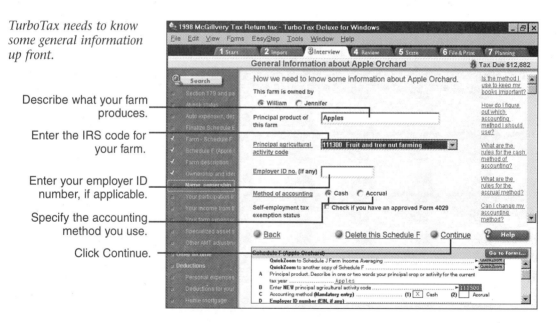

9. If you materially participated in this farm, click **Yes**. If you own the farm but don't work on it, click **No**. For more information on material participation in a business, see Chapter 7, "1099-MISCs and Schedule C (for the Self-Employed)."

10. Enter your income from the sale of produce, livestock, and other products you purchased and sold, along with the total cost of what you sold.

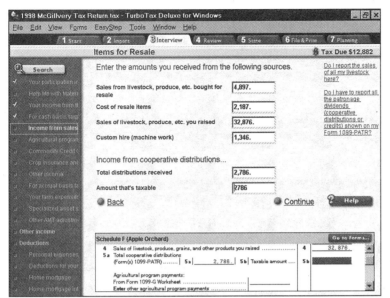

*Record your various sources of income.*

11. Enter income you received from the sale of livestock and produce you raised, along with any work-for-hire payments you received and payments from a cooperative. Click **Continue**.

12. If you received any agricultural payments from the government reported to you on form 1099-G, click **Yes**.

13. Enter the payer's name, click **Continue**, and enter the amount of the payment(s).

14. Click **Agricultural payment** or **Federal disaster payment** to specify the type of payment received, and then click **Yes** to report the payment on the current Schedule F.

15. When you are done entering information about government payments you received, click **Done with 1099-Gs**.

16. Enter the amount of any additional agricultural payments you received that were not reported to you on forms 1099-G, and click **Continue**.

17. If you received any Commodity Credit Corporation (CCC) loans, enter the requested information and click **Continue**.

18. If you received any crop insurance or disaster relief payments, click the check box options to indicate the types of payments you received, click **Continue**, and enter the requested information. (If you already entered values from all your 1099-MISC and 1099-G forms earlier, don't enter this information again.)

### Purchased or Raised?

Income you receive from reselling livestock or crops you purchased is handled differently than income from livestock you raised or crops you grew. Make sure you enter the right numbers in the blanks in steps 10 and 11.

**Defer Payments**

If you use the cash method of accounting, you might be able to postpone reporting the payment as income to 1999 if you received the payment in 1999 for your 1998 crop. However, you must be able to show that the income from this crop would have been reported in 1999. This practice is a little risky, as well. For instance, if you sell your 1998 crop, and the buyer can't pay you for it, you lose. You can also lose out if you prematurely agree to the sale and the price of your crop rises.

**19.** Continue working through the Interview until you have answered all the income-related questions.

The Interview proceeds to ask you about any additional sources of income and then leads you through a long series of questions to gather information about your expenses. By following the Interview, you can be assured that you will account for all eligible deductions. The following sections provide additional information about farm-related expenses and payments.

# Logging Payments and Expenses

Running a farm requires some hefty expenditures for everything from big-ticket items, such as farm machinery, to the seed and fertilizer you use to grow your crop. If you managed to stay organized throughout the year, accounting for these expenses will be pretty straightforward (though time consuming). To help you gather the records you need and take advantage of all eligible expenses, read through the following list of common farm expenses:

➤ Farm tools and equipment, including harnesses and branding tools.

➤ Car and truck expenses.

➤ Breeding fees.

➤ Conservation fees. (If you perform land conservation activities, such as conditioning the soil or digging drainage ditches, that conform to a government land conservation program, you can deduct the cost of those activities up to 25% of your farm income.)

➤ Seed and fertilizer, including crop-dusting fees.

➤ Dues to farming organizations.

➤ Fence and road repair.

➤ Food for livestock, including hay.

➤ Pasture and land rental, including rental property you used in exchange for a portion of a crop.

➤ Room, board, and health benefits provided for hired hands.

➤ Storage fees.

➤ Insurance premiums (other than your personal or family health insurance).

➤ Mortgage interest and any interest on loans used to purchase business assets (assets used to produce income).

➤ Utilities related to the operation of your farm. Utility expenses for personal use are not deductible.

➤ Veterinary bills.

As you work through the Interview, TurboTax displays screen after screen of text boxes for nearly every farm expense imaginable. Don't worry if a specific expense doesn't appear on the list—at the very end, TurboTax asks if you have any additional expenses the Interview missed and gives you the opportunity to report those expenses.

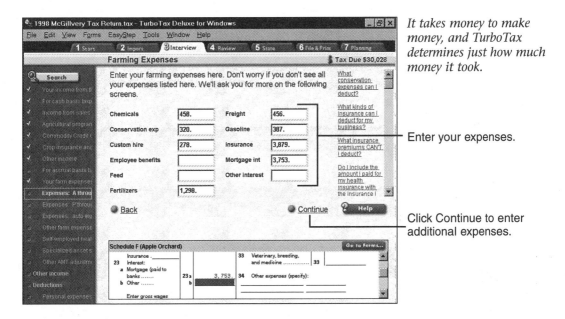

*It takes money to make money, and TurboTax determines just how much money it took.*

Enter your expenses.

Click Continue to enter additional expenses.

# Depreciating Livestock, Machinery, and Other Farm Assets

Chapter 8, "Depreciating Your Old Stuff," covered most of the issues related to depreciation, but a few issues relate specifically to farm assets, including livestock, machinery, and agricultural structures (such as chicken coops). The trouble is that TurboTax isn't very farmer-friendly. Although it provides a fairly comprehensive list of asset categories, the list leaves off the variations for depreciating livestock and other key farm assets.

**Don't Be Fuelish**

Keep track of the amount of cash you paid for all the fuel you pumped into your tractor and other farm equipment. The government gives you a credit for any federal tax you paid on that fuel.

115

When you finish entering your farm expenses, the Interview leads you through the process of recording information about your depreciable assets. You must describe the asset, specify the date you placed it in service, and enter its cost. When you get to the part that asks you to pick an asset category, scan the list to see if the asset is included (for example, farm machinery is on the list). If the asset is not listed, click **Other** at the end of the list and enter the requested details to tell TurboTax how to calculate depreciation for this asset. The following table should help.

## Table 9.1 Depreciation Categories for Farm Assets

| Asset Type | Asset Class |
|---|---|
| Cows (dairy or breeding) | 5-year property |
| Goats or sheep (breeding) | 5-year property |
| Hogs (breeding) | 3-year property |
| Racehorses | 3-year property if more than two years old when placed in service, 7-year property if under two years old when placed in service |
| Other horses | 3-year property if more than 12 years old when placed in service, 7-year property of under 12 years old when placed in service |
| Farm machinery | 7-year property |
| Cotton ginning equipment | 7-year property |
| Drainage facilities | 15-year property |
| Farm buildings | 20-year property |
| Horticultural structures | 10-year property |
| Fences | 7-year property |
| Grain bin | 7-year property |
| Logging equipment | 5-year property |
| Over-the-road tractors | 3-year property |
| Fruit-bearing trees or vines | 10-year property |
| Heavy-duty trucks | 5-year property |

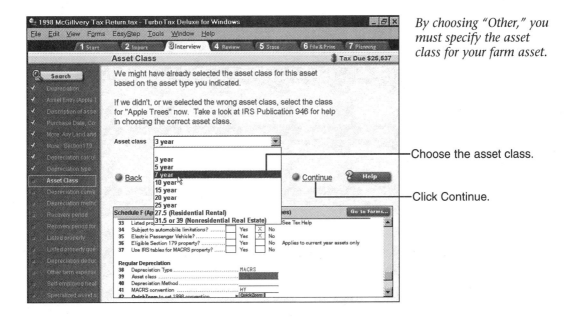

*By choosing "Other," you must specify the asset class for your farm asset.*

Choose the asset class.

Click Continue.

# How Much Did You Make?

After you have completed Schedule F, TurboTax calculates the net profit you received from farm activities and inserts the total on Schedule F, line 36; form 1040, line 18; and Schedule SE, line 1. Schedule SE calculates the amount of self-employment tax you must pay. This tax can really hit you where it hurts. When you're self-employed, you pay both halves of the social security and Medicare taxes, which is roughly equivalent to 15.3%. When you work a regular job, your employer foots half the bill. For the gruesome details about the self-employment tax, see "The Increased Tax Burden for the Self-employed," in Chapter 16.

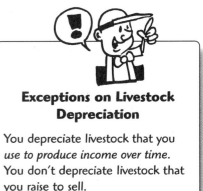

**Exceptions on Livestock Depreciation**

You depreciate livestock that you *use to produce income over time.* You don't depreciate livestock that you raise to sell.

*TurboTax calculates the net profit from your farm and transfers the total to form 1040.*

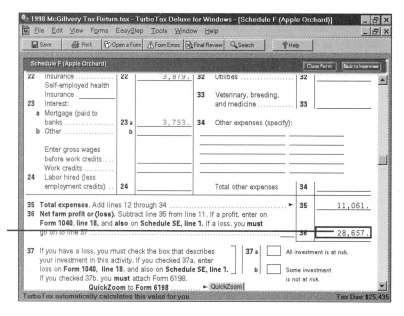

Net farm profit

## Still on Track?

At this point, you should be nearly finished entering your income. If you have any income from royalties or rental property, move on to Chapter 10. To report income from other sources, see Chapter 11. Before you move on, however, make sure you have done the following:

### Don't Forget Section 179

When reporting depreciation, don't forget about the Section 179 deduction. You can deduct up to $18,500 of your depreciable assets as direct expenses rather than depreciating the assets over time. Most buildings are excluded from the Section 179 deduction, but single-purpose agricultural buildings do qualify. See "Don't Want to Depreciate? See Section 179," in Chapter 8.

➤ Determined if income averaging would lower your tax bill. See "Income Averaging Is Back!" on page 110.

➤ Picked the best accounting method for your farm and specified the method you use in TurboTax. See "Pick Your Accounting Method: Accrual or Cash?" on page 111.

➤ Reported all your farm income on Schedule F. See "Plowing Through the Income Section on Schedule F," on page 111.

➤ Entered all your farm expenses and payments on Schedule F. See "Logging Payments and Expenses," on page 114.

➤ Entered the required information for depreciable farm assets. See "Depreciating Livestock, Machinery, and Other Farm Assets," on page 115.

➤ Determined your net profit from farming activities. See "How Much Did You Make?" on page 117.

# Chapter 10

# Rentals and Royalties for Landlords, Authors, and Inventors

---

### In This Chapter

➤ Report royalties received from your creations

➤ Tap the royalties from wells, mines, timber, and other resources

➤ Play Monopoly with your rental properties and draw the tax card

➤ Pay for your next vacation by renting out your vacation home

➤ Trim your net profit from rental income with a few savvy deductions

➤ Meet Schedule E face to face

---

You've worked hard and managed to create or purchase a few items of value. Maybe you patented a process for using tap water as heating fuel, struck oil in your back yard, or had the foresight to buy a vacation home in southern Florida. Whatever the case, you have something valuable, something you can charge other people to use, something that can earn you money while you perfect your golf stroke.

When you're done counting your money at the end of the year, you must report your good fortune to the IRS and pay a tax on it. You do this by filling out Schedule E, Supplemental Income and Loss. Of course, TurboTax guides you step-by-step through the process of completing Schedule E, so you don't need line-by-line instructions. However, there are a few intricate issues related to royalties and rentals and a handful of tricks for maximizing your deductions. This chapter provides the background material you need and a list of deductions to get you started.

# Keeping Track of Royalty Payments

When you hear the term "royalties," you probably think of Stephen King or Danielle Steel, who have received millions of dollars in royalties from their creations. But royalties also apply to songs, original artwork, fees you receive from the people pumping oil out of your well, and anything else (except rental property) that earns income without your having to do work. Following is a list of royalty producers you might or might not have considered:

➤ Patents—If someone pays you a license or rental fee for using a patent you own, the fee is a royalty.

➤ Original creations—These creations may consist of published works (including books), original artwork, and songs.

➤ Movie rights—You can sell the movie or television rights for a composition you own. In addition, you might sell a juicy personal story that ends up as an *ABC Sunday Night Special.*

➤ Oil wells—If someone pumps oil out of an oil well you own, and then pays you a portion of the profits from the sale of the oil, you're receiving royalties. If you run the oil well, the income you receive is not a royalty—it's business income.

➤ Forests—If you own some land populated by trees, and you let people harvest the trees and pay you an amount determined by the harvest, you're receiving royalties. If you cut down the trees and sell them yourself, you have income from sales, not royalties.

➤ Coal—If you own a coal mine and receive payments from a mining company for mining that coal, you're receiving royalties. If you run the coal mine and sell the coal yourself, you have business income, not royalties.

**Self-employed Receiving Royalties?**

If you're self-employed and receiving royalties related to that work, you report royalties from you work on Schedule C, not on Schedule E. If your main income comes from another source, and you're picking up this royalty income from something you do on the side, report the royalty income on Schedule E. Also, if you're receiving royalty income from something that a long-lost relative created, report it on Schedule E.

You typically receive reports of royalty income on 1099-MISC (for standard royalties from published works) or Form K-1.

## *Offsetting Your Royalties with Deductions*

When you start receiving royalties, it's easy to overlook your deductions. The money is flowing in and you don't have to work at it, so why worry? To help reduce the tax bill on your royalties, hunt down any qualifying deductions. Here's a list of possible deductions that might help get those creative juices flowing:

➤ Office supplies used to create the work, as well as other office expenses

➤ Computer expenses, software, musical equipment, or other equipment required to create the product

➤ Advertising fees to promote the work

➤ Travel fees for marketing or promoting the work

➤ Legal and accounting fees

## Exhaustible Resources: The Depletion Deduction

When you're receiving royalties for exhaustible resources, such as coal, oil, gas, and timber, you can claim a deduction for depletion. This is a fairly complex calculation that requires you to estimate the remaining portion of the resource (*cost depletion*) or the portion that was used (*percentage depletion*). (Percentage depletion is not allowed for timber.) If you have royalties from exhaustible resources, you should find the numbers you need on the K-1 you received. If you did not receive a K-1, consult a qualified accountant to determine how to perform the required calculations. After you have the numbers, TurboTax leads you through the process of entering them.

# Rental Income for Slum Lords and Lasses

Whether you rent out the other half of a double or own an apartment complex, you must report the income you receive from your rental properties and (for your own benefit) claim any qualifying deductions.

As long as you have kept a detailed record of damage deposits and rental payments you received, reporting rental income is fairly straightforward. You enter the address of each rental property you own and enter the total income you received from each property. However, there are a few issues that might trip you up and generate more questions than answers. The following sections clarify these issues.

**Depletion and the Alternative Minimum Tax**

When your deductions exceed limits in certain categories, your income might qualify for the *alternative minimum tax* (AMT). This tax ensures that people who report a high gross income and a low net income still pay their fair share of income tax. One of the areas that places you at risk for the AMT is the deduction for depletion. To learn more about the AMT, see "What's with This Alternative Minimum Tax?" in Chapter 16, "More Taxes (As If You Weren't Paying Enough)." For now, just enter the numbers and let TurboTax determine if the AMT applies to your situation.

## What's Rental Income, and What's Not?

Is a damage deposit rent? How about reimbursements from tenants? These questions muddy the waters. Use the following list to determine which payments you must report as income:

➤ Damage deposits that are earmarked to be returned to the tenant at the end of the lease, assuming the tenant does not trash the joint, are not income. Don't report a damage deposit as an expense when you return it. If you keep a portion of the damage deposit for cleaning fees or repairs; report it as income, and report your cleaning fees and repairs as expenses.

➤ Damage deposits that are earmarked to be used as the tenant's last month's rent are income. Report the income in the year in which you receive the payment.

➤ Labor and repairs in lieu of rent are income. For example, if you give your tenant a free month's rent for painting the house, you report that as income and deduct the fair market cost of the paint job as an expense. It seems silly, but that's how it works.

➤ Payments the tenant makes to you to reimburse you for repairs, utilities, and other expenses are income. When you actually pay the bills, you can deduct your payments as expenses.

## Fourteen Days or Fewer? Don't Bother

You live in Louisville, Kentucky, and you rent out your upstairs for one week during the Kentucky Derby. Surely the government will want a piece of the action, right?

Wrong. It's just too much trouble for you and the IRS to deal with the all the paperwork, depreciation calculations, and other messy accounting issues. Pocket the money and be thankful that you're finally getting a legal break.

Now, if your renters trash your house, don't try to claim a deduction. As far as the feds are concerned, that's your loss.

## Did You Live There? Get Out Your Calculator

If, at some time during the year, you resided in the property you rented, your deductions might be limited. Here's the rule: If you lived in the residence for 14 days or over 10% of the total number of days you rented it out (whichever number is larger), the IRS considers the property to be a rental property, but you cannot claim a loss on the property. In other words, you can claim deductions, but the amount you deduct cannot exceed the amount you receive in rent. If you let your relatives live in the residence for free, count the days they occupied the residence as if you had lived there.

If you rented out a portion of a multi-unit residence and lived in another portion of it, your tax situation becomes a little more complicated. You must list deductions for your portion of the property on Schedule A, and list the rental portion of the property on Schedule E. Following is an example for a three-unit dwelling in which you occupy one of the units:

|            | Total  | Schedule A Deduction | Schedule E Deduction | Non-deductible Expense |
|------------|--------|----------------------|----------------------|------------------------|
| **Taxes**        | $900   | $300                 | $600                 | $0                     |
| **Interest**     | 1,200  | 400                  | 800                  | 0                      |
| **Repairs**      | 660    | 0                    | 440                  | 220                    |
| **Depreciation** | 300    | 0                    | 300                  |                        |

# Rental Payments from Your Vacation Getaway

Your new vacation home set you back quite a bit, so you've decided to recoup some of the expense by renting it out for a few weeks every year. Good idea. By renting out your vacation home, you not only get a little extra cash, but the IRS lets you deduct a good chunk of your mortgage interest, taxes, and other expenses. Here's what you need to know:

➤ If you rent out your vacation home for fewer than 15 days, pocket the money and call it even. You can't deduct your expenses.

➤ If you rent out the vacation home for 15 days or more and you stayed in the home for more than 14 days or over 10% of the total number of days it was rented (whichever is greater), then it's not rental property, and you can't claim a loss on it. However, you can still deduct a portion of your expenses from the rental income you received. When counting the days, omit days when the home was vacant or you were working on it full-time.

➤ If you occupied the vacation home for 14 days or less than 10% of the total number of days it was rented, then it is rental property and you can claim a loss, assuming your expenses exceed the rental income.

**Vacation Home Tax Strategy**

If you use your vacation home over 10% more than any tenants use it, claim expenses on Schedule E to lower your reported rental profit to as close to zero as you can get. You can't claim a loss, so if your expenses exceed your rental income on Schedule E, you won't see any additional tax benefit. If possible, move excess expenses (such as mortgage interest and property taxes) to Schedule A, so you can use them as personal deductions.

At this point, you're probably wondering why I said that renting out your vacation home is such a good idea. In addition to receiving the extra rental income, you receive the following benefits:

➤ You allocate your vacation home's operating expenses based on the percentage of the total time the home was occupied. For example, if you rented it out for 48 days and used it yourself for 48 days, you rented it out 50% of the time, so you can deduct 50% of the expenses.

➤ You can claim a deduction for property taxes and mortgage insurance on both Schedule E and Schedule A. If you rented out the home for 48 days, you would deduct 48/365 (or 13%) of your mortgage interest and property taxes on Schedule E, reducing your taxable rental income. You would then deduct 87% of your property taxes and mortgage interest on Schedule A to increase your itemized deductions.

## A Word About Losses and Carryovers

You might not realize it, but when you rent out your vacation home or half of your double, you're creating your very own *tax shelter*. The government doesn't like tax shelters, because they enable taxpayers to legally avoid paying taxes on something that's generating income.

In 1986, Congress passed a law that was intended to do away with tax shelters. The IRS considers renting out property to be a *passive activity* and might limit the amount you can claim as a loss. If you're claiming a loss from your rental property, you might have to complete Form 8582, Passive Activity Loss Limitations, unless *all* of the following conditions hold true:

**Tax Shelter**

A tax shelter is any investment that enables you to deduct expenses that exceed your investment. The IRS frowns on tax shelters because they enable you to reduce your taxable income.

➤ Income from your rental property is the only income you receive from a passive activity. In other words, you receive rental income, but you don't receive income from partnerships, S corporations, or estates, as explained in Chapter 11, "What Else Constitutes Income?"

➤ You were actively involved in the management of your rental properties. You didn't just sit back and collect the money. Active involvement includes finding and approving tenants, drawing up rental terms, hiring people to clean and repair the rental units (or doing it yourself), and writing the checks.

➤ The loss you are claiming is $25,000 or less. If you share ownership of the rental property with someone who is filing a separate tax return, the limit is $12,500 or less.

➤ You had no other passive activity losses for rental property in a previous year that exceeded the deduction limit.

➤ Your modified adjusted gross income is less than $100,000, or $50,000 if you are married filing separately. If you make any more than that, your loss limit is reduced by fifty cents on a dollar for every dollar in excess of $100,000 (or $50,000 if married filing separately).

➤ If you are married and filing separately, you and your spouse did not live together for the entire year.

If you work through the TurboTax interview, you don't have to concern yourself too much with these issues. Just answer the questions. Based on your answers, TurboTax determines the limits that apply to you and performs the necessary calculations.

# Jotting Down Your Income on Schedule E

If you received a 1099-MISC reporting your royalty payments, you might have entered most or all of your royalty income in Chapter 7, "1099-MISCs and Schedule C (for the Self-Employed)" (refer to the section called "Completing Form 1099-MISC"). If you haven't yet entered that income, scroll up in the Interview Navigator, click **Form 1099-MISC, Miscellaneous Income**, and type the required entries. After you have typed the numbers from your 1099-MISC into TurboTax, TurboTax asks if you want to list the income on Schedule C or E. Choose **Schedule E**.

To enter income you received from rental property that was not reported to you on a special form, take the following steps:

1. In the Interview Navigator, click **Your business, rental, and farm activities**.
2. Click the check box next to **Rental or royalty property – Schedule E** and click **Continue**.
3. Click **Rental property** to specify that you received rent.
4. If you sold the property in 1998, click **Yes**. Otherwise, click **No**.
5. Click **Continue**.
6. Type a brief description of the property and its address.
7. If the rental property is a *dwelling unit* (as opposed to a motel room), click **Yes**. Otherwise, click **No**. Click **Continue**. TurboTax asks if you want to review the tax rules for rental property.
8. To review the tax rules, click **Yes, review the rules**, and read through the rules. Otherwise, click **No, skip the rules**, and proceed to step 9.
9. Click the option to specify whether you or your family resided in the rental property for part of 1998 and the amount of time you occupied the residence. Click **Continue**.
10. If you used the rental property for more than 15 days in 1998, enter the number of days you rented out the property and the number of days you resided in it. Click **Continue**.
11. Continue with the Interview to enter any income you received from the rental property and any expenses you incurred, as explained in the following section. The steps in the Interview vary depending on the answers you provided for previous questions.

*TurboTax can determine your allowable deductions based on the time you used the property and rented it out.*

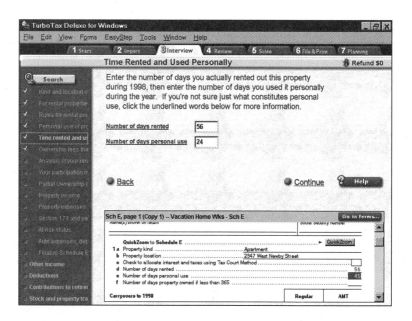

*Enter the income you received from this property.*

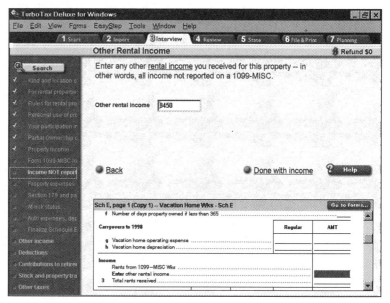

When you have finished entering income and expenses for one of your rental properties, the Interview asks if you have another rental property you need to report. Repeat the previous steps to enter information about additional rental properties.

# Trimming Your Rental Profits by Claiming Expenses

Although rental property can earn a substantial amount of income, it costs money to purchase, improve, and maintain your property. To keep more of your rental income, you should deduct all elligible expenses on your tax return. Read through the following list to make sure you haven't overlooked any qualifying deductions:

➤ Advertising—To keep your rental properties populated, you might need to advertise in the local papers, post flyers in the neighborhood, or pay a commission to a real estate agent. Any money you spend on finding tenants is deductible.

➤ Cleaning—If you pay a cleaning service to clean apartments or other living units, the cleaning fees are deductible.

➤ Condominium fees—If you rent out your condo and you pay fees for maintenance and upkeep, don't forget to deduct those fees.

➤ Collection fees—If a tenant fails to pay rent and you must hire a collection service to strong-arm the tenant, those fees are deductible.

➤ Insurance—Any insurance payments are deductible.

➤ Management fees—If you hire someone to manage your rental properties (someone who will find tenants and clean and maintain the properties), those fees are deductible.

➤ Mortgage interest—Any mortgage interest you paid on rental property in 1998 is fully deductible.

➤ Property taxes—If your state or local government is hitting you up for property taxes on your rental property, make sure you deduct it.

➤ Lawn care and landscaping—Don't overlook the costs of maintaining the land on which your rental property sits. Landscaping costs are deductible.

➤ Repairs and maintenance—Unless you really are a slum lord, you probably paid for repairs and maintenance in 1998. However, if your tenants paid for the maintenance, you can't deduct the costs unless you reported the amount your tenant paid as rental income.

➤ Utilities—If you pay the utilities out of your rental income, the utilities are deductible. If the tenant pays you for utilities and you pass those payments onto the utility company, the payments are not deductible.

➤ Wages—If you hire workers to help you manage, clean, repair, or improve the property, those wages are deductible.

➤ Legal and accounting fees—If you had to hire a lawyer to solve an issue dealing with the property or with a troublesome tenant, deduct those fees as expenses. You can also deduct any fees paid to an accountant for managing the finances related to the rental property.

➤ Depreciation—As your rental properties age, their value is reduced, and you can claim the reduction in value as an expense. See Chapter 8, "Depreciating Your Old Stuff."

When you are done entering your income for one of your rental properties, the Interview leads you through the process of recording any common expenses for rental properties. If you have expenses that are not listed, you can enter them as other expenses at the very end.

TurboTax calculates the total income or loss from each rental property and inserts the net income or loss for each property on line 22 of Schedule E. TurboTax then adds up the numbers from all your rental properties, inserts the total on line 26, and carries the total to form 1040, line 17.

### Land Doesn't Depreciate

According to the IRS, land doesn't depreciate. When calculating depreciation, subtract the value of the land from the overall cost of the property. This number is on the assessment or real estate appraisal you received when you purchased the property.

*TurboTax prods you to enter expenses for each rental property.*

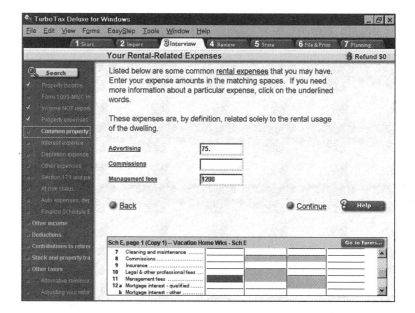

## Still on Track?

At this point, you should have accounted for all your main sources of income. In the next chapter, you'll tie up any loose ends so that you'll be ready to start focusing on personal deductions. Before moving on, make sure you're still on track and have done the following:

➤ Categorized your royalty income as business income or supplemental income. See "Keeping Track of Royalty Payments," on page 120.

➤ Accounted for all royalty income that you need to report on Schedule E. See "Keeping Track of Royalty Payments," on page 120.

➤ Claimed all deductions related to your royalty income. See "Offsetting Your Royalties with Deductions," on page 120.

➤ Understand all the rules for reporting rental income and qualifying deductions. See "Rental Income for Slum Lords and Lasses," on page 121.

➤ Determined what is considered rental income. See "What's Rental Income, and What's Not?," on page 122.

➤ Entered income from rental and royalty property on Schedule E. See "Jotting Down Your Income on Schedule E," on page 125.

➤ Pared down your rental income by deducting all eligible expenses. See "Trimming Your Rental Profits by Claiming Expenses," on page 127.

**Limited Losses and Carryovers**

Losses on rental property can be severely limited, especially on vacation property. However, you can carry over the losses from one year to the next. If you use TurboTax every year and transfer data from your previous year's tax return, TurboTax will handle the carryovers for you.

# Chapter 11

# What Else Constitutes Income?

### In This Chapter

➤ Howdy, partner! K-1 forms and other partnership issues

➤ Report income from S corporations and estates

➤ Alimony income—the best part of a broken marriage

➤ Scholarships, for higher education and higher taxes

➤ Taxes on swaps, trades, and barters

➤ The jury's out and taxes are due

You had a simple year. You held a full-time job, avoided the tumultuous stock market, and the closest you came to any farming activity is growing tomatoes in your back yard. If that's the case, skip this chapter and shift your focus to deductions in Chapter 12, "Income Reduction Through Deductions."

But maybe 1998 was a little more complicated. Perhaps you decided to form a corporation to reduce taxes, or your ex finally started sending you alimony payments. Maybe you decided to go back to school and received the scholarship for which you applied, or you had jury duty and they paid you just enough money to complicate your tax return.

Whatever the case, you have a source of income that's a little less common, and you need to account for it. Well, you've come to the right place. This chapter shows you how to tie up all the loose ends and complete the process of recording your income.

# Schedule K-1 for Partnerships, S Corporations, and Estates

If you received any income from a partnership, S corporation, or estate, you should receive a K-1 form at the end of the year, reporting the amount of income you received or the amount the partnership or corporation lost. Because partnerships and S corporations are not taxed, the government taxes the income that each partner or member of the corporation receives.

The only complicated aspect of form K-1 is the determination of whether the income is from a passive or nonpassive activity (is that an oxymoron or what?!):

➤ If you are a working partner or a shareholder in an S corporation, your income is considered nonpassive. In other words, did you work or just count money? We'll look at this in detail later in this section.

➤ If you are a partner in name only, your income is passive and any loss you report from the partnership or S corporation might be limited.

➤ In most cases, if you are a beneficiary of an estate or trust, you are not an active participant in managing the estate or trust, so you report gains and losses as passive.

Are you still unsure? The following is a list of tests to determine if you are a passive or nonpassive partner. If you can answer "Yes" to *any* of the following questions, you are considered to be an active (nonpassive) partner:

➤ Did you participate in the activity for more than 500 hours in 1998?

➤ Did you do all the work in the partnership, even if it took you less than 500 hours?

➤ Did you participate in the activity for more than 100 hours *and* did the time you participated equal or exceed the time put in by every participant? If anyone else did more than you (come on, be honest), answer "No."

➤ Did you actively participate in two or more partnerships for more than 100 hours each, *and* does the total time you participated in all partnerships add up to more than 500 hours? For example, if you invested in five businesses and worked 101 hours in each business, the IRS considers you an active participant overall. This is called *grouping activities*. Now, if you worked 120 hours in four businesses and 90 hours in the fifth, you would have to answer "No" to this question, because you failed to work over 100 hours in the fifth business.

➤ Did you actively participate in the activity for 5 of the last 10 tax years? The five years do not need to be consecutive.

➤ Did you actively participate in a personal service activity (for example, health, law, architecture, consulting, or accounting) for 3 of the last 10 tax years? Again, the years do not need to be consecutive.

➤ Did you actively participate in the activity regularly for more than 100 hours since you became a partner?

**At Risk?**

The TurboTax Interview will ask you if any of your investment in the partnership or corporation is *at risk*. An investment is at risk only if it is possible for you to personally lose money you have invested. Why does the IRS want to know this? Because some sly business people have been known to claim losses from a partnership or S corporation that exceed their personal investments. For instance, if the partnership or S corporation loses $10,000 and the person invested only $5,000, the IRS doesn't want the person claiming a $10,000 loss. At risk rules are fairly complicated, so consult an accountant if you need to split hairs.

## Passive Activity Rules and Limitations

When you claim a passive loss, the IRS is less than sympathetic. It figures that because you were making money without lifting a finger, the loss isn't of a personal nature and it shouldn't reduce your taxable income. To prevent taxpayers from claiming excessive passive losses, the tax code disallows passive losses unless you have enough passive income to offset the loss. In a way, the government treats passive income and loss just like gambling income and loss. Of course, there are a couple ways to claim passive losses:

➤ If you have two or more passive activities, you can deduct the loss from one passive activity against the gain from another. However, you cannot claim a net loss—the passive loss from one source cannot exceed the passive income from another.

➤ If you have only one passive activity, you can carry any loss over to the following year and deduct it from the gain for that year. You can continue to do this from one year to the next until you have deducted the entire loss, or until you dispose of the property or relinquish your role in the partnership or S corporation.

➤ If your passive activity consists of owning rental properties, you should be aware of additional rules, as explained in "Rental Income for Slum Lords and Lasses," in Chapter 10, "Rentals and Royalties for Landlords, Authors, and Inventors."

## *Reporting Partnership Income and Losses in TurboTax*

Entering your income from partnerships in TurboTax is fairly simple. All you have to do is enter the name of the partnership, enter the numbers from your K-1 form(s), and answer a few additional questions. The following steps show you how to get started:

1. In the Interview Navigator, click **Tax documents you received**, click **Schedule K-1 for partnerships**, and click **Continue**.

2. If desired, click the **Play** button to watch the Partnership K-1s video. Then, click **Continue**.

3. Enter the name of the partnership and click **Continue**.

4. Enter the ID number for the partnership and its tax shelter ID number. The tax shelter ID number is the most important of the two; it tells TurboTax to generate form 8271, Investor Reporting of Tax Shelter ID Number. By failing to submit this form, you could be subject to a $250 penalty.

*TurboTax wants the name, rank, and ID number for your partnership.*

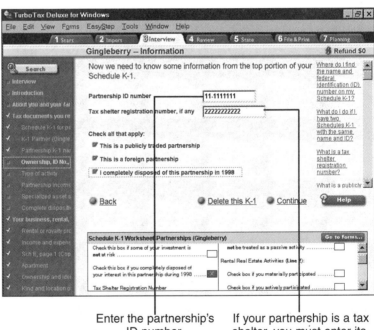

Enter the partnership's ID number.

If your partnership is a tax shelter, you must enter its tax shelter ID number.

5. Click any of the following check box options that apply to the partnership:

➤ This is a publicly traded partnership—Click this option if the partnership is traded on an established securities market. TurboTax does not create a form 8582, Passive Activity Loss Limitations for publicly traded partnerships. Instead, it performs the required calculations in the background and displays the results on a worksheet. Don't worry—TurboTax keeps track of the limitations on losses.

➤ This is a foreign partnership—Click this option if the partnership was created outside of the United States. Although the partnership might not be required to file a tax return, you must report your portion of the income.

➤ I completely disposed of this partnership in 1998—Click this option if you sold your interest in the partnership to a non-relative. This tells TurboTax that any losses you've been carrying over from year to year due to the passive loss limitations can finally be deducted in full.

6. Click **Continue**.

7. Click the option that best describes the activity in which this partnership was involved: **Trade or business**, **Rental real estate**, or **Other rental activity**. Click **Continue**.

8. Now for the $64,000 question: Did you materially participate in this partnership? By now you should know the answer, so place your right hand on the Bible and click **Yes, I materially participated** or **No, I didn't materially participate**. (If this is a publicly traded partnership, TurboTax skips this question.)

9. If you clicked **No**, TurboTax asks if the partnership activity was related to an oil or gas property (in which case, the passive activity limitations do not apply). Click **Yes** or **No**. TurboTax displays a list of check boxes like the ones that appear on your K-1 form.

10. Click the check box next to every item in the list that has a value on your K-1 form. Click **Continue**. (This makes it possible for the Interview to save you time by skipping entries that don't apply to you.)

11. Continue with the Interview, entering the requested values and information from your K-1 form. The steps vary depending on the boxes you checked in step 10.

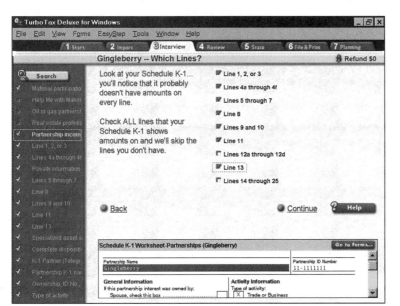

*The Interview wants to know which boxes are filled in on your K-1 form.*

135

# Reporting Income from S Corporations

The steps you take to report income from S corporations are nearly identical to the steps for reporting income from partnerships, although the information you enter is a little different. To get started, scroll up or down in the Interview Navigator, click **Tax documents you received**, click **Schedule K-1 for S corporations**, and click **Continue**. You have to enter some preliminary information, such as the S coporation's name, ID number, and tax shelter ID number, before the Interview gets down to the nitty gritty of asking for the numbers.

*After you've identified the S corporation, the Interview leads you through the process of entering the numbers.*

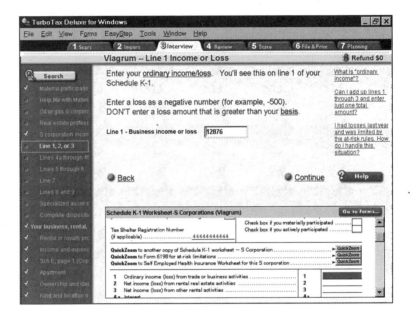

# Lucky You! A Beneficiary of an Estate or Trust

A person commonly sets up an estate to deal with the messy details of distributing his assets after his death or after he files for bankruptcy. The trustee of the estate must file form 1041 to report any gains or losses from the estate and sends you a form K-1 to report any payments made to you, a beneficiary of the estate.

Trusts are similar in that they distribute funds to various beneficiaries, although the funds or assets can be distributed before or after an individual's death. With a trust, the owner of the assets transfers ownership of assets to an intermediary, called the *trustee*, who then distributes the assets to the beneficiaries according to the rules stated in the trust.

Well, that's all very interesting, but how do you report this transfer of assets or cold, hard cash? To get started, scroll up or down in the Interview Navigator, click **Tax documents you received**, click **Schedule K-1 for estates or trusts**, and click **Continue**. In the Interview Navigator, click **Schedule K-1 for estates or trusts**, and then follow the Interview's lead. There's nothing tricky here; just transfer the information as it appears on the paper copy of the K-1 form into TurboTax.

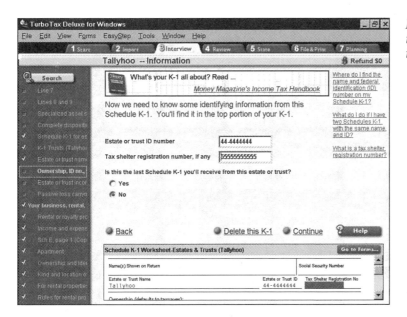

*Enter the numbers from the K-1 for your estate or trust into the blanks.*

# Tying Up the Loose Ends with "Other" Income

If you have any other income that doesn't fall into any of the other major categories, click **Other Income** in the Interview Navigator and click the check box next to each type of income you received. This includes alimony, income from fellowships and scholarships, carryover income and losses from previous years, and barter income. Click **Continue**. The following sections provide additional details about these other sources of income.

### Smart Interview

Keep in mind that TurboTax uses the Smart Interview System to streamline the Interview. If you don't click a check box next to an item, the Interview won't prompt you to enter the required information.

## *Yes, Alimony Is Income*

You cleaned house, hosted dinner parties, raised the kids, cleaned up after the dog, and managed the finances while your spouse climbed the corporate ladder and then decided to dump you. Fortunately, the courts decided that you deserved some financial support (alimony) while you're rebuilding your career. Unfortunately, the tax code requires someone to pay taxes on that money—and that's typically the recipient.

I say "typically," because divorces have been known to become a little messy. Sometimes, the alimony recipient gets into a financial bind, decides that the payer should pay the taxes, and conveniently forgets to report the alimony as income. Or, the payer gets remarried, has additional bills to pay, and decides—despite the divorce decree that specifies otherwise—to claim alimony payments as a deduction.

### Exchange Your Social Security Numbers

Make sure you and your ex have each other's social security numbers. You must enter these numbers on your tax returns, so the IRS can make sure that the alimony payments on both of your returns match.

So, what are the rules covering alimony? In most cases, the payer deducts the alimony payments on his tax return and the recipient claims the payments as income. If you're the recipient, you must claim the payments as income if the payments meet *all* the following requirements:

➤ The payments are in cash or the equivalent (a check or money order). If your ex gives you a dog in lieu of a cash payment, that doesn't count.

➤ The divorce decree specifies that alimony payments are required. If your ex gives you money just to be nice, the payment doesn't count as alimony.

➤ Payments must total more than $15,000 per year and continue for at least three years. Payments of your spouse's legal fees and lump sum property settlements are not alimony.

➤ The payment cannot be for child support. Child support payments are not tax-deductible and the money received is not taxable income.

➤ The divorce decree does not specifically state that the payer must pay the taxes due. If there is no such clause in the decree, the payer can deduct alimony payments and the recipient is required to report the payments as income.

➤ The payer and recipient cannot reside in the same house or file their tax return jointly. (You two lovebirds just couldn't stay apart, could you?)

➤ The divorce decree did not state that payments must continue after the death of the recipient. Duh!

*Although the divorce might have been messy, reporting the alimony you received is a no-brainer.*

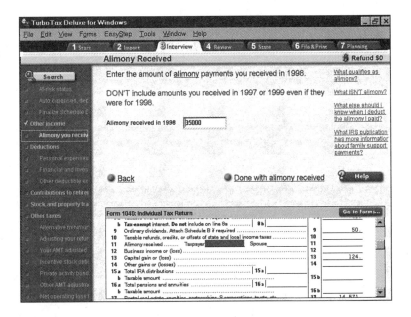

If you're paying alimony, see "Getting Back Some of Your Alimony Payments," in Chapter 12, for instructions on how to claim your alimony payments as a deduction.

To report alimony payments you received in TurboTax, scroll down in the Interview Navigator to **Other Income** and click **Alimony you received this year**. Click **Continue**. To learn more about alimony income, click the **Play** button to view the video clip; otherwise, click **Continue**. Type the total amount of money you received in the form of alimony payments, and then click **Done with alimony received.**

## Scholarships, Fellowships, and Other Freebies

Don't freak out over the heading. Most scholarships, fellowships, student loans, and VA educational benefits are tax-free, as long as you use the money for education. To determine if the money you received is, in fact, tax-free, make sure you follow the rules. To be tax-free, the following must be true:

➤ You are a candidate for a degree at an educational institution. You can't just take classes without a goal in mind.

➤ You use the funds you receive for educational expenses, including tuition, enrollment fees, books, supplies, and equipment required for your course of study.

➤ If you receive VA benefits for education, you use the funds for education or training.

The IRS is a little tougher when it comes to grants. In general, grant money is income and is taxable if *any* of the following holds true:

**Reported on W-2?**

If the funds you received for education or training came from your employer and are already accounted for on your W-2, don't report this money as income again.

➤ You use the grant to pay for room, board, travel, research, clerical help, or late night trips to the pizza joint.

➤ You use the grant to purchase equipment and supplies not required in your course of studies, including surfboards.

➤ You use the grant to pay tuition or fees if the terms of the grant specifically state that this is not a valid use of the money.

➤ You received the grant (or a portion of it) as payment for services.

➤ You won the grant as a scholarship, and the rules did not specifically state that the funds were to be used for educational purposes.

If you determined that the funds you received are non-taxable, skip this part of the interview. You don't want to report non-taxable income. However, if you realize that the entire scholarship, fellowship, or grant (or a portion of it) is taxable, enter the taxable amount in TurboTax. In the Interview Navigator, click **Scholarships and fellowships**, enter the amount that represents the taxable portion of the money you received, and click **Done with scholarship income**.

*Enter only the taxable portion of the money you received from the scholarship, fellowship, or grant.*

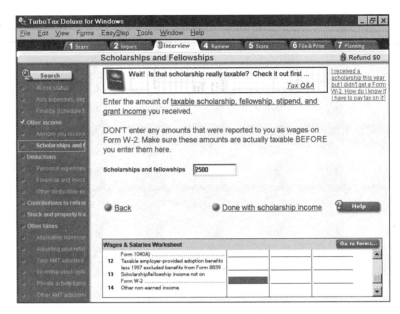

## Reporting Income from Losses Deducted in Past Years

Remember that $200 you loaned to your neighbor a couple years ago that you were sure you'd never see again? Well, your neighbor finally shows up and hands you the two hundred smackers. Is this income? If you reported the $200 as a loss in a previous year, then you must report it as income this year. The same holds true for other losses you claimed in earlier years. For instance, if you thought someone had stolen a thousand bucks from your secret hiding place, reported it as a loss, and then discovered it at the bottom of your sock drawer, you must report it as income.

To report this income that once was lost and now is found, click in the Interview Navigator and click one of the following options:

➤ Reimbursements of expenses deducted in an earlier year—Click this option if you were reimbursed for medical expenses, taxes, business or moving expenses, loss from a theft or casualty, or any other losses you deducted in a previous year. Follow the Interview to enter the requested information. (If you received a tax refund that you already reported on form 1099-G, don't report it here.)

### No Tax Benefit?

Report losses you recovered only if you saw a tax benefit from that loss in the year you claimed it. For example, if you had to pay for medical expenses because your insurance company lost your claim, but the expense did not push you over the 7.5% limit required for you to take advantage of your medical expenses, don't claim the payment from the insurance company when you receive the money.

➤ Recovery of a bad debt deducted in an earlier year—Click this option if you personally loaned someone some money, deducted it as a loss, and then received the payment this year. Enter the amount you were repaid and click **Done with bad debt recoveries**.

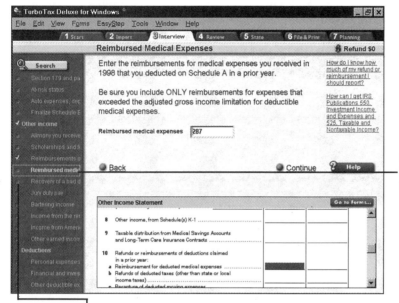

*If you claimed a loss in a previous year and then recovered that loss in 1998, report it as income.*

Click to report a reimbursement of an expense.

Click to report a loan payment you received for a debt you had previously reported as a loss.

## Raking in the Big Bucks from Jury Duty

When you serve on a jury, you typically receive some nominal fee that doesn't even come close to what you'd earn by putting in a normal day's work. However, you're still required to report the money you receive as income.

To report income from jury duty, click in the Interview Navigator and click **Jury duty pay**. Enter the amount you received and click **Done with jury duty pay**.

If you handed over your jury duty pay to your employer, the Interview will later ask you to report this same amount as an adjustment to your income. To enter this amount yourself, pull up form 1040, scroll down to line 31, and enter the amount on the **Other Adjustments to Income Smart Worksheet**, line C.

## *Bartering and Other Under-the-table Income*

In a cash-based economy, the government earns revenue whenever cash changes hands. Your employer pays you for your services, and the government taxes your income. When you have your car fixed, the government taxes the mechanic's income. When a transaction occurs in which cash doesn't change hands, the government gets a little testy. If you remodel your mechanic's kitchen in exchange for a rebuilt engine, no money changes hands, but the government still requires you and the mechanic to pay taxes on the fair market value of the transaction.

To report your income from a barter transaction, you might need to consult with your trade partner on the fair market value of whatever service or product the person provided to you. You can expect the person to give you a funny look and question your sanity, but if you want to keep the transaction legal, you'll need to know the value of what you received as payment. After you've obtained the number you need, click in the Interview Navigator and click **Bartering income**. Enter the fair market value of the goods or services you received and click **Done with bartering income.**

## *Income That the Feds Didn't Even Consider*

The IRS provides a fairly comprehensive list of income sources, but it might have omitted something. To cover all the bases, the IRS included a couple categories to help tie up any loose ends. If you have income from any personal property you rented, click **Income from the rental of personal property** in the Interview Navigator and enter the requested information.

For income from any other source, click **Other earned income** and fill out the form to describe each income source and the amount you received from each source.

# Still on Track?

At this point, you should have accounted for income from every source imaginable, and TurboTax should display an enormous amount for the taxes due. Fortunately, you'll begin to whittle down your income in Part 3, "Deductions, Credits, and Other Ways to Reduce Taxes," by claiming eligible deductions. Before you move on, however, make sure you've done all of the following to complete this chapter:

➤ Determined if the income you received from a partnership, S corporation, or estate is passive or nonpassive. See "Schedule K-1 for Partnerships, S Corporations, and Estates," on page 132.

➤ Reported any income or loss from a partnership reported to you on form K-1. See "Reporting Partnership Income and Losses in TurboTax," on page 134.

➤ Reported any income or loss from an S corporation reported to you on form K-1. See "Reporting Income from S Corporations," on page 136.

➤ Entered any income or loss from an estate or trust reported to you on form K-1. See "Lucky You! A Beneficiary of an Estate or Trust," on page 136.

➤ Reported any qualifying alimony payments you received as income and entered the social security number of your ex. See "Yes, Alimony Is Income," on page 137.

➤ Entered any income from scholarships, fellowships, or grants that qualifies as taxable income. See "Scholarships, Fellowships, and Other Freebies," on page 139.

➤ Entered income from any losses or bad debts you deducted in a previous year. See "Reporting Income from Losses Deducted in Past Years," on page 140.

➤ Entered any income you received by serving on a jury, even if you passed the money on to your employer. See "Raking in the Big Bucks from Jury Duty," on page 141.

➤ Received your honesty badge for reporting the fair market value of any product or service you received in exchange for another product or service you supplied. See "Bartering and Other Under-the-table Income," on page 142.

➤ Reported as income the five bucks you found in the parking lot and other income that didn't fall into any of the other categories on form 1040. See "Income That the Feds Didn't Even Consider," on page 142.

# Part 3

# Deductions, Credits, and Other Ways to Reduce Taxes

*We don't pay taxes. Only the little people pay taxes.*

*—Leona Helmsley*

*Filing a tax return is like haggling over prices at a Mexican market. You list your income, the IRS shoves a tax rate schedule in your face showing your tax liability, and the game begins. Now it's your move. Your job is to pare down that reported income to lower the adjusted gross income, which the IRS uses to calculate your tax. You do this by claiming deductions, including medical expenses, contributions, mortgage interest, business expenses, and capital losses.*

*After you've lowered your adjusted gross income and determined the amount of taxes due, you can reduce your tax liability even further by taking advantage of credits, such as credits for child care, the new child tax credit, and education credits.*

*If you claim enough deductions and credits to owe nothing in taxes, you get to join the ranks of the "big people" and hobnob with the likes of Leona Helmsley, but hopefully not in a federal prison.*

# Chapter 12

# Income Reduction Through Deductions

## In This Chapter

➤ Take advantage of the fact that your house is a money pit

➤ Learn why most people throw away their medical receipts

➤ Make charity begin at home with a deduction for your contributions

➤ Avoid paying taxes on your taxes

➤ Recoup some of the alimony you paid

The government treats each taxpayer as an insular business. It doesn't tax *all* your income. It taxes only your net profit, which the government refers to as your *adjusted gross income* (or AGI, for short). With that in mind, your goal as a taxpayer is to reduce your AGI for the year to the lowest possible level allowed by law. You do this by claiming deductions.

The government allows you to deduct all sorts of expenses, including the interest on your home, medical bills in excess of 7.5% of your AGI, charitable donations, alimony payments, property taxes, state and local taxes, and some unreimbursed employee business expenses. Unfortunately, the government doesn't allow you to deduct expenses for other essentials, such as food, gas, clothing, electricity, and fun stuff like vacations.

This chapter gives you a start on your deductions, showing you how to enter information about the major eligible deductions. Later chapters in this part cover minor deductions, major credits, and additional income and expenses you might have overlooked.

## Standard Deduction or Itemized Deductions?

The IRS gives you a choice. The first option is to take the standard deduction: $4,250 (individual), $6,250 (head of household), $7,100 (married filing jointly or qualified widower), or $3,550 (married filing separately). The other option is to *itemize* your deductions—come up with your own number based on your expenses. Obviously, the first option is easiest, but by taking it, you might shortchange yourself. Unless you're really lazy or you think that the government needs the money more than you do, at least try to itemize your deductions to determine if itemizing will help reduce your tax bill.

# It Pays to Own a Home

Your real estate agent just talked you into buying more house than you can comfortably afford. Every month, you stare at your mortgage statement in disgust, as you see your hard-earned dollars float away in interest payments. Your stomach cramps whenever you see how much you're paying in property taxes. When the toilet backs up, the roof leaks, and your lawn gives way to grubs, you begin to dream about the good old days when you rented an apartment.

Buck up, little homeowner. It's tax time. Now that money pit can actually help you save some money by giving you the big, fat deduction you need to make itemizing your deductions a worthwhile endeavor.

The following two sections explain the ins and outs of homeowner's deductions, to give you a realistic view of the tax breaks associated with owning a home. If you're in a hurry and none of this interests you, grab form 1098 and your property tax statement and meet me in the third section, "Entering Your Homeowner's Deductions in TurboTax."

## *What's Deductible, and What's Not*

Most people describe homeownership as a state of being somewhere between ecstasy and nirvana, especially when tax time rolls around. The truth is that unless you have a mortgage of more than $100,000 at more than 7% interest, your mortgage interest alone probably won't do you much more good than the $7,100 standard deduction. But it will give you a good start on your itemized deductions.

When you're looking at your home through deduction-colored glasses, here's what you'll see as allowable deductions:

➤ Mortgage interest—Any interest you paid on the money you borrowed to purchase your home is deductible.

➤ Points—If you paid points to reduce the interest percentage, those points are deductible in the year you paid them. The payment of points can become very complicated if the seller paid points on your mortgage or you paid points to refinance. See the next section, "More About Points," for details.

➤ Mortgage interest and points on a second home—Yep, you can own two money pits and get a real big deduction.

➤ Late payment charges—If you send in your payment late and have to pay a fee for it, count the fee as interest.

➤ Property taxes—If you paid property taxes or if your mortgage company paid your taxes out of an escrow account, those taxes are deductible. Don't deduct the entire amount you contributed to the escrow account; deduct only the amount that was paid in property taxes in 1998. This amount should be listed on the 1098 you receive at the end of the year.

➤ Interest on a home-equity loan—Long ago, the feds phased out deductions for interest on personal loans, except for mortgage interest. Two of the few remaining ways to get a tax deduction for money you borrow is to refinance your home or to take out a home-equity loan. You can use the money for anything, including paying off the balance on your high-interest credit cards.

➤ Business use of your home—If you run a business from your home, you might be able to deduct a portion of your mortgage interest, property taxes, utilities, and other home-related expenses as business expenses. See Chapter 7, "1099-MISCs and Schedule C (for the Self-Employed)," for details.

➤ Personal losses—If your home was damaged and the insurance didn't cover the cost of the repairs, you can claim the amount you paid out of your pocket as a casualty loss. Likewise, if someone stole stuff from your house that your insurance did not cover in full, you can claim the loss as a deduction. See "Taking the Bite Out of Thefts and Casualties in Chapter 13, "Additional Deductions You May Have Overlooked."

**Paying Interest Doesn't Pay**

Paying interest doesn't benefit you, even if it does give you a tax break. You'll receive bigger benefits and a sense of accomplishment by paying off your mortgage early.

## More About Points

Lenders commonly charge borrowers *points*, fees that the borrower must pay up-front to secure the loan. One point equals one percent of the loan amount. If you take out a $200,000 mortgage, one point would be $2,000. However, one point doesn't necessarily reduce the interest percentage by 1%. For example, a mortgage company may charge 2 points for a 1.25% interest reduction. To further confuse matters, a point may be used to reduce the interest percentage (in which case it is deductible) or be charged as a non-deductible service fee.

Deducting points can be very easy. If you purchased your home in 1998 and this is your primary or secondary residence, the deductible points (points paid as advanced interest to reduce the interest rate) are fully deductible in 1998. Points paid as a service charge are not deductible. The payment of points must conform to the following rules to qualify as deductible:

➤ You use your principal residence (main home) as collateral. When you purchase a home, you essentially give the lender the right to take possession of your home if you fail to pay off the loan.

➤ The practice of charging points is normal for your geographical area.

➤ The points paid do not exceed the average for your area.

➤ The points are calculated as a percentage of the loan amount and are designated as "points," "loan origination fees," or "loan discount" on the loan statement.

➤ You pay the points directly to the lender.

➤ You pay the points out of your pocket and not from any of the funds acquired through the loan. For instance, if you refinance a $90,000 mortgage for $92,000 and use the extra $2,000 to pay for closing costs and points, the points are not deductible.

In addition to those standard IRS conditions, there are several other twists and turns of which you need to be aware when deducting points:

➤ If you purchased a new home and the seller paid the points, you get to deduct them. The seller gets a break by deducting the amount of the points paid from the total price of the residence, thus reducing the reported profit from the sale.

➤ If you refinanced and paid points simply to reduce the interest rate on your mortgage, you must deduct the points over the life of the loan. For example, if you refinanced and took out a 15-year mortgage, you must deduct 1/15 of the points each year over the life of the loan. In the first and last years of the loan, you must prorate your deduction. For example, if 1/15 of the points you paid comes to $300 annually, and you secured the loan in July, 1998, then you deduct $25 per month for a total of $150 this year.

➤ If you refinanced to improve your home, you can deduct the points in full in 1998. If you used a portion of the money for something else, you can fully deduct a percentage of the points that's equal to the percentage of the money you rolled back into your home. For any money you did not use to improve your home, you must deduct the points over the life of the loan.

**Selling Your Home**

If you refinanced your home and have been deducting points over the life of the loan, when you sell your home you can fully deduct the remaining amount you paid in points.

## Entering Your Homeowner's Deductions in TurboTax

Fortunately, TurboTax can handle all the messy tax issues related to mortgage interest, points, and property taxes. Make sure you have the 1098 form from your bank or mortgage company along with your year-end property tax statement. Then, take the following steps to enter the required information:

1. Scroll down in the Interview Navigator and click **Deductions**. TurboTax displays a list of items that qualify as personal deductions.

2. Click the check box next to each deduction for which you qualify. If you're not sure, click the check box anyway. Click **Continue**.

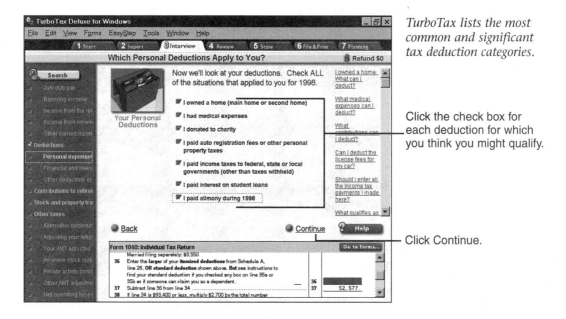

*TurboTax lists the most common and significant tax deduction categories.*

Click the check box for each deduction for which you think you might qualify.

Click Continue.

3. Click **Continue** and read through the information about mortgage deductions until TurboTax displays a list of check box options for forms you might or might not have.

4. Click the check box next to each option that describes the forms you have or the situation that applies to you. Click **Continue**.

5. For each 1098 form you received, type the name of the lender and the amount of mortgage interest and deductible points you paid. Click **Continue**.

6. Enter the amount you paid in real estate or property taxes on your main home and second home (if you have one). Click **Continue**.

Yep, that's it. TurboTax transfers the numbers you entered to the appropriate lines on Schedule A, totals your personal deductions up to this point, determines if your personal deductions exceed the standard deduction allowed for your filing status, and transfers the larger of the two numbers to form 1040. If you paid more in mortgage interest and points than the amount allowed for your standard deduction, you should see the taxes due number dip or the refund number increase.

*Enter the total amount of mortgage interest and deductible points you paid in 1998.*

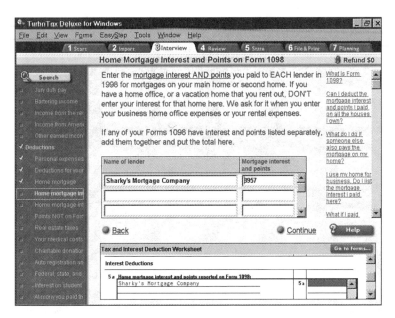

# Medical Deductions: Don't Get Your Hopes Up

You've been stuffing your medical receipts in a folder all year in the hopes that you'll get a big tax deduction at the end of the year. Well, unless you and your family members were really ill, don't expect too much. Before you can deduct a single penny, your medical and dental bills must exceed 7.5% of your AGI. For a modest AGI of $50,000, your medical bills would have to exceed $3,750!

## What's Deductible, and What's Not

In general, any payment you make to a licensed doctor, dentist, or medical professional (including chiropractors and eye doctors) and any expenses from *prescription* drugs are deductible. In addition, you can deduct 10 cents per mile for commuting between your home and the doctor's office or hospital, or the exact amount you spend to take a taxi or bus (include any expenses for parking fees, tolls, and lodging). You cannot deduct any of the following expenses:

➤ Health insurance premiums paid out of a cafeteria plan or medical savings account—You already received your tax break by paying these bills with pre-tax dollars.

➤ Over-the-counter medicines, such as aspirin—In case you haven't noticed, the government has been approving more and more medicines for over-the-counter sales. I wonder why?

➤ Elective or cosmetic surgery—Expenses for cosmetic surgery are deductible only if the surgery is performed to correct a congenital abnormality or disfiguring disease. Generally, liposuction and face-lifts don't qualify.

➤ Consultations with unapproved alternative healthcare physicians—The government does allow deductions for some alternative treatments, such as acupuncture.

➤ Stop-smoking and weight-loss programs—These are only deductible if prescribed by the doctor to treat a serious condition. For instance, if the doctor prescribes a stop-smoking program because you just had a heart attack, the expense is deductible. If the doctor signs you up for Weight Watchers because she thinks you're obese, the expense is nondeductible.

➤ Special diets—The government figures that you need to eat no matter what, so replacing one food with another doesn't entitle you to a tax deduction.

**Reimbursed Expenses**

The IRS gets really upset if you claim a medical expense for which you were reimbursed. If you paid for medical or dental care and your insurance company reimbursed you for it, it's no longer your expense. However, include reimbursed expenses in the total; TurboTax will subtract any payments you received from your insurance company from this value.

## *Entering Your Medical and Dental Expenses in TurboTax*

Although the deduction for medical bills is limited, don't give up. Get out your calculator and stack of medical and dental bills, and add them up. Don't forget to include the amount you paid for medical and dental insurance, assuming it wasn't paid out of a cafeteria plan or medical savings account. When you have the total, take the following steps to enter the numbers in TurboTax:

1. In the Interview Navigator, click **Your medical costs for 1998**.

2. If desired, click the **Play** button to check out the video clip. Otherwise, click **Continue**.

3. Type your medical expenses in the blanks and click **Continue**.

4. If you paid insurance premiums with after-tax dollars (not from a cafeteria plan or medical savings account), enter the amounts in the **Medical insurance premiums** and **Qualified long-term care premiums** text boxes.

5. If your insurance company or medical savings account reimbursed you for any of the expenses included in the amount you entered in step 3, enter the reimbursement amounts in the appropriate text boxes. Click **Continue**.

*TurboTax gathers information about your medical and dental expenses.*

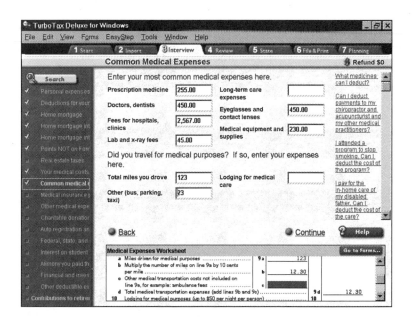

*Enter the amounts you paid for health insurance and the amount you received as reimbursement for expenses.*

Enter your health insurance premiums.

Enter the amount your health insurance company paid you to cover expenses.

Click Continue.

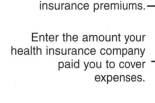

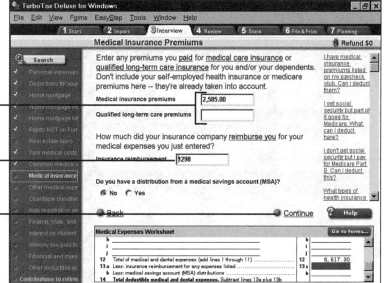

**6.** Enter descriptions and amounts for any other qualified medical expenses you paid in 1998 and click **Done with medical expenses.**

# When It's Better to Give Than to Receive

You've been generous this year, tithing to your church and giving donations to schools and other tax-exempt organizations. Now it's time to take advantage of the tax break you deserve. The only complicated part of claiming deductions for charitable contributions is in determining which organizations qualify as tax-exempt. In general, contributions to the following organizations are fully deductible:

➤ Churches and other religious organizations

➤ Federal, state, and local governments, not including taxes you paid (I know it's tempting)

➤ Nonprofit schools

➤ Public parks and recreational facilities

➤ Service organizations, such as the Red Cross, the Salvation Army, and Goodwill

➤ Girl Scouts and Boy Scouts

➤ War veterans groups

➤ Out-of-pocket expenses you pay when doing volunteer work for a nonprofit organization

### Up to 50% of Your AGI

If you give away more than 50% of your AGI (fat chance, right?), any amount over the 50% AGI limit is not deductible. For some organizations, including most war veterans groups, the limit is 30% of your AGI. Most people don't come close to these limits, but I thought I'd mention them.

To qualify as tax-exempt, the organization must file for approval (and receive it) from the federal government. If you have any questions concerning an organization to which you contribute, ask the organization to send you a copy of its tax exemption certificate. You can obtain a list of tax-exempt organizations from the IRS by calling 1-800-829-3676 or (if you have Internet access) by connecting to www.irs.ustreas.gov/ prod/search/eosearch.html and searching for the organization by name.

When claiming deductions for charitable contributions, it's your responsibility to keep detailed records of your contributions. To learn more about the types of records and receipts you need to keep, turn to "Reaping the Rewards of Your Donations," in Chapter 2.

To record your charitable contributions in TurboTax, take the following steps:

1. In the Interview Navigator, click **Charitable donations**.

2. If desired, click the **Play** button and dance to the little ditty about charitable donations. Otherwise, click **Continue**.

**3.** Click the check box next to the description of each type of donation you made: cash, non-cash, and volunteer expenses.

**4.** If you gave away more than $500 in non-cash items (for example, a truckload of stuff you dropped off at Goodwill or a valuable painting), click the corresponding option button. Click **Continue**.

**5.** If you made cash contributions, enter the name or a description of each organization and the total you contributed to each organization. Click **Continue**.

*Enter the name and contribution amount for each organization to which you gave a cash donation.*

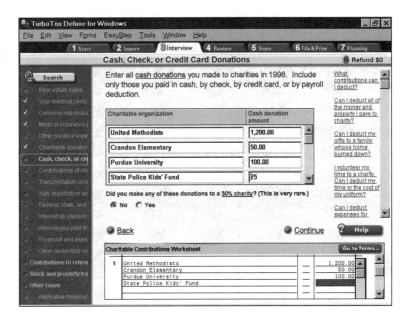

**6.** If you donated property to any organization, including clothes, capital gains from investments, paintings, or anything else of value, enter the name of the organization and the value of the donated item(s), and select the type of donation:

➤ **A** 50% donation—In this case, you could just leave the Type box blank. Most gifts to charity are covered by the 50% AGI limit. This doesn't mean you get credit for only 50 cents on a dollar. It affects you only if you give away more than half of your AGI.

➤ **B** 30% donation—This type of donation is rare, and is used only for some war veterans groups and nonprofit cemeteries.

➤ **C** Capital gain donation to 30% charity—This type of donation is for property that has increased in value since you purchased it. By donating the property, you get to deduct its fair market value and you don't have to pay capital gains tax on the amount that it increased in value.

➤ **D** Capital gain donation to 20% charity—This type of donation is the same as option C, but your donation deduction cannot exceed 20% of your AGI.

7. Click **Continue**.

8. If you put any mileage on your car commuting to or running errands in volunteer service, enter the number of miles and other travel costs you personally paid.

9. If you donated money in past years that you could not deduct because it was over the 30% or 50% limit, click **Yes**, click **Continue**, and enter the amount. Otherwise, just click **Continue**.

# Deducting the Taxes You've Already Paid

You pay taxes every day you live and breathe. The government levies taxes on the registration and license for your car, the gas you use to power it, most items you purchase, your house and the land on which it sits, and your income. In many cases, the government taxes your money twice. For instance, the government taxes your income, and later when you purchase gas for you car, the government taxes your purchase. In other cases, the federal government gives you a break by allowing you to claim a tax as a deduction.

In addition, if you sent estimated tax payments to the IRS or your state's revenue service, you must record those payments so that TurboTax can credit your bill. Although estimated taxes are not deductions, TurboTax lumps all these paid taxes together in the Interview, so make sure you have the records for your estimated tax payments on hand.

The following sections explain the deductible and non-deductible taxes you might have paid in 1998, provide a brief background on estimated tax payments, and show you how to enter the taxes you've paid in TurboTax.

## Deductible Taxes

I don't want to depress you, but there are a host of taxes you cannot deduct: auto license fees not marked as property taxes, pet licenses, taxes on cigarettes and alcohol, sales tax, utility taxes, tolls and users fees, and hunting and fishing licenses. The following list shows taxes you *can* include as personal deductions:

➤ Property taxes—You might have already entered the amount of property taxes you paid on your home. You can also deduct property taxes you paid for your recreational vehicles, including a boat or RV.

➤ Automobile license fees—You can deduct only the personal property tax amount listed on your registration. This amount is typically designated as "personal property tax" or "auto license fee." Most states don't charge a property tax on cars. If you leased your car, check with the dealer to find out how much of your bill was handed over as a property tax.

### 1998 Taxes Paid in 1999

When claiming a deduction for state and local taxes paid in 1998, you cannot deduct any payments you made in 1999. For example, if you submit your estimated tax payment for the fourth quarter of 1998 on January 15, 1999, that payment is deductible on next year's tax return, not on your 1998 tax return. Now, if you submitted a state or local estimated tax payment for the fourth quarter of 1997 at the beginning of 1998, you can deduct that amount on this year's return.

➤ State income taxes—You can deduct the amount of state income taxes you paid in 1998. If you received a state tax refund from a previous year in 1998, and you claimed a deduction in that year for the state taxes you paid (by itemizing), you must report that refund as income in 1998.

➤ Foreign taxes on interest and dividends—If you received a 1099-INT or 1099-DIV reporting gains from foreign investments, and you paid foreign taxes on those investments, you can deduct the taxes.

## Adjusting Your Tax Bill for Estimated Tax Payments

The government grabs its money before most taxpayers get to see it by withholding taxes from their paychecks. However, if you're self-employed or you have a good chunk of investment income, your withholdings might not cover your tax bill, and you could face a penalty when you file your tax return. To prevent this from happening, you should send estimated tax payments to the federal and state government quarterly.

If you didn't pay estimated taxes in 1998, there's not much you can do about it at this point. To plan for next year, see "Calculating and Paying Estimated Taxes," in Chapter 22, "Tax Planning for 1999." If you paid estimated taxes, don't expect the government to let you know how much you've sent in. Get out your checkbook and determine the total yourself. Then, move on to the following section to enter the amount in TurboTax.

## Entering Your Tax Payments in TurboTax

Whew! All these details about taxes you've paid and deductible and non-deductible taxes can make your head spin. Just grab your records and take the following steps to enter the numbers in TurboTax:

1. In the Interview Navigator, click **Auto registration and other personal property taxes**.

2. Enter the amount of personal property taxes you paid on your car or recreational vehicle. Click **Continue**.

3. Click the check box next to each item that describes the type of tax payment you made in 1998, including estimated taxes, taxes from previous years, and any fee you submitted to file for an extension. Click **Continue**.

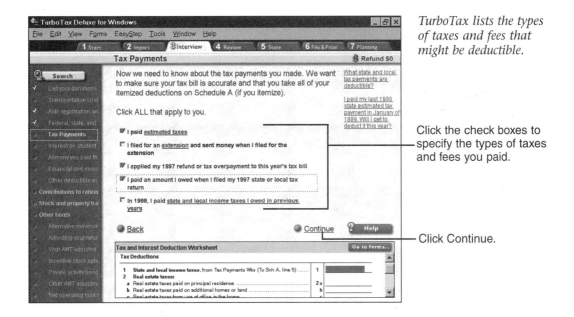

*TurboTax lists the types of taxes and fees that might be deductible.*

Click the check boxes to specify the types of taxes and fees you paid.

Click Continue.

4. If you clicked **I paid estimated taxes** in step 3, click the check box next to each type of estimated tax payment you made in 1998, including any estimated tax payment you submitted in 1998 to pay the fourth quarter estimated tax for 1997. Click **Continue**. (If you send in one estimated tax payment that is applied to both your state and local tax bill, do not check the box next to **Local for 1998**; include it as part of your state estimated tax payments.)

5. Enter the date and the estimated tax payment you sent to the IRS in each quarter (your federal estimated tax payments).

6. Click **Done with federal estimated taxes**.

7. Enter the date and the estimated tax payment you sent to your state's revenue service each quarter (your state estimated tax payments).

8. Click **Done**.

9. If you sent in separate estimated taxes to your county or local revenue service, enter the date and the estimated tax payment you paid each quarter (your local estimated tax payments).

10. Click **Done**.

11. If you paid your 1997 fourth quarter state or local estimated taxes in 1998, enter the amounts of those payments, specify the state or locality, and click **Continue**.

12. Proceed through the Interview to enter any additional information about filing fees for extensions, tax refunds to which you were entitled last year but chose to apply to this year's taxes, and any amount you had to pay when you filed your 1997 state and local tax return.

159

*TurboTax leads you through the process of recording your 1998 estimated tax payments.*

Enter the date on which you submitted the payment.

Enter the amount of the payment.

Click Done with federal estimated taxes.

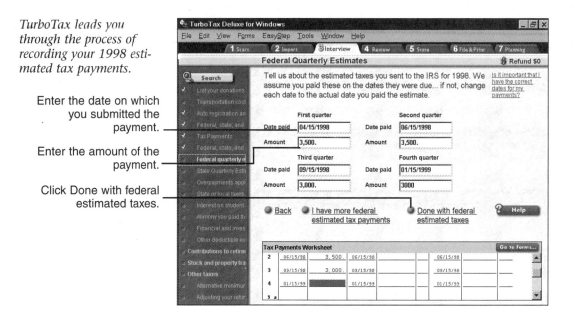

# Getting Back Some of Your Alimony Payments

You thought it was over after the judge granted the divorce. Little did you realize that the divorce was only the beginning. Now, you're sending a monthly check to your ex and kicking yourself for not drawing up a prenuptial agreement. To rub it in, your ex probably sends you a post card from a different Caribbean island each month.

Well, it's tax time, and although you can't get that money back from your spouse, you can report the payments on your tax return and reduce your tax bill. To enter the total you paid in alimony, scroll down in the Interview Navigator, click **Alimony you paid this year**, and click **Continue**. Type your ex's social security number (this is very important) and the total amount you paid to your ex in 1998. If you omit the social security number, you might face a $50 fine, risk losing the deduction, and not be able to pass Go and collect $200 or whatever the deduction might be.

# Still on Track?

At this point, you should begin to see the refund amount displayed in the upper-right quadrant of your screen steadily rising (or the taxes due steadily falling) as you claim deductions. Before you start thinking about additional deductions, make sure you've accounted for the major deductions covered in this chapter:

➤ Did you deduct mortgage interest and qualifying points you paid in 1998 on your first or second home? See "It Pays to Own a Home," on page 148.

➤ Did you report the total amount you paid in medical and dental bills, including your insurance premiums? See "Medical Deductions: Don't Get Your Hopes Up," on page 152.

➤ Did you account for all your charitable donations, including cash and non-cash contributions? See "When It's Better to Give Than to Receive," on page 155.

➤ Did you deduct any property taxes you paid on your car? See "Deductible Taxes," on page 157.

➤ If you paid estimated taxes, did you enter your 1998 federal, state, and local estimated taxes in TurboTax? See "Adjusting Your Tax Bill for Estimated Tax Payments," on page 158.

➤ If you're paying alimony as required by a divorce or separation decree, did you enter your total 1998 alimony payments? Did you remember to enter the social security number of your ex? See "Getting Back Some of Your Alimony Payments," on page 160.

# Chapter 13

# Additional Deductions You May Have Overlooked

---

### In This Chapter

➤ Deduct business expenses even if you're not self-employed

➤ Invest with borrowed money and deduct the interest

➤ Deduct losses from thefts or casualties—the IRS does care

➤ Lose your job, move, claim a deduction

➤ A handful of miscellaneous (yet legal) deductions

---

When you start talking with your friends and neighbors about taxes, it's easy to become annoyed. They'll tell you about the whopping refund they're expecting and brag about the godlike skills of their accountant. You begin to wonder how much they had withheld from their paychecks and where they came up with all those deductions. As you see the delivery guys dropping off a hot tub at the neighbor's house, you begin to suspect that they did something sinister, something very illegal.

And then you start thinking, "Why can't I do that?"

Well, this chapter doesn't tell you how to evade taxes, but it does reveal some deductions you might not have considered, deductions that are perfectly legal and legally correct. Think of this as the I-didn't-know-you-could-deduct-*that!* chapter.

# Business Expenses for Non-business Owners

Whatever you do for a living, you have some expenses that your company or organization doesn't pay for. Teachers buy pens, pencils, paper, boxes of tissues, grade books, software, and other supplies. Service people might have to purchase their own tools and pay to have their uniforms cleaned. In any occupation, you might have to pay union dues, purchase trade journals, or take courses to keep abreast of the current trends.

These expenses add up and can cut deep into your adjusted gross income, but are they deductible? That depends. Non-reimbursed employee business expenses are lumped with other miscellaneous expenses, and the total must exceed 2% of your AGI before you'll see any benefits. In addition, the expense must qualify as an actual business expense. Use the following list as your guide:

➤ Union dues—If the union dues are used for lobbying or other political activities, they are not deductible. In that case, you're just investing money to get a raise instead of to improve working conditions and improve your professional skills.

➤ Dues to professional organizations.

➤ Professional journals related to your occupation.

➤ Small tools required for you to perform your job.

➤ Professional licenses.

➤ Continuing education costs—The training classes or courses you take must help you keep working in the same field; they do not apply if they help you change careers. The idea here is the assumption that you already have a marketable skill, and it's not essential that you acquire a new skill to secure a livelihood.

➤ Job-related insurance, including malpractice insurance.

➤ Overnight travel expenses related to your job.

➤ Auto expenses or a mileage deduction for use of your car—You can't claim a deduction for commuting; but if you run errands, visit clients, or use your car to travel from one work site to another, you can deduct 32.5 cents per mile or a percentage of the actual cost of using your vehicle that's equal to the percentage you use the vehicle for business. See "Your Car Could Save You Some Cash," in Chapter 7, "1099-MISCs and Schedule C (for the Self-Employed)," for details.

➤ Uniforms—If your employer requires you to wear a uniform that you wouldn't be caught dead wearing outside of work, you can deduct the cost of the uniform and any money you spend to have it cleaned. If your employer simply has a dress code to ensure that everyone looks professional, you can't deduct the cost of your clothes or cleaning expenses.

➤ Safety equipment.

➤ Job hunting costs—These costs are deductible only if you're looking for a job in the same field, and this is not your first job. The feds have no sympathy for those who choose to change careers. (In addition, if you have been unemployed for a long period of time, your job hunting expenses might be disallowed.)

### Look at Your W-2

If your employer included the amount paid to you as reimbursements for expenses in Box 1 of your W-2 form, don't enter the reimbursement amounts again in TurboTax. You already entered them when you completed the W-2 worksheet. Otherwise, you'll be paying taxes twice on that money.

➤ Employee home office—Only if required by your employer for the convenience of your employer. For example, if your company requires that you telecommute, and you must sacrifice a portion of your precious living space and income to set up and maintain that office, it's a deductible expense. You can also deduct business-related phone calls and depreciation on a home computer or cellular phone, assuming you paid for them.

➤ Medical exams required by your employer—Most employers pay for these exams, but if you must pay out of your own pocket, take the deduction.

➤ Security clearance and bond fees—If you pay to become bonded or receive security clearance, the fees are deductible.

To deduct non-reimbursed employee business expenses, you must complete form 2106, Employee Business Expenses. Never fear—the TurboTax Interview will ask you all the right questions and plug in the numbers where they need to go:

1. In the Interview Navigator, click **Other deductible expenses**.

2. Click the check box next to **I paid for business expenses related to my employment**. While you're at it, click the check box next to any of the other options that apply to you. Click **Continue**.

3. Enter any qualifying expenses you paid out of your own pocket for union dues, subscriptions, uniforms, or job searches for your current occupation. Click **Continue**.

*TurboTax displays one screen after another of employee business expenses.*

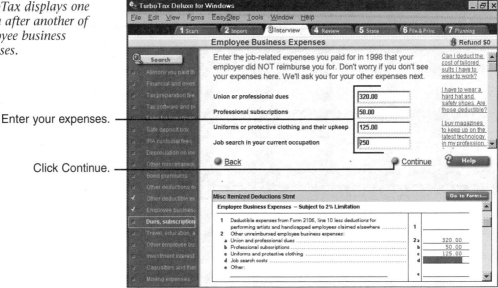

Enter your expenses. ————

Click Continue. ————

4. If you paid and were not reimbursed for any job-related expenses including travel, entertainment, education, business use of your car, or a home office, click **Yes**. Otherwise, click **No** and skip to step 16.

5. Type a brief description of your occupation (for example, **Plumber**) and click **Continue**.

6. Enter any job-related expenses you paid for business gifts or education, and click **Continue**. (If you are married filing jointly, you must also specify whether the expenses are for your job or your spouse's job.)

7. If you have any assets you used to perform your job (a car, computer, tools, machinery), click the check box next to each situation that applies to you. Click **Continue**.

8. Proceed through the Interview and enter information for all the job-related assets you own or have sold in 1998. To learn more than you probably want to know about depreciation, see Chapter 8, "Depreciating Your Old Stuff."

9. When you're done entering information for all your job-related assets, click **No, done with assets**.

10. If you sold one of the assets, follow the Interview to record information about the sale of the asset. TurboTax will determine your net profit or loss from the sale and include it in your return.

11. If you indicated that you want to claim the home office deduction, the next screen introduces this deduction. Click **Continue**.

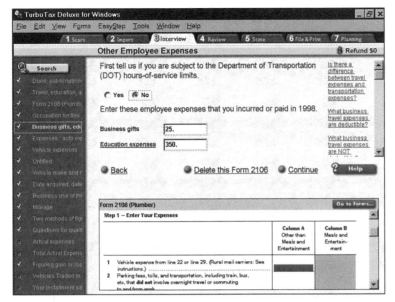

*Enter your job-related expenses.*

12. The Interview introduces some of the disadvantages of claiming a home office deduction and asks if you still want to claim the deduction. If you do, click **Yes**.

13. Enter your address, click **Continue**, and answer the questions posed by the Interview. See "SOHO Deductions for the Home Office," in Chapter 7 for details. When you're done, click **No, done with home office**.

14. Enter any job-related parking fees, overnight travel expenses, or expenses for meals and entertainment for which you were not reimbursed, and click **Continue**.

15. If you have any additional job-related expenses, enter a description for and the amount of each expense. Click **Done with employee business expenses**.

# Saving a Little on Your Investment Loans

On Wall Street, you can be heavily in debt, but as long as you can get your fingers on a loan, you can profit considerably (or lose your shirt). When you borrow money to invest in any moneymaking venture, the government allows you to deduct the interest you paid on your debt.

### Tax-Free Bonds and Tax-Deferred Accounts

If you borrow money and use it to purchase tax-free bonds or to invest in an IRA or other tax-deferred account, the loan interest is not deductible.

The only catch is that you can deduct interest only up to the amount of income you made through your investment. So, if your investments broke even or lost money, you're out of luck. However, you can carry over interest deductions from one year to the next; for example, if your investments broke even in 1997 and you paid interest on money you borrowed for those investments, you can deduct the unclaimed interest in 1998.

To enter the amount of interest you paid on investment loans, take the following steps:

1. In the Interview Navigator, click **Investment Interest Expense**.

2. When asked if you have any investment interest to deduct, click **Yes**.

3. Type any investment interest you paid on money borrowed to purchase or create something from which you received royalty income.

*Enter the amount of interest you paid on money borrowed to purchase each investment.*

Enter any investment interest you paid to acquire royalty property.

Enter a description of the investment.

Type the amount of interest you paid.

Click Continue.

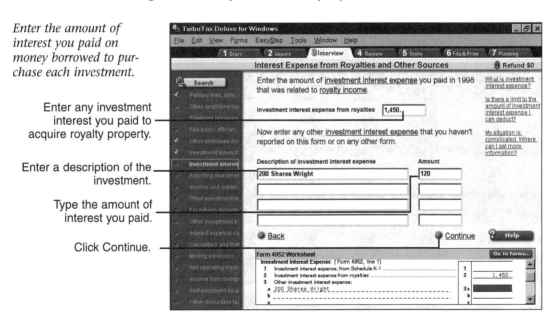

4. In the text boxes for investment income expenses, type the name of each investment and the amount you paid on the money you borrowed to purchase the investment. Click **Continue**.

5. If you have any alternative minimum tax interest expenses, enter the expenses and click **Continue**.

6. In the rare case that you have investment income from a business that is not a passive activity and in which you did not materially participate, enter your income and expenses from the business. Click **Continue**.

7. If you have any other investment *income*, enter a description of each investment income source and the amount you received. (You should already have entered these amounts in Chapter 6, "1099s for Interest, Investments, and Capital Gains.") Click **Continue**.

8. Enter any alternative minimum tax adjustments that apply to you and click **Continue**.

9. Proceed through the Interview to enter any additional information about investment expenses and adjustments, until you reach the Carryover screen.

10. If you had any investment interest that you could not claim in 1997 due to limitations, enter that amount and click **Done with investment expenses**.

# Taking the Bite Out of Thefts and Casualties

When someone rips you off or a natural disaster turns your dream home into a big box of toothpicks, you can deduct a portion of your loss on Schedule A. Here's what you need to know:

➤ The catastrophic event must be sudden, unexpected, and unusual. The fact that your 30-year-old plumbing had to be replaced or termites chowed down on your house is a *gradual* disaster. Disasters from volcanic eruptions, tornadoes, hurricanes, fires, and just about anything else that's been covered in a Hollywood movie is considered sudden, unexpected, and unusual.

➤ You must automatically subtract $100 from each loss. If someone stole your $300 mountain bike, the most you could possibly deduct would be $200.

➤ You must automatically subtract 10% of your AGI from your total losses. If your AGI is $80,000, you can claim losses only in excess of $8,000. In short, your loss on that $300 mountain bike is *your* loss unless you've had additional losses that can boost you over the 10% AGI hump.

➤ You must subtract any insurance payments you received as reimbursement for the loss.

**Keep Records**

If you suffered a qualifying loss, get some proof. For thefts, a police report is sufficient. For natural disasters, keep any insurance records, newspaper clippings, and bills for repairs. Take pictures. Better yet, videotape your residence inside and out and all your valuable possessions, and store the tape in a safe-deposit box, just in case anything happens. When disaster strikes, videotape the devastation (assuming your camcorder survived the disaster).

➤ Your loss is based on your basis in the property or its fair market value, whichever is less. For instance, if someone stole the computer for which you paid $3,000, but the value of the computer when it was stolen was only $1,000, you deduct $1,000 minus $100 minus 10% AGI. Don't hold your breath.

➤ If the loss is business related, go back to Chapter 7, and deduct your loss as a business expense and you might actually get a break. Don't include it as an itemized deduction on Schedule A, where losses are so limited.

To enter your losses from casualties and thefts, take the following steps:

1. In the Interview Navigator, click **Casualties and thefts** and click **Continue**. TurboTax displays a caution telling you to stop if you're claiming a loss from business assets.

2. To claim your personal property losses, click **Continue**. TurboTax displays some introductory information about form 4684, Casualties and Thefts.

3. Click **Ready to start Form 4684**.

4. Proceed through the Interview to enter the requested information for each loss, including a description of the item, its value, and any amount you were reimbursed for it.

You can record up to four losses on form 4684. If you have additional losses, the Interview will lead you through the process of creating the additional forms you need.

# The Relocation Allocation: Moving Expenses

You just moved out to sunny southern Florida. Can you deduct your moving expenses? Maybe. If you moved out there because you're company relocated or because that's the only place that hires alligator wrestlers, you can deduct your moving expenses. But the move must meet the following conditions:

➤ Your move must be job related—If you moved to a better school system or because you've always wanted to live in San Francisco, you can't deduct your moving expenses. The trick is to always link your moves to a job change or relocation.

➤ You must move at least 50 miles—Add 50 miles plus the distance (in miles) your old house was from your old job. You must move at least that far from your old house to your new house.

➤ You must work at the new job for at least 39 weeks—Assuming you're an employee, you must work full time for at least 39 weeks at the new job for the 12 months you live in the new home. If you're self-employed, you must work full time for 39 weeks of the first 12 months *and* 78 weeks of the first 24 months.

➤ Exception for workers living in foreign countries—If you work in a foreign country and decide to retire in the States, you can deduct your expenses for moving back to the States, even if the move is not job-related.

If your moving expenses qualify, you can deduct only the cost of moving your belongings from your old home to your new home and the costs of travel and overnight lodging required for expediting the move. In addition, if your move is job-related, make sure you deduct any qualifying job search expenses, as explained previously in this chapter in the section "Business Expenses for Non-business Owners." If you pay for temporary lodging while your house is getting built, that's not deductible.

To enter your moving expenses, take the following steps:

1. In the Interview Navigator, click **Moving expenses**, and then click **Continue**.

2. Read through the list of conditions that make it unnecessary to file form 3903 and click **Continue**.

3. Type the name of the new company that hired you (or type **Self-employed**) and click **Continue**.

4. Click the check box next to each option that relates to your moving expenses, to ensure that your moving expenses are deductible. Click **Continue**.

5. Assuming you've met the time requirements explained earlier, click **Yes**, **I pass the time test**.

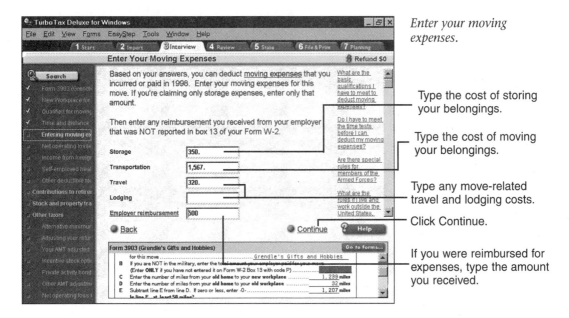

*Enter your moving expenses.*

Type the cost of storing your belongings.

Type the cost of moving your belongings.

Type any move-related travel and lodging costs.

Click Continue.

If you were reimbursed for expenses, type the amount you received.

6. Enter the number of miles that your old home is from your new workplace and the number of miles from your old home to your old workplace. Click **Continue**.

7. Enter the expenses you incurred for storage, transportation, travel, and lodging and the amount your new employer reimbursed you for these costs. Click **Continue**. TurboTax displays a summary of your moving expenses.

8. Click **Continue**.

9. Assuming you have no other moving expenses to report, click **No, I'm done with 3903**.

# In the Hole? Claim a Net Operating Loss

When your personal expenses exceed your income, you can pretend that you're a business and claim a net operating loss (NOL, for short). This is a pretty rare and complicated tax issue that's best handled by a qualified accountant. In most cases, a person suffers an NOL when a business the person owns loses more money than the person earned as income from the business and any other sources.

To claim an NOL, go to the Interview Navigator, click **Net operating losses**, and follow the Interview. To take advantage of the NOL, you must first divvy up the loss over the past three tax years. Then, you must project the remaining loss forward over the next 15 years. In short, you don't get to deduct the loss completely in 1998. Don't worry—TurboTax will serve up the required forms and help you fill them out.

# Still on Track?

At this point, your Schedule A should be packed with enough deductions to lift you over the standard deduction hump. If not, you can at least celebrate the fact that you're healthy, haven't lost much from theft or casualties, and don't own more house than you can afford. In addition, the following chapters help you trim more from your tax bill. For now, make sure you've done the following:

➤ Taken advantage of your employee business expenses for which you were not reimbursed. See "Business Expenses for Non-business Owners," on page 164.

➤ Accounted for any interest on loans used for investments. See "Saving a Little on Your Investment Loans," on page 167.

➤ At least attempted to take a deduction for any losses from casualties or thefts. See "Taking the Bite Out of Thefts and Casualties," on page 169.

➤ Determined if your moving expenses qualify as deductible, and entered your deductible moving expenses in TurboTax. See "The Relocation Allocation: Moving Expenses," on page 170.

➤ Determined if you experienced a net operating loss in 1998 and, if you did, completed the required forms in TurboTax. See "In the Hole? Claim a Net Operating Loss," on page 172.

# Chapter 14

# Getting a Tax Break with Retirement Investments

## In This Chapter

➤ Maximize your long-term investments by using tax-free dollars

➤ Learn the difference between a standard and a Roth IRA

➤ SEP, KEOGH, and other tax-saving acronyms

➤ Push the contribution limits for tax-deferred investments

➤ Add your medical savings account to your retirement plan

At some point in your life, you might consult with a personal financial manager. This person will take two hours to tell you three things: draw up a budget, pay off your credit card debt, and *pay yourself first.* The pay-yourself-first rule doesn't mean you should treat yourself to a shopping spree or buy a new car. Paying yourself consists of setting aside a fixed amount of money each month or each paycheck for investments. By investing, you use your money (instead of your valuable time) to make money.

Although you can invest your money in numerous ways, investments fit in two general categories: taxed and tax-deferred. If you're investing to earn income that you can spend right away or in the near future, the government taxes the money you invest and any income you earn from the investment. With tax-deferred investments, the government doesn't tax the money you contribute or the income you earn from the investment until you start taking the money out.

### April 15, 1999 Deadline

You can contribute to your retirement account up until April 15, 1999 and claim the contribution as a deduction on your 1998 tax return. This can increase your refund enough to take the sting out of the contribution or significantly reduce the amount of taxes you owe.

### Stick with Your Employer's Plan

Because the IRS rules for IRAs are fairly complex and could cause you to inadvertently contribute beyond the limit that is deductible, it makes sense to invest as much as possible in an employer's plan before you invest any additional money in an IRA.

Because the government has a hands-off policy when it comes to tax-deferred investments, IRAs and other types of tax-deferred accounts have become the most popular tools for building future wealth. This chapter shows you how to put these tools to work for you and take advantage of the tax savings in 1998 and beyond.

# Traditional IRAs: Save Now, Pay Later

This whole tax-deferred investment party began with IRAs (individual retirement accounts). According to Congress, the idea behind IRAs is to enable taxpayers to set up their own retirement savings plans when their employers offer no retirement benefits. (I suspect the real reason Congress set up IRAs is because it knew that social security was going to go bust, and it wanted to cushion the blow—but I can't prove it.)

At any rate, IRAs and other tax-deferred plans do enable individuals and couples to set aside money before taxes and watch their investments grow tax-free. Before you rush out and set up an IRA, read through the following sections to make sure you qualify and to determine how much you can contribute to it each year.

## *Sorry, You Don't Qualify*

Any taxpayer with more than $2,000 in income or alimony may contribute up to $2,000 to an IRA, but part or all of that $2,000 might not qualify as deductible. In general, if you are not covered by an employer's retirement plan, you can deduct the full $2,000. BUT, it's not that simple. The IRS has rules:

➤ You must have income in the form of a regular salary, commissions, tips, self-employment earnings, or alimony. If your sole source of income is from investments, you don't qualify.

➤ If you're single, covered by a retirement plan, and your modified AGI is less than $30,000, you qualify. If your modified AGI is between $30,000 and $40,000, your contributions are limited, as explained in the following section. Anything over $40,000, and you no longer qualify. If you are not covered by a retirement plan at work, ignore this rule.

➤ If you're married filing jointly, only one of you is covered by a retirement plan, and your modified AGI is less than $150,000, the person who is not covered by a retirement plan gets a full $2,000 deduction. If your combined AGI is between $150,000 and $160,000, your contributions are limited. If your AGI is over $160,000, you're out of luck. Again, if neither of you is covered by a retirement plan at work, each of you can contribute up to $2,000 (completely deductible) to an IRA.

To calculate your modified AGI, fill out the following form:

| | |
|---|---|
| Enter your AGI from line 32 of your 1040. | 1_____ |
| Add your IRA contribution. | 2_____ |
| If you worked in a foreign country, add the income you earned from that job. | 3_____ |
| If you had interest on Series EE savings bonds, add the exclusion you claimed from form 8815. | 4_____ |
| If you received adoption assistance, add the exclusion you claimed. | 5_____ |
| Write down the total. This amount is your modified AGI. | 6_____ |

## Contribution Limits

The maximum deductible amount you can possibly contribute to an IRA is $2,000. However, if you fall into one of the categories described in the previous section, your deductible contributions might be limited. The first limitation is based on your AGI—your IRA contribution cannot exceed your AGI. Like that's gonna happen!

The second limitation comes into play only if your modified AGI falls in the gray (*phaseout*) area: $30,000 to $40,000 for singles or $150,000 to $160,000 for married couples. If your income falls in this range, fill out the following form to determine your maximum deductible IRA contribution:

| | |
|---|---|
| Enter one of the following: $40,000 if single or $160,000 if married filing jointly. | 1_____ |
| Enter your modified AGI (as calculated in the previous section). | 2_____ |
| Subtract your modified AGI (line 2) from the value on line 1. | 3_____ |
| Divide the amount on line 3 by $10,000. | 4_____ |
| Multiply the amount on line 4 by $2,000. This is the largest deductible amount you can contribute to your IRA. If you're married, each person can contribute this amount. | 5_____ |

# 401(k), SEP, Keogh, and SIMPLE Retirement Contributions

Although IRAs get all the press, their limitations and complicated rules have made them nearly obsolete. More and more companies are offering their own retirement plans in the form of 401(k)s or SIMPLE (Savings Incentive Match Plan for Employees) plans, and self-employed individuals can set up their own SEP (Simplified Employment Pension) or Keogh accounts. All these options enable you to contribute amounts that are way beyond the IRA contribution limits. The following list provides brief descriptions of these retirement plans:

**Keogh Deadline**

You can contribute to an existing Keogh plan as late as April 15, 1999 and deduct your contribution. However, the plan must have been set up by December 31, 1998 or you're out of luck.

**Change Jobs? Rollover!**

When you change jobs or resign and become self-employed, do NOT take your money out of the company's retirement plan until you have another retirement plan in which to put it. Then, complete the necessary paperwork to rollover funds from one plan to the other. If the plan writes you a check, they're required to deduct 20% in taxes from the amount.

➤ 401(k)—401(k)s are typically set up by companies employing more than 100 workers as a way to provide employees with non-taxed, deferred pay. With a 401(k) plan, you can make a tax-deductible contribution of up to $10,000 per year to the plan. In addition, most companies offer matching contributions of 50 cents or more for every dollar you contribute, up to 6% of your salary.

➤ SIMPLE—SIMPLE plans are 401(k)s for small companies (those employing fewer than 100 workers). Your contribution to a SIMPLE plan must be determined as a percentage of your salary and cannot exceed $6,000 per year.

➤ SEP—A Simplified Employee Pension plan is ideal for individuals who are self-employed and don't want to wrestle with a lot of paperwork. With an SEP plan, you can contribute up to 15% of your net self-employment income minus your SEP contribution and half of your self-employment tax up to $24,000. This works out to a little over 13% of your net earnings.

➤ Keogh—Keogh plans are complicated SEP's with higher limits. You can make deductible contributions of up to 25% of your net self-employment income minus your Keogh contribution minus half of your self-employment tax, up to $30,000. This works out to about 20% of your net earnings.

If you're an independent contractor or small-business owner, you should set up an SEP, SIMPLE, or Keogh plan immediately, even if you don't have much money to invest. If you earn more in a particular year than you ever imagined you would, these plans can help you keep that hard-earned cash. Consult with a personal financial manager, accountant, or mutual fund company to learn how to set up your account.

# I Invested Too Much. Now What?

After reading about all about the deductible limits on your retirement contributions and realizing that you can deduct only a portion of your contributions, you might feel as though you've been scammed. Don't fret. Although your contribution might not be fully deductible, your investment earnings are not taxed until you withdraw the money. In short, contributing more than is deductible is not bad, as long as you don't exceed the absolute limit (for instance, $2,000 for an IRA).

If you make contributions beyond the amount that's deductible, keep a record of your contributions and list the deductible and nondeductible portions of your contributions. You must submit form 8606, Nondeductible IRAs—Contributions, Distributions, and Basis, with your tax return to report the nondeductible portion of your contribution. TurboTax will automatically create this form for you, if necessary, and fill in the required information.

**$2,000 IRA Limit**

Under no circumstances can you contribute more than $2,000 to an IRA in a single year. Any additional money you contribute is called an *excess contribution*, subject to a 6% penalty. To avoid the penalty, withdraw any excess contributions (and any earnings from those contributions) before the April 15th filing deadline and report the amount you withdrew as income. TurboTax will help determine if you made excess contributions based on the information you enter.

# Roth and Education IRAs: Pay Now, Save Later

In an effort to further inflate stock prices, Congress has given taxpayers two new IRAs: the Roth IRA (named after Senator William Roth, Jr.) and the Education IRA. Unlike the standard IRA, which allows you to make tax-deductible contributions, these IRAs do not provide you with an immediate tax benefit. However, the IRA's earnings grow untaxed and you can withdraw your money untaxed if your withdrawals meet the required conditions.

## Roth IRAs

Although standard IRAs are still the best way to set aside retirement income, Roth IRAs provide a good way to save some money if you're planning on buying your first home five years from now, need some tax-free cash in your early retirement years, or you want to set up your own life-insurance policy.

Individuals can contribute up to $2,000 per year in a Roth IRA, and if you keep the money in the account for at least five years, you can withdraw it without paying taxes on your withdrawals under the following conditions:

➤ You use the money to purchase your first home. You can withdraw up to $10,000 tax-free. (This rule holds for standard IRAs, too.) The IRS has some specific conditions for qualifying as first-time home buyers, so consult with an accountant to determine if you qualify.

➤ You reach age 59 1/2. This rule makes the Roth IRA excellent for the first few years of retirement. By drawing tax-free dollars from your Roth IRA, you can leave money in your standard IRA or other retirement accounts so it can continue to grow.

➤ You are disabled.

➤ You die. Why would you care about this? Well, you can shovel money into a Roth IRA and use it as additional life insurance.

**Laws Change**

When you plan for the future, realize that laws change. Currently, you can withdraw money tax-free from a Roth IRA when you reach the age of 59 1/2, but if the U.S. has a budget crisis somewhere down the road, you can bet your bottom IRA dollar that the laws will change to allow that money to be taxed.

There are some limitations on how much you can contribute to a Roth IRA. First, your contributions to a standard IRA and Roth IRA cannot together exceed $2,000. To qualify for the full $2,000, your modified AGI must be less than $95,000 (if filing singly) or $150,000 (if married filing jointly). If your modified AGI is above $110,000 (filing singly) or $160,000 (married filing jointly), then you don't qualify. If your AGI is anywhere in between, you're in the phaseout range and must calculate your allowable contribution as discussed earlier in this chapter.

## Education IRAs

Personally, I think the best way to save for education is to not save at all. Put some money aside for retirement, keep a little in savings, and by the time your kids are old enough for college, things will work out. If you're rich, you can pay for their schooling. If you're poor or your kids are real smart or are great athletes, they'll get scholarships, grants, or other financial aid. If they need a little extra, they can get low-interest loans.

The trouble is that the more we all save for education, the more the educational institutions jack up their costs, and the less likely it is that individual students will qualify for assistance. Just think about it, if your kid has $30,000 in education IRAs, do you think your kid will get one dime's worth of assistance until the institution milks that fund dry? Of course not.

Well, so much for the sermon. If you're worried about the high costs of education, then you can set aside some money in either of two ways (but not both):

➤ Contribute to a qualified state tuition program—In short, you pay tuition in advance and then your child withdraws it tax-free to pay for tuition costs. Read the fine print. If your kid decides to join the circus instead of going to college, you might lose a little money.

➤ Contribute to an education IRA—You can contribute up to $500 per child per year. The contribution is nondeductible, but the investment grows tax-free until your child withdraws the money for tuition, books, and other fees.

# Medical Assistance Via MSA

A medical savings account (MSA, for short) is a relatively new (circa 1997) scheme that enables you to make tax-deductible contributions to an account and then use those tax-free dollars to pay your medical bills. Think of it as another way to circumvent that 7.5% AGI hurdle you have to leap before you get to deduct any of your medical expenses.

Like a cafeteria plan or FSA (flexible spending account), an MSA enables you to pay medical bills with pretax dollars. Unlike a cafeteria plan or FSA, an MSA is not subject to the "use it or lose it" rule. This enables you to use the funds in your MSA as supplemental retirement income.

Of course, every tax deduction comes with a set of rules and limitations:

➤ You must have a health insurance plan with a high deductible—at least $1,500 for individual coverage or $3,000 for family coverage.

➤ The most you can contribute to the MSA per year is 65% (single) or 75% (family) of your coverage.

➤ Amounts you withdraw for qualifying medical expenses are tax-free.

➤ Amounts you withdraw for nonqualifying expenses are subject to both income tax and a 15% penalty. Ouch!

➤ If your situation changes and you become covered by another health plan, anything left in the account is subject to income tax and the 15% penalty. At this point, it's best to spend as much of the money as you can on new glasses, braces for your kids, and other qualifying medical and dental expenses.

➤ At age 65, you can withdraw the funds for any purpose. Withdrawals are subject to tax but no penalties.

# Entering Your Retirement Contributions

If you contributed to a retirement plan in 1998 or want to test the waters and see the effect of a contribution on your tax return's bottom line, take the following steps:

1. In the Interview Navigator, click **Contributions to retirement plans, IRAs and MSAs**.

2. Click the check box next to each type of retirement account you contributed to in 1998. Click **Continue**.

3. If you made an IRA contribution, you can play the video (if desired); then, click **Continue**.

*TurboTax lists the retirement account types.*

Click the check box next to each type of retirement account in which you invested.

Click Continue.

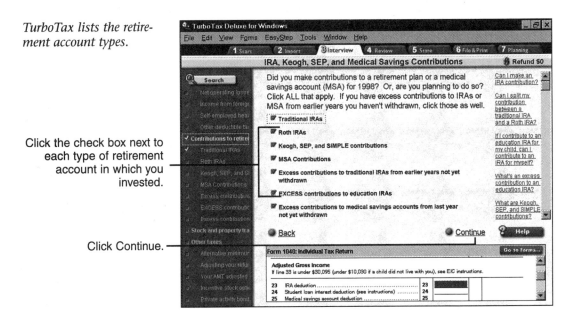

4. If you or your spouse (if you're married) contributed to a standard IRA in 1998, read the introductory blurb and click **Continue**.

5. Enter your contribution and your spouse's contribution (if you're married) to a standard IRA in 1998.

6. If you transferred any funds from your standard IRA to a Roth IRA, enter the amount transferred in the **Recategorized contribution** text box.

7. Enter your basis in the IRA as of the end of 1997. This is the non-deductible amount you contributed from the time you started the IRA to the end of 1997, not counting any earnings that were reinvested. (This amount should be listed on the 1997 form 8606, line 12.) Click **Continue**.

8. Answer any additional questions to indicate if you or your spouse was covered by an employer's retirement plan. TurboTax uses this information to determine

the amount of your contribution that is deductible. Click **Continue**. If you indicated in step 2 that you contributed to a Roth IRA, TurboTax asks the amount you contributed.

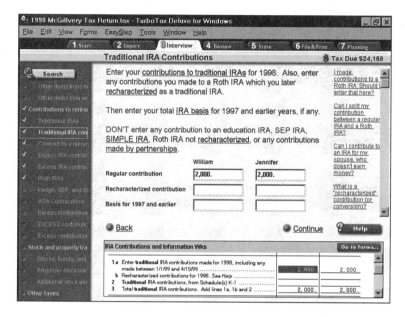

*TurboTax collects the information about the contributions you made in 1998.*

9. Enter the amount of your contribution for you and your spouse (if you're married). Click **Continue**, and respond to any additional questions about your Roth IRAs.

10. If you (or your spouse) contributed to an SEP, Keogh, or SIMPLE plan, click the check box next to the name of each person who contributed and click **Continue**.

11. Click in the text box for the type of plan to which you contributed and enter the total amount of the contribution. (If you plan on investing additional money by April 15th and want to claim a deduction for it in 1998, be sure to include the amount in the total and make sure you actually deposit that money by April 15th.) Click **Continue**.

12. If the Interview prompts you to enter an adjustment to your self-employment income, enter the desired adjustment and click **Continue**. (This is rare, but if you're running two businesses and one suffers a loss while the other turns a profit, you might need to enter a number to offset the loss and provide yourself with a higher limit for your deductible contributions.)

**Biggie Size It!**

To have TurboTax determine the maximum amount you can contribute to a Keogh or SEP plan based on your earnings, click the **Maximize** check box next to the type of plan in which you participate.

*If you invested in an SEP, SIMPLE, or Keogh plan, enter the amounts here.*

Enter the amount you contributed.

Click the Maximize check box to have TurboTax calculate your maximum deductible contribution.

Click Continue.

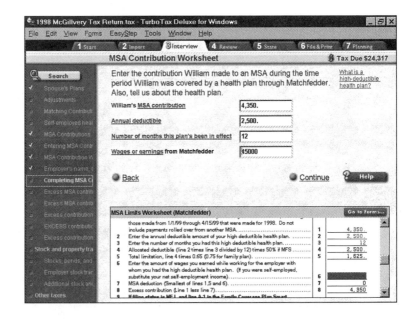

**13.** To enter any MSA contributions you made in 1998, click **MSA Contributions** in the Interview Navigator.

**14.** When asked if you made any contributions to an MSA in 1998, click **Yes** and click **Continue** until you reach the Employer screen.

**15.** Enter the employer's name or your name (if you're self-employed) and click **Continue**.

*Enter the total amount you contributed to your MSA in 1998 (or the amount you will contribute by April 15, 1999).*

**16.** Enter your deductible, the number of months you've had the health plan, your income, and the type of coverage: Self or Family. Click **Continue**.

**17.** Enter your total contributions for 1998 and any part of 1999 up to April 15th, the annual deductible, the number of months the plan has been in effect, and your wages or earnings from this employer. Click **Continue**.

**18.** Assuming this is the one and only MSA to which you contributed, click **No, I'm done with the worksheets**.

## Still on Track?

Contributing to a tax-deferred retirement account is one of the best ways to build wealth for your future. If you haven't contributed this year, there's still time. Get a hold of some money and contribute it by April 15th. Then, make sure you've taken the following necessary steps to claim your deduction:

➤ Determined if you qualify for a tax-deductible contribution to a standard IRA. See "Sorry, You Don't Qualify," on page 174.

➤ Determined your limit on tax-deductible contributions to a standard IRA. See "Contribution Limits," on page 175.

➤ Figured out how to contribute a higher percentage of your income by starting your own retirement plan. See "401(k), SEP, Keogh, and SIMPLE Retirement Contributions," on page 176.

➤ Figured out what to do if you made excess contributions to your retirement account. See "I Invested Too Much. Now What?," on page 177.

➤ Understood the benefits of Roth and Education IRAs over standard IRAs and vice versa. See "Roth and Education IRAs: Pay Now, Save Later," on page 177.

➤ Discovered an additional way to save on taxes with an MSA. See "Medical Assistance Via MSA," on page 179.

➤ Recorded any contributions to retirement or medical savings accounts in TurboTax. See "Entering Your Retirement Contributions," on page 180.

# Chapter 15

# More Income and Loss Via Stock and Property Transactions

> **In This Chapter**
>
> ➤ Account for profits and losses from the stuff you sold
>
> ➤ Calculate profits and losses from sales
>
> ➤ Account for depreciation of your assets
>
> ➤ Sell your house, make lots of money, and avoid taxes
>
> ➤ Sell your business and claim the profit or loss

You've been buying stuff for years—a house, furniture to fill your house, land, stocks, equipment, tools, and anything else that you just couldn't pass up when you walked down the sales aisle. Your portfolio is a mess, your house is packed, and you currently rent an entire strip of storage units out in the country.

When you decide to start clearing things out and selling off your possessions, you might need to pay taxes on any profits or want to claim deductions for your losses. This chapter deals with the tax issues involved in the sale of property and assets, including your home, and shows you how to enter profits and losses in TurboTax.

## Calculating Your Profit or Loss

You would think that calculating a profit or loss would be easy. You bought a computer for $3,000, sold it for $500, and lost $2,500, right? You bought a car at an auction for $2,500, sold it for $6,700, and made a profit of $4,200, correct?

Well, that's not exactly the case.

### What About Sales Tax and Shipping?

When calculating the cost basis of an asset, include sales tax, shipping, installation charges, and any other expenses directly related to the purchase and setup of the asset.

The purchase price is only the beginning. This is the asset's *cost basis*. To this amount you must add the cost of any improvements and additions you made to the property. For example, you might have installed a new hard drive and more memory in the computer before you sold it, or you might have built a sun room on the back of your house before putting it on the market. This gives you the asset's *revised basis*.

No, you're not done yet. Now, you must deduct any depreciation expense you claimed for the asset over the life of the asset. This gives you the asset's *adjusted basis*. If you completely depreciated the asset or claimed its entire cost (and the cost of improvements) as a Section 179 expense, the adjusted basis is zero and the money you received when you sold the property is taxable profit.

To determine your profit or loss on a sale, you subtract the adjusted basis from the asset's selling price. If the number is positive, you made a profit and must report the profit as income. If the number is negative, you suffered a loss and might be able to claim the loss as an expense or deduction.

# Direct Sales: Property, Stocks, and Bonds

Chapter 6, "1099s for Interest, Investments, and Capital Gains," shows you how to report income from the sale of stocks, bonds, and other investments, assuming you received a 1099 reporting your profit or loss. In this section of the Interview, TurboTax double-checks to make sure you have entered this information and reported any income from the sale of investment property. Take the following steps:

1. In the Interview Navigator, click **Stock and Property Transactions**. The Interview displays a long list of items related to profit or loss from investment sales.

2. Click the check box next to each item that describes an asset or investment you sold in 1998. Click **Continue**.

3. If you had any transactions related to your employer's stock purchase plan, click the check mark next to each type of plan and click **Continue**. Read the blurb about employee stock purchase plans, and click **Continue**. Otherwise, click **No employer's stock plan transactions** and skip to step 8.

4. Click the check mark next to each type of transaction you made—**I PURCHASED stock...** or **I SOLD stock...**—and click **Continue**.

5. Enter the requested dates of the transactions: the date the stock was available, the date you purchased it, and the date you sold it (if you sold it). Click **Continue**.

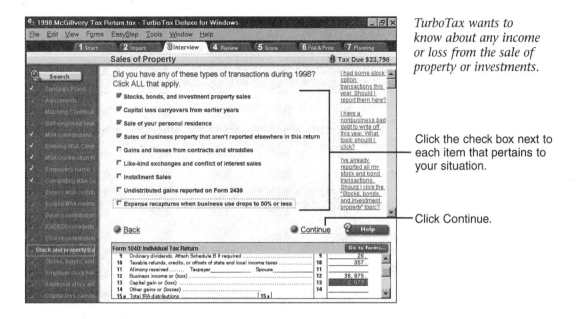

*TurboTax wants to know about any income or loss from the sale of property or investments.*

Click the check box next to each item that pertains to your situation.

Click Continue.

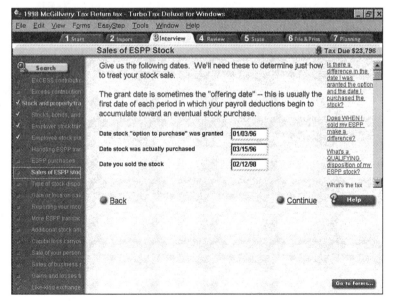

*If you purchased stock through your employer and sold it, enter the requested information.*

**Disqualifying Disposition**

A *disqualifying disposition* is the total amount you received as a discount on the stocks you purchased through your employer's plan. This is recorded as income on your W–2. How the IRS came up with this term, I don't know.

6. Enter the requested amounts to specify the number of shares you sold, the market price of the stock, the price you actually paid, and the total amount you received from the sale of the stock. Click **Continue**. TurboTax calculates and displays your net gain from the sale.

7. Click **Continue**.

8. If you have any other stock, bond, or investment income to report that you had not entered in Chapter 6, enter the requested information for each transaction, including a description, the dates you purchased and sold the stock or investment property, the purchase and sale price, and the type of transaction.

9. Click **Done with this stock sale**.

# Capital Loss Carryovers from 1997

Whenever you have a capital loss from the sale of investment property or stocks, you can claim your loss as a deduction, up to $1,500 (if single) or $3,000 (if married filing jointly). If your total capital loss exceeds the limit, you can carry that loss over to the next year.

If you used TurboTax last year and transferred information from last year's return, TurboTax automatically carries over the nondeductible portion of your capital losses to this year's return. If you did not transfer information from last year's return, this amount should be listed on last year's return. To carry over capital losses, take the following steps:

1. In the Interview Navigator, click **Capital loss carryovers from earlier years**.

2. Enter the long-term and short-term capital losses you want to carry over from 1997 into the appropriate text boxes.

3. Click **Done with capital loss carryovers**.

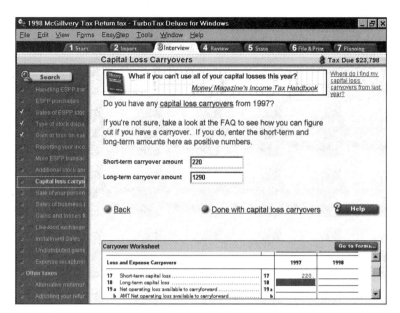

*If you couldn't deduct capital losses on your 1997 tax return, deduct them on this year's return.*

# Did You Sell Your Home Last Year?

One of the best investments you can make, purchasing a home, just got better. The average home not only provides you with a place to live, increases in value nearly 10% annually, and provides self-employed taxpayers with additional deductions, but also the profit from the sale of a home is no longer taxed, up to $250,000 (if you're single) or $500,000 for married couples ($250,000 for each qualifying spouse). Of course, there are a couple rules:

➤ Only your primary residence—If you have a second home or vacation home, the profit is taxed.

➤ Two of the last five years—You must have lived in your home for two of the last five years. If you purchase a home, live in it for 18 months, and sell it, you must report your profit as income.

➤ Exceptions—If your move is job- or health-related, the two-year rule is waived and you can prorate the exclusion. For instance, if you lived in the house for 12 months, the exclusion is half: $250,000 for married couples or $125,000 for singles.

**Keep Your Receipts**

Whenever you pay for a home improvement, keep your receipts. These receipts are your proof that you invested additional funds in your home and helped reduce the reported profit from the sale of the home. You might not think you'll see a $500,000 profit from your home, but if you got a good deal on your home and stay put for 20 years, your profit might exceed that amount, the law might change, or your state might levy a tax on the sale.

189

Your real estate agent should be able to determine if you need to report the sale of your home. If you must report the sale, your real estate agent should issue you a form 1099-S containing the numbers and dates you must enter.

## Calculating Your Net Profit

When you sell your home, you don't determine your profit simply by subtracting what you paid for the home from its sale price. You must determine your *adjusted basis* in the home, including the amount you paid for it plus the following expenses:

**Business Use of Your Home**

If you used a portion of your home as an office or rental property and were *entitled* to depreciate that portion of your home (whether you deducted for depreciation or not), you must treat the sale of the business portion of your home separately. You subtract the depreciation from your adjusted basis in the property, thus increasing your net profit on that portion of your home. This profit is taxable income. Don't worry about the details. If you claimed a deduction for the business use of your home, TurboTax handles all the details.

➤ Inspections—The cost of home and termite inspections you paid for when purchasing the home you're selling add to the adjusted basis of the home.

➤ Loan fees—If you paid any fees to secure your mortgage, including a credit report or escrow fee, add those fees to the adjusted basis of the home.

➤ Reports and recording fees—If you had to pay for a title policy, appraisal, or other report, the cost is added to the adjusted basis of the home.

➤ Real estate commission—If you purchased the home through your real estate agent, the agent might have charged you a commission. If the seller paid the commission, you cannot include it as part of the adjusted basis of the home. However, when you sell the home, you can deduct the amount you paid in commissions as part of the cost of selling the home.

➤ Home improvements—Improvements (not repairs) include room additions, landscaping, fencing, garage, wall-to-wall carpeting, central air conditioning, and appliances. You cannot add the cost of normal repairs and maintenance. For example, installing central air conditioning in a house that never had it adds to your adjusted basis in the home, but replacing an old central air conditioning system does not.

You further decrease your net profit from the sale by subtracting the costs of preparing the home for sale and selling the home. Following is a list of common expenses:

➤ Painting

➤ Planting flowers

➤ Decorating

➤ Repairs

➤ Real estate commission

➤ Recording fees

➤ Legal fees

To determine your net profit from the sale of your home, take the sales price minus your adjusted basis in the home, minus expenses for preparing the home for sale, minus the cost of selling the home.

## Entering the Sales Figures in TurboTax

If you sold your home in 1998, chances are you won't have to pay taxes on your profit. However, you must enter information about the sale in TurboTax, so it can determine if tax is due and complete the required forms. To enter information about the sale of your home, take the following steps:

1. In the Interview Navigator, click **Sale of your personal residence**.

2. If you received a form 1099-S from your real estate agent, click **Yes, I received Form 1099-S**. Otherwise, click **No, I did NOT receive Form 1099-S** and answer the questions to determine if you must report the sale of your home.

3. Click **Continue**.

4. Type the address of the home you sold and click **Continue**.

5. Answer the questions posed by TurboTax to determine if you must report the sale of your home under the old tax rules, and then click **Continue**.

6. To take advantage of the $250,000 or $500,000 exclusion, click **Yes, I want to use the exclusion**. (If you prefer to pay more income tax, click **No, I'll skip the exclusion and report my gain**.)

7. Type the date on which you purchased the home and the date on which you sold it. Click **Continue**.

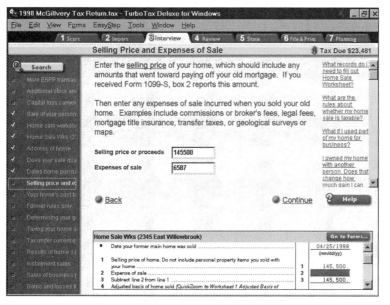

*Enter the sale price and expenses you paid to sell your home.*

191

8. Enter the sale price of the home and any expenses you paid to sell the home, including real estate commissions, legal fees, and title insurance. Click **Continue**.

9. When asked if you want to complete the worksheet for determining the basis of your home, click **Use the worksheet to figure my tax cost**.

10. Enter the original cost of the home (what you paid for the home, not including improvements) and any postponed gain from the sale of your previous home. For example, if you made $20,000 from selling a home five years ago and chose to carry over that gain, enter it here. Click **Continue**.

11. Proceed through the Interview to enter the information TurboTax needs to determine the net profit from the sale. At the end of the grilling Interview, TurboTax displays the adjusted basis of your home.

### Postponed Gain

When you sell your home and purchase a new home of equal or greater value, you may carry over your profit indefinitely until you purchase a home of lesser value or decide not to purchase a home. The government taxes your profit only when you have the actual profit in hand. If you carry over a profit from a previous sale, this is added to the profit from the sale of your current home. With the new tax law allowing you to earn $250,000 or $500,000 on the sale of a home without paying taxes, carrying over profits is nearly obsolete. However, if you sold a home you owned for less than two years, you might want to carry over the profit.

12. Continue with the Interview to specify how you want to report the profit from the sale of your home and complete this section of the Interview. Using your answers and filing status, TurboTax determines if the profit is taxable and completes the required forms.

13. When you're done, click **No, done with home sales**.

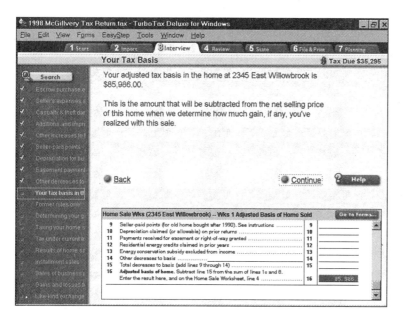

*When you're done entering the requested information, TurboTax calculates the adjusted basis of your home.*

# Profit or Loss from the Sale of Business Property

Nobody can say that TurboTax isn't thorough. If you have a business or farm, you already entered information about your business assets earlier in the Interview, including information about the disposal (sale) of any assets. However, if you sold an asset that didn't quite conform to the questions earlier in the Interview, the Interview wants to know about it:

1. In the Interview Navigator, click **Sales of business property that aren't reported elsewhere**.

2. Click **Continue with sales of business property**.

3. Click the check box next to each type of business property you sold: **Property Class 1** or **Property Class 2**. Click **Continue**.

4. Click the option to specify whether or not the property was sold at a gain. If you clicked **Yes**, proceed to step 5. If you clicked **No**, go to step 12. (Keep in mind that you calculate gain by subtracting the adjusted basis of the property, including depreciation, from the sale price.)

5. Type a description of the property and click **Continue**.

### Section 1231 Gains and Losses

Section 1231 applies to the gains and losses from special business assets, such as timber, coal, iron ore, crops that were not harvested, and livestock used for draft, breeding, dairy, or sporting purposes. In short, unless you are a person who participates in these types of businesses, you can probably ignore this part of the Interview.

6. Enter the date you acquired the property, the date you sold it, the price at which you sold it, the price you paid for it, and the depreciation you claimed over the years you owned it. Click **More about this sale**.

7. Click the option that best describes the type of property and click **Continue**.

8. If you used the ACRS or MACRS method of depreciation, enter any excess depreciation you claimed on this property after 1975. Click **Continue**.

9. Answer any additional questions to help TurboTax determine if you are recording this sale as a result of a casualty or loss and whether you sold the asset on an installment basis. (If a business asset is stolen or destroyed, you can claim your deduction by recording the disposition of the asset as a sale.)

10. To enter information about the sales of other business assets, click **Yes, more gain properties to enter** and repeat steps 5 to 9. Otherwise, click **No, done entering gain property sales**.

11. Click **No, I'm done with special property gain sales**.

12. Enter a description of any Class 2 property you sold (at a gain or loss) and any Class 1 property you sold at a loss, the date you acquired it, the date you sold it, and the sale price. Click **Enter cost and depreciation**.

13. For each asset you entered in step 12, enter the cost of the asset, any amounts you claimed for depreciation in previous years, and the type of sale. Click **Done entering Class 2 sales**.

14. If you have any Section 1231 losses from previous years that you could not deduct because you had no Section 1231 gains to offset the losses, enter the losses. Click **Done with business property sales**.

# Other Profits and Losses

At the end of the property-and-stock-transactions section of the Interview are four transactions that you probably already have entered earlier in the Interview or that don't apply to you. However, you should check them out in case you overlooked them earlier:

➤ Gains and losses from contracts and straddles—Gains and losses from contracts are reported on form K-1 for partnerships and S corporations. Gains and losses from straddles should be reported on form 1099-B. If you have a profit or loss from a contract or straddle that was not reported to you, enter the information here.

➤ Like-kind exchanges and conflict of interest sales—A like-kind exchange is a transaction without gain or loss that consists of swapping two assets that are in the same asset category (for example, you trade your condo in Bermuda for a condo in Florida). A conflict of interest sale is a transaction you're forced to make because you received a certificate of divestiture from the Office of Government Ethics.

➤ Installment sales—If you sell something and agree to have the buyer pay you in installments rather than all at once, you can choose to report the payments as income when you receive the payments rather than at the time of the sale. By recording the sale as an installment sale, you can spread out your reported income from the sale over two or more years.

➤ Undistributed gains reported on form 2439—If you received form 2439 from a trust fund that does not pay distributions on capital gains, report the capital gains here.

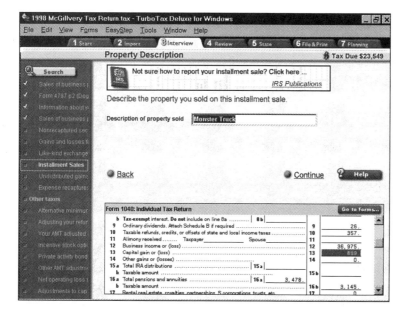

*Got any other income or losses?*

## Still on Track?

If you sold anything for a profit in 1998, TurboTax should now have the information it needs to calculate your profit and report it on your income tax return, so you can pay additional taxes. The next chapter brings more bad news, introducing additional taxes that might apply to your situation. Before you move on, make sure you've done the following:

➤ Calculated the net profit from the sale of an asset. See "Calculating Your Profit or Loss," on page 185.

➤ Reported profits or losses from the sale of stocks, bonds, and property for which you did not receive a form 1099. See "Direct Sales: Property, Stocks, and Bonds," on page 186.

➤ Accounted for any capital loss carryovers that were nondeductible in previous years. See "Capital Loss Carryovers from 1997," on page 188.

➤ Entered the income or loss from a sale of your primary residence. See "Did You Sell Your Home Last Year?," on page 189.

➤ Entered your income or loss from the sale of business assets. See "Profit or Loss from the Sale of Business Property," on page 193.

➤ Accounted for gains or losses from any additional transactions, including contracts and straddles, installment sales, and sales resulting from a conflict of interest. See "Other Profits and Losses," on page 194.

# Chapter 16

# More Taxes (As If You Weren't Paying Enough)

---

### In This Chapter

➤ Taxes for people who are rich enough to hire a nanny, chauffeur, and other helpers

➤ Self-employment taxes—another reason to find a real job

➤ The alternative minimum tax, for those with too many deductions

➤ Richie Rich's guide to the kiddie tax

➤ More taxes for those who just don't pay enough

---

TurboTax isn't done yanking money out of your wallet. Just when you thought you had accounted for all your taxable income and taxes due on that income, the TurboTax Interview hits you with a second round of taxes. Not only must you pay taxes on the money *you* earn, but you might also have to pay taxes on the unearned income of your kids, chip in extra to cover social security and Medicare if you're self-employed, and pay FICA for any household employees. And if you claimed *too much* in deductions, you might come face to face with the evil alternative minimum tax.

This chapter explains these additional taxes and provides a few techniques for limiting the amount you must pay. As for the taxes that you cannot avoid, this chapter shows you how to enter the required information in TurboTax, so it can properly calculate your tax burden.

# Paying for the Hired Help: The Nanny Tax

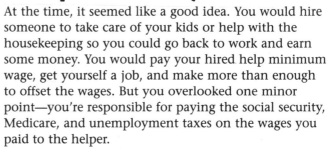

**Your Withholding Must Cover the Cost**

Although the feds don't require you to submit quarterly payments for your household employees, your withholding and estimated tax payments must be sufficient to cover the bill. Otherwise, you're charged a penalty at tax time.

At the time, it seemed like a good idea. You would hire someone to take care of your kids or help with the housekeeping so you could go back to work and earn some money. You would pay your hired help minimum wage, get yourself a job, and make more than enough to offset the wages. But you overlooked one minor point—you're responsible for paying the social security, Medicare, and unemployment taxes on the wages you paid to the helper.

Welcome to the nanny tax.

If you paid someone more than $1,100 to work in your home (or as your chauffer or groundskeeper) in 1998, you owe the government 15.3% in taxes on those wages. In addition, if you paid the person more than $1,000 in any quarter, you must pay federal unemployment tax. You do have the option of withholding half the money from your employee's paycheck to pay these taxes, but it's your door the IRS is going to knock on if these taxes aren't paid.

**Check Your Insurance Coverage**

If you hire someone to work in your home, make sure your insurance policy covers household employees. If Junior bites the nanny and your nanny decides to sue, you could lose a lot of money.

## *Calculating the Wages Subject to Social Security and Medicare*

The only difficult part about paying social security, Medicare, and federal unemployment (FUTA) taxes for your employees (in addition to coming up with the money) is calculating the amount of wages that are subject to these taxes:

➤ Social security wages—Add up the wages you paid to all employees to whom you paid more than $1,100 in 1998. (If you withheld taxes from the pay, include the amount you withheld.) Omit the wages of any employees who earned less than $1,100, payments to your kids under the age of 21, and payments to students under the age of 18. If you paid anyone more than $68,400, subtract the amount that's over $68,400. That's the maximum amount of income that the government taxes for social security.

➤ Medicare wages—Add up the wages you paid to all employees whom you paid more than $1,100 in 1998. (If you withheld taxes from the pay, include the amount you withheld.) Omit the wages of any employees who earned less than

$1,100, payments to your kids under the age of 21, and payments to students under the age of 18. Unlike social security, Medicare taxes have no upper wage limit, so all pay (even over the $68,400 social security limit) is taxable.

➤ Federal unemployment wages—The first $7,000 in wages paid to any household employee is subject to federal unemployment tax. To determine the total amount due, add up all the wages paid to all employees whom you paid over $1,100 in 1998, excluding all those wages you excluded when determining the amount due for social security.

### State Unemployment Taxes

Check with your state's tax office to determine if you must submit quarterly unemployment contributions for your household employees. Although the IRS does not require you to pay quarterly, most states do.

The government allows you to come up with the money for paying social security and Medicare taxes in either of two ways. You can withhold half of the amount due from your employees' paychecks or pay the taxes in full yourself. The second option is a little easier; you simply pay the person a little less and foot the bill for the taxes. If you pay the full amount yourself, you must include the employee's share of these payments (7.65%) as income when determining the amount of social security and Medicare tax that's due.

### Hiring Through an Agency

If you hire the nanny or other household worker through an agency and you pay the agency, the agency is the employer and is responsible for paying the tax.

## Entering Information About Household Employees in TurboTax

The good news is that you don't have to mess with separate tax returns for reporting wages for your household employees, and you need not submit quarterly reports and payments for social security and Medicare. You can enter it on your 1040 by completing Schedule H in TurboTax:

1. In the Interview Navigator, click **Other taxes**, make sure **Taxes for household employees (the Nanny Tax)** is checked, and click **Continue**.

2. Click **Continue**.

3. If you paid any one person more than $1,100 (excluding your spouse, your kids under the age of 21, or a student under the age of 18) to work in your home in 1998, click **Yes**. Otherwise, click **No** and pour libations to the tax gods.

4. Enter your federal employer identification number. (You get one of these by filing a form SS-4 with the IRS. If you're in a hurry to submit your return, apply for the ID number and type **Applied for** in the blank.) Click **Continue**.

5. Enter the wages that are subject to social security tax and Medicare tax, any amount you withheld from the pay to pay these taxes, and any advances you paid to employees as advances on earned income credit. Click **Continue**.

Enter the total amount subject to social security tax.

*TurboTax gathers the information it needs to determine taxes due for your hired hands.*

Enter the total amount subject to Medicare.

Enter any amount withheld from your employee's pay to pay taxes.

Enter any earned income advances you paid.

Click Continue.

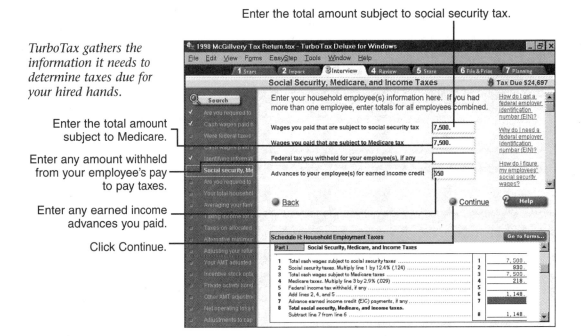

### Hire a Kid

Wages you pay to your kids under the age of 21 or students under the age of 18 are exempt from the nanny tax.

6. If you paid more than $1,000 to any household employee in a single quarter of 1998, click **Yes** and continue to step 7. Otherwise, click **No** and skip to step 9. The Interview asks you three questions about how you paid unemployment taxes in 1998.

7. Click the option buttons to answer the questions about how you paid unemployment taxes for 1998. Click **Continue**.

8. Enter the requested information about the state to which you paid unemployment taxes, including the amount you paid. If you did not pay state unemployment taxes, fill in as much information as possible and leave the last box blank. Click **Next state**.

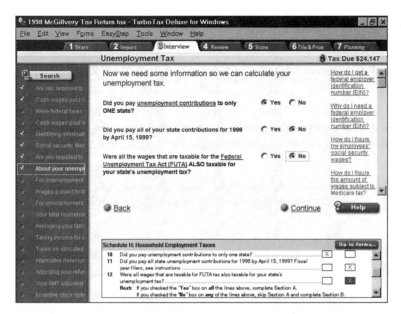

*If you paid any state unemployment taxes for household workers, answer these questions.*

9. Enter the total wages you paid to household employees that is subject to FUTA tax. Click **Continue**. TurboTax displays the amount of additional tax you owe.

10. Click **Done with household employment taxes**.

# The Increased Tax Burden for the Self-employed

When my employer gave me the opportunity to become self-employed, I was elated. No more commuting. No more office politics. No more trying to look busy when the boss passed by my office. Working at home would bring the freedom I always wanted and break the shackles that chained me to corporate America.

Then, I looked closely at my taxes. The 28% income tax bracket didn't bother me too much. I would certainly have enough deductions to cover my income tax bill. It was that other number, the 15.3% in self-employment taxes that would surely kill me. 28% plus 15.3% was 43%! How could the government possibly get away with that?! And why did so many of my friends and relatives believe that being self-employed was a *good thing*?

Well, it's not quite that bad. The IRS does give you a little break by allowing you to deduct half of the self-employment tax you pay from your gross income, so at least you don't have to pay income tax on your self-employment tax, but the bite still hurts.

If there's anything positive to say about self-employment tax, it is that if you must pay it, TurboTax probably already calculated the amount due and rolled it into the total taxes you owe. To check out the bite that self-employment tax takes out of your income and enter any other income that might be subject to self-employment tax, take the following steps:

1.  In the Interview Navigator, click **Other taxes**.

2.  Click the check box next to **self-employment tax** and click **Continue**. TurboTax displays the amount it calculated that you owe in self-employment tax and asks if you have any other self-employment income that might be subject to self-employment tax.

*Your self-employment tax can significantly add to your tax bill.*

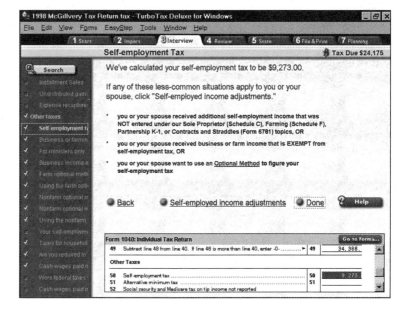

3.  To enter additional self-employment income that you have not yet reported, click **Self-employed income adjustments** and proceed with step 4. Otherwise, click **Done**.

4.  Enter any self-employment income or income from farming that you had not reported earlier and click **Continue**. TurboTax updates the amount of self-employment tax and displays the result.

5.  Click **Done with self-employment tax**.

### Why Is the Self-employment Tax So Much?

When you have a normal job, your employer pays half of your social security, Medicare, and federal unemployment tax, which comes to 7.65% of your income. Your employer withholds the other 7.65% from your paychecks. When you're self-employed, you act as employer and employee, and the government socks you with a bill for the whole 15.3%.

# What's with This Alternative Minimum Tax?

You worked for two sleepless days, tracking down every deduction imaginable, and managed to match each dollar in income with a dollar in deductions. Your tax bill is zero and every penny your employer withheld in taxes, every penny you sent in estimated taxes, is now on its way home to daddy, right?

Wrong!

To prevent rich folks from claiming too much in deductions and losses, as well as close some of the gaping loopholes in the current tax code, Congress cooked up the alternative minimum tax (or AMT). I guess it was just too much trouble to come up with something logical like a flat tax. At any rate, if your deductions exceed certain pre-established limits, the AMT kicks in to make sure you're paying income tax. Any of the following deductions or income might put you at risk of facing the AMT:

➤ Deductions for home equity mortgage interest not used to improve your home

➤ Deductions for taxes you paid

➤ Excessive depreciation deductions

➤ Medical and dental expenses exceeding 10% of your AGI

➤ Incentive stock options that your company paid you as alternative income

➤ Legal fees associated with tax-sheltered farm activity

➤ Losses claimed from some passive-activity sources, such as an oil or mining business

➤ Excessive deductions for charitable donations of valuable property

### Defer Deductions

The only way to avoid the AMT is to defer deductions for those items that could trigger an AMT. For example, if you are claiming a large Section 179 expense, depreciate your assets rather than claim the depreciation all at once.

Of course, TurboTax determines (from the information you entered) if you might need to pay the AMT. To check out what TurboTax has determined and to enter any additional information if you do qualify, take the following steps:

1. In the Interview Navigator, click **Alternative Minimum Tax (AMT)**. If TurboTax has determined that you are probably not subject to AMT, TurboTax displays a message asking if you want to complete form 6251 now to report additional information.

2. If you think you may be subject to AMT, click **Yes** and proceed to step 3. Otherwise, click **No**, and you're done.

3. If desired, click the **Play** button to watch the video clip about AMT. Then, click **Continue**.

4. Enter the amount of mortgage interest you paid on money borrowed for anything but home improvements. (The information that TurboTax prompts you to enter might vary, depending on the entries in your return.) Click **Continue**.

*TurboTax can calculate the AMT you must pay, if any.*

Enter the amount of mortgage interest for money you didn't use to improve your home.

Click Continue.

5. If you entered the sale or exchange of any asset other than those recorded under Business, Rental, Farm, Installment Sales, or Schedule K-1, enter the gain/loss difference for AMT purposes and click **Continue**. (Click the **gain/loss difference** link for details.)

6. If you exercised any incentive stock options that were not reported to you on a form K-1, enter the total discount you received when you purchased the stock (the market value of the stock minus the amount you paid for it). Click **Continue**.

7. Enter any adjustment or tax preference amounts that apply to the AMT, as shown in the following figure. Click **Continue**.

8. Enter any net operating losses you are carrying over from prior tax years to your 1998 return and any adjusted net operating loss for AMT. (The adjusted net operating loss adds any miscellaneous deductions and tax payments that contribute to your net operating loss, to reduce the reported loss.) Click **Continue**.

9. Enter any required AMT adjustments to short- or long-term capital gains or losses. Click **Continue**.

10. Enter any required AMT adjustments for Section 1250 capital gains and click **Continue**.

11. If prompted, enter any required AMT adjustments for capital gains you chose to report as investment income. Click **Continue**.

12. If you reported paying any foreign taxes, enter any AMT adjustments for those deductions and click **Continue**.

13. TurboTax displays the AMT you owe. Click **Done with AMT**.

**More Questions?**

These steps lead you through the basic Interview sequence for reporting information needed to calculate your AMT. However, the Interview process might ask different questions depending on the information contained in your return.

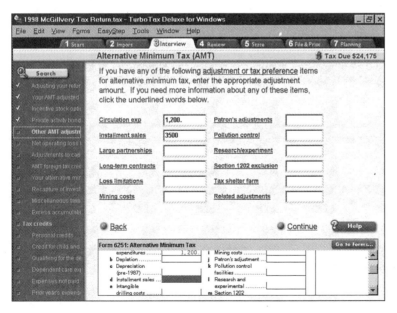

*Enter amounts for any tax preference items that apply to your situation.*

# Paying Your Children's Taxes: The Kiddie Tax

When your kid can't even keep his room clean and he's pulling down $20,000 a year, the government gets a little suspicious. They think that maybe you rich parents are trying to avoid taxes by shifting your income to your kids. But you wouldn't think of doing *that*, would you?

To discourage parents from shifting the income to their children, the tax code requires you to report a child's income in excess of certain amounts on your tax return and pay taxes on that income. Here are the tax rules that apply to a child's income:

➤ Your kid must file his own return if there was federal income tax withheld from the child's pay, the child paid estimated taxes for 1998, or the child overpaid taxes in 1997 and chose to apply the excess to the 1998 tax bill.

➤ If your kid must file a tax return, he gets a standard deduction of $700. Or, your kid can itemize deductions on Schedule A.

➤ If your kid is under the age of 14 and makes more than $1,400 in interest or investment income, he must pay income tax on the excess amount at your tax rate. If your child has no earned income, the first $700 of unearned income is not taxed, the second $700 is taxed at the child's rate, and any amount over that is taxed at your highest marginal tax rate.

➤ If your kid is 14 years or older, the kid can file his own tax return and pay taxes separate from yours.

## Shifting Income Can Hurt You Later

When you shift your income to your kids, it shows up as their savings. If your child applies for financial aid to attend a college, the financial aid office is going to look at your kid's net worth and expect your kid to contribute his share of tuition and expenses. Most financial aid programs expect students to contribute a higher percentage of their savings than they expect from the parents.

In most cases, you're better off having your child file a separate return. When you include your child's income on your return, you increase your AGI and risk moving yourself into a higher tax bracket, exceeding deduction limits, limiting your deductible for IRA contributions, and facing additional limits. The major benefit of including your child's income with your own is convenience—you don't have to file a separate tax return for your child. However, there are a couple additional benefits, such as raising your charitable contribution limit and being able to claim capital losses against capital gains on your child's investments.

If you decide to include your child's income on your return, TurboTax can perform the required calculations for determining the additional taxes due. Many of the questions refer to items that are included on 1099s your child received to report income from dividends, interest, and investments, so have these forms handy. Then, take the following steps to punch in the numbers:

1. In the Interview Navigator, click **Taxing income for children under 14**.

2. Click **Include my children's income on my return**. (These steps assume you are reporting your child's income on your return. If you would rather have your child file his own return, click **I'll report my children's income on their own returns** and complete a separate tax return for your child later.)

3. Type your child's first name and click **Continue**.

4. Click the check box next to each item that describes your child's income level, age, and tax status. Your answers to these questions tell TurboTax whether your child qualifies to have his income reported on your return. Click **Continue**.

5. Enter your child's last name, middle initial, and social security number. Click **Continue**.

6. Enter the child's income from interest only. Do not include dividends or capital gains; TurboTax will lead you through the process of entering that income later in the Interview. Click **Continue**.

7. Enter any adjustments to your child's interest income, including tax-exempt interest reported on form 1099-INT. Click **Continue**.

8. Enter amounts for any tax-exempt interest, exempt-interest dividends, and passive-activity bond interest your child received in 1998. Obtain this information from the 1099 or K-1 forms your child received. Click **Continue**.

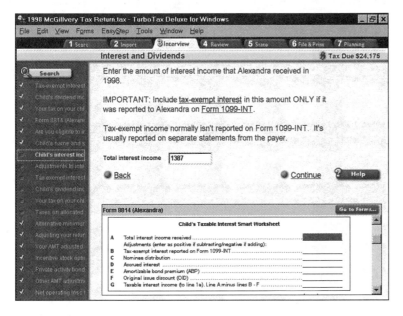

*Enter the total interest and dividends your child received.*

### Nominee Distributions

Nominee distributions are amounts paid to you but earned from someone else's money. For example, if you have a savings account that you share with someone else and the bank pays dividends in your name, the portion of the dividends that belongs to the other person are your *nominee distributions*. You report them on your return, but they get subtracted later, so you're not taxed on them. Because most kids have their own accounts, they rarely see nominee distributions.

9. Enter the total gross dividends your child received in 1998, along with amounts for any nominee or nontaxable distributions.

10. Enter the total capital gains earned from your child's investments. Click **Continue**. TurboTax performs the required calculations and displays the amount of tax due and how it is broken down.

11. Click **Done with this Form 8814**. TurboTax asks if you need another form 8814 (for instance, if you need to enter income for another child).

12. To enter information for another child, click **Yes, start a new Form 8814 for another child** and repeat steps 3–11. If you have no other child's income to report, click **No**.

*TurboTax shows you just how much money your kid's nest egg is going to cost.*

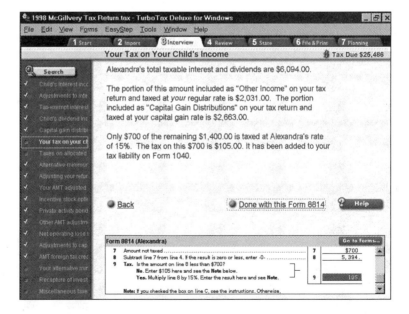

# Taxes You Can Probably Ignore

You paid income tax, social security, Medicare, the nanny tax, the alternative minimum tax, and taxes on your kids' income. If taxes haven't wiped you out, yet, there's more. Near the end of the "Other taxes" section of the Interview, click **Miscellaneous taxes** to see if you have any other income that the feds want to tax. Here, you can enter the following amounts:

➤ Excess benefits tax—If your company chose to lavish benefits on you rather than pay you in cold, hard cash, you might be taxed on your benefits. Like the tax on stock options, this tax applies mostly to upper management. Working stiffs rarely see *excess* benefits, unless they have a really good union.

➤ Accumulation distributions from trusts—If you are the beneficiary of a complex or accumulation trust that pays you distributions, you must include those distributions as income. If you already entered this information in Chapter 11, "What Else Constitutes Income?," in the section called "Lucky You! A Beneficiary of an Estate or Trust," don't enter it again.

➤ The Did-we-miss-anything? category—If the IRS missed anything on which you should be taxed but the government forgot to ask, enter it here. You wouldn't want to pass up the opportunity to pay yet another tax, would you?

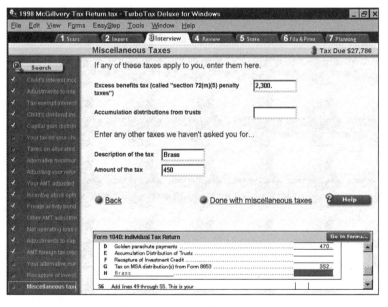

*If you have other income or benefits the Interview didn't ask you about, enter it here.*

# Still on Track?

Fortunately, the additional taxes described in this chapter apply to relatively few taxpayers. However, if you got hit by another tax in this chapter, you'll be happy to hear that the next chapter returns to the process of trimming your tax bill. Before you move on, make sure you've done the following:

➤ If you hired any household help in 1998, you paid taxes due on the wages you paid. See "Paying for the Hired Help: The Nanny Tax," on page 198.

➤ If you are an independent contractor or small-business owner, you paid your fair share of self-employment tax. See "The Increased Tax Burden for the Self-employed," on page 201.

➤ You determined if you are subject to the alternative minimum tax and completed any required AMT paperwork. See "What's with This Alternative Minimum Tax?," on page 203.

➤ You paid any taxes due on your kid's income or decided to have your kid file his own tax return. See "Paying Your Children's Taxes: The Kiddie Tax," on page 206.

➤ You ignored any additional taxes that probably don't apply to you. See "Taxes You Can Probably Ignore," on page 209.

➤ You decided to give up your worldly belongings and join a monastery. See ya later!

# Chapter 17

# Making the Most of the IRS Tax Credits

## In This Chapter

➤ Understand why a credit is worth more than a deduction

➤ Have a kid? Collect $400

➤ Get money from the IRS even if you don't make enough to pay taxes

➤ Get credit for your babysitting and daycare bills

➤ Grab more credits if you're old or disabled

➤ Take advantage of business credits when the feds toss you a bone

Is there anything on a tax return that's better than a deduction? Yes, a *credit*! With deductions, you chip away at your taxable income and then calculate the tax on what's left. With a credit, you lop dollars right off the amount of taxes that are due. For instance, if you have kids and you qualify for the child care credit, you get to cut $400 per kid off your tax bill. That's $400 for each kid, right back in your pocket!

Although TurboTax might have already decided the tax credits to which you're entitled and subtracted the amounts from your tax bill, this chapter explains the available credits and shows you how to check them out in TurboTax. This gives you the confidence that TurboTax is doing its job and making sure you get back what you deserve. And if you don't qualify for tax credits this year, this chapter helps you plan ahead for next year.

# Parents Only: The Child Tax Credit

Nobody has kids just to get a tax break, but having children sure helps when you're filing your income tax return. Not only are you allowed a deduction for each of your children, but Congress has sweetened the pot in 1998 by giving parents a $400 tax credit for each child. That's more than enough to cover the five bucks a week you pay out in allowance. In 1999, the tax credit will jump to a whopping $500 per child!

**Borderline Income Levels**

If your AGI is right on the threshold of $75,000 or $110,000, revisit the personal deductions section of the Interview and see if you can come up with any additional deductions that can lower your AGI.

So, what's the catch? This child tax credit does have a couple limitations:

➤ The child must be under the age of 17 at the *end* of the year.

➤ You must be able to claim the child as an exemption. See "Claiming Kids and Other Dependents," in Chapter 4, "Okay, Let's Get Started."

➤ If you are filing as single or head of household, your credit is reduced by $50 for each $1,000 of your AGI that exceeds the following threshold: $75,000 for single or head of household or $110,000 for married filing jointly ($55,000, if married filing separately).

Based on the information you entered early in the Interview, TurboTax determines if you qualify for the credit, performs the required calculations, and subtracts the qualifying child tax credit from your tax bill on form 1040. To check out the total credit to which you are entitled, click in the Interview Navigator and click **Child tax credit**. If "Child tax credit" is not listed, click **Personal Credits**, click the **Child tax credit** check box, and click **Continue**.

*Check out your child tax credit and give your kid a big kiss.*

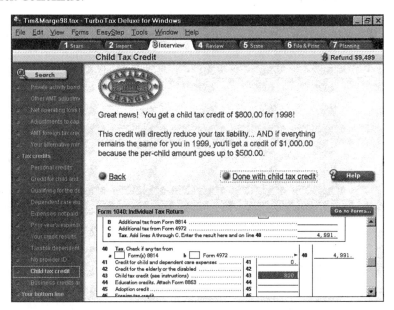

# The Earned Income Credit: Do You Qualify?

If you barely make enough money to cover your bills, either you have too many bills or you're not earning much. The government won't help you if you're simply spending beyond your means, but it does lend a hand if you hold down a paying job but just don't earn very much. The help comes in the form of the earned income credit (EIC, for short). With the earned income credit, the government gives you credit against the taxes you paid. If you qualify, EIC can substantially increase your tax refund and can even return a profit. That's right, by qualifying for EIC, it's possible that the government will pay *you*.

Don't start spending the money yet. Qualifying for the earned income credit is tough. Here are the conditions, and you must meet *all* of them:

➤ You must have worked sometime in 1998 and earned some money.

➤ You must be at least 25 years of age and under 65 years of age *or* had a dependent child living with you for more than six months in 1998. Grandchildren and stepchildren count. The child must be under the age of 19 (or 24, if a full-time student) at the end of the tax year or must have been permanently and totally disabled at any time during the tax year.

➤ You must have paid for at least half of the cost of maintaining your home or renting a home or apartment.

➤ Your earned income *and* your AGI must be less than $26,473 (if you have one dependent child), $30,095 (two children), or $10,030 (no child).

➤ If you are married, you and your spouse must file jointly.

➤ Your investment income cannot exceed $2,250.

➤ You cannot be listed as a qualifying child on the tax return of someone else who is claiming earned income credit.

➤ Two people cannot claim the same qualifying child for the earned income credit (unless, of course, you're married filing jointly). The person with the highest income gets to claim the child.

➤ You cannot claim the foreign income exclusion.

➤ You must be a resident of the United States or married to a United States citizen.

Do you think you qualify? TurboTax can help you determine if you qualify and calculate the amount of your earned income credit. Take the following steps:

1. In the Interview Navigator, click **Earned income credit**. (If "Earned income credit" is not listed, click **Personal credits**, click **Earned income credit**, and click **Continue**.) If your income level disqualifies you for the credit, TurboTax lets you know. Otherwise, TurboTax displays a list of items that may automatically disqualify you for the credit.

2. Click the check box next to any description that pertains to you and click **Continue**.

### Getting an Advance on Your EIC

You can submit a W-5 form for an advance on your EIC for the year 1999. You must have one or more qualifying children and you can receive a maximum of 60% of available credit for one qualifying child. If you received an advance in 1998, be sure to report it as income, as explained in Chapter 5, "W-2s for Salaried Employees."

3. If you entered information for your children, open the drop-down list and choose the item that best describes your child. Click **Continue** and repeat this step for any additional children.

4. Read the blurb about earned income credit, play the video (if desired), and click **Continue**.

5. If you did time in a penal institution, or received payments from the Federal Assistance for Needy Families program, enter any amounts you were paid for your services. If you were paid for performing services for other inmates, I don't want to hear about it. Click **Continue**.

6. If you or your spouse received non-taxable earned income (deferred compensation, military housing, and so on) in 1998 that you have not already entered in TurboTax, enter a description of the income and the amount you received. Click **Continue**.

7. TurboTax calculates your earned income credit, inserts the number on form 1040, line 59a, and pats you on the back. This amount is counted as a tax payment, as if you had sent money to the IRS, so if the amount exceeds your tax bill, the IRS pays you! Click **Done with earned income credit**.

*TurboTax displays your earned income credit. Rejoice and be merry!*

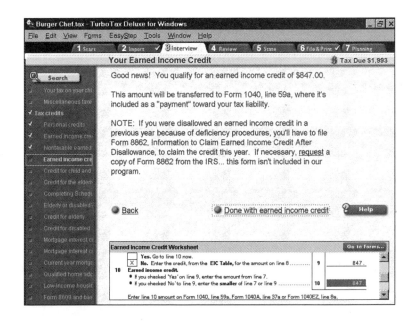

# Child and Dependent Care Credit

If you paid someone to care for your rugrats (under the age of 13) or other qualifying dependent while you worked, looked for a job, or went to school, you get an additional credit: the child and dependent care credit. This credit is intended to offset the cost of caring for your dependents while you earn a buck.

Based on your income, you can claim a credit for 20% to 30% of the amount you paid to have someone care for your child or dependent. For instance, if your AGI is over $28,000 and you paid $4,000 for childcare, you get a credit of $800. That's $800 subtracted from your tax bill or added to your refund.

You already should have entered all the information TurboTax needs to determine if you qualify for this credit and calculate your credit for child and dependent care. If you haven't entered this information, go back to the section in Chapter 4 called "Claiming Kids and Other Dependents." Or, click in the Interview Navigator, click **Credit for child and dependent care expenses**, and follow the lead.

### A Live-in Nanny?

If you hired a nanny or other person to provide care for a child or other dependent in your home, and you paid the person more than $1,100 in 1998, you might owe additional taxes on the wages you paid that person. See "Paying for the Hired Help: The Nanny Tax," in Chapter 16, "More Taxes (As If You Weren't Paying Enough)."

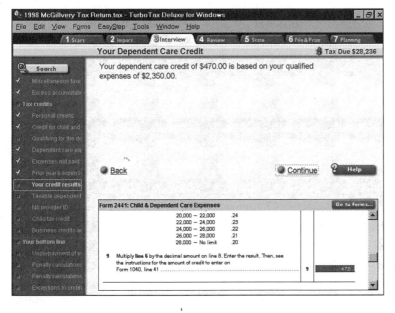

*TurboTax informs you of your qualifying credit for child and dependent care.*

# It Pays to Be Smart: Education Credits

Although I've criticized the United States throughout this book for overtaxing its citizens, I still think the U.S. is the land of opportunity. Anyone with a little ambition and some intelligence can live comfortably and steadily climb the socio-economic ladder. And given the amount of financial aid available, anyone with a high school diploma can get a college education.

To make it even easier for families and students to afford the cost of higher education, Congress has introduced two new education tax credits in 1998:

### Student Loan Interest Deduction

In addition to the new credits, a student or parent can deduct up to $1,000 in interest paid on student loans. The student must attend school at least part-time and the deduction is allowed for the first 60 months in which you must pay interest. The phase-out range is $40,000 to $55,000 AGI (single) and $60,000 to $75,000 (married filing jointly).

➤ Hope Scholarship Credit—The Hope Scholarship Credit provides a tax credit for the cost of higher education for the first two years after high school. This credit covers 100% of the first $1,000 of tuition and fees (excluding room and board) and 50% of the second $1,000 for any one student per year. In short, each student attending college (or the student's parent) gets a $1,500 credit. The student must attend a qualifying institution at least part-time and may not have a conviction for a state or federal drug offense. (I guess first-degree murder is okay.)

➤ Lifetime Learning Credit—The Lifetime Learning Credit provides a tax credit for the cost of higher education for any year after high school. The credit covers 20% of the first $5,000 of tuition and fees for any one student, up to $1,000 total credit per year. However, you can claim only those expenses paid after June 30, 1998. The Lifetime Learning Credit doesn't stop after the first two years of college.

You can claim either credit for more than one student in a year. For instance, if you have three kids attending college at least part-time, you can claim $1,500 for each of your children, for a total $4,500 credit. However, you cannot claim both the Hope Scholarship and Lifetime Learning Credit for a single student in the same year. The most logical way to use these credits is to claim the Hope Scholarship Credit for the first two years and the Lifetime Learning Credit for any years after that.

Of course, there are a couple limitations in addition to those mentioned in the previous list. First, the credits are disallowed if, during the same year, any funds are withdrawn from an education IRA to cover education expenses. Second, the credits are phased out at $40,000 to $50,000 (single) and $80,000 to $100,000 (married filing jointly).

To claim your prize, or at least find out if you qualify for one of the education credits, take the following steps:

1. In the Interview Navigator, click **Education Credits**.

2. If desired, click the **Play** button and watch the video clip about education credits. Click **Continue**.

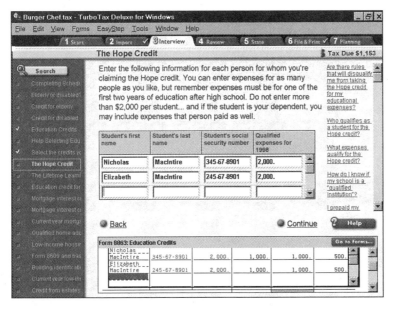

*Take advantage of the most lucrative education credit for which you qualify.*

3. Click **Choose my credits**.

4. Click the check box next to **The Hope Credit**, **The Lifetime Learning Credit**, or both. Click **Continue**.

5. If you chose the Hope Credit, enter each student's name, social security number, and qualifying expenses for the Hope Credit. (Do not exceed $2,000 for each student.) Click **Continue**.

6. If you chose the Lifetime Learning Credit, enter each student's name, social security number, and qualifying expenses for the Lifetime Learning Credit. (Expenses before June 30, 1998 do not qualify.) Click **Continue**.

7. TurboTax performs the required calculations and displays the total amount of your credit. Click **Done with education credits**.

# Credits for the Elderly and Disabled

If you're old *and* disabled, you have enough going against you, and the government doesn't want to kick you when you're down. Instead of clipping your retirement and disability income with yet another tax, the government is willing to give you a break, under certain conditions (all conditions must be met):

➤ You must have been "permanently and totally disabled" at the time you retired. This basically means that because of your physical or mental condition, you can't hold down a paying job and that a doctor has certified that your condition has lasted or will last for at least 12 months, or will lead to your death.

**217**

➤ You received taxable disability income in 1998, typically from a former employer's disability plan.

➤ By January 1, 1998, you had not reached your employer's mandatory retirement age.

The tax credit is limited by the amount of income you earn from other sources, including social security, but TurboTax is quite capable of calculating your tax credit based on the income you've entered so far. Just take the following steps:

1. In the Interview Navigator, click **Credit for the elderly or the disabled.**

2. If you are married filing jointly, click the check box next to your name, your spouse's name, or both of your names to specify who qualifies for the credit. Click **Continue**.

3. Enter the amount that you (and your spouse, if you are married and filing jointly) received in veteran's pension and other nontaxable pensions, annuities, and disability benefits. Click **Continue**.

4. Type the amount that the person claiming the credit received in disability income. Click **Continue**.

*Enter the amount received in disability income.*

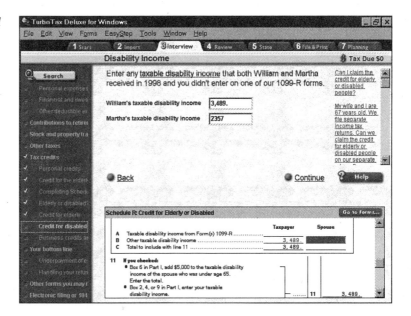

5. Click the option buttons to specify if you ever attached a doctor's statement claiming permanent and total disability on a previous return and if the condition results in the person's inability to engage in substantial, gainful activity. Click **Continue**. The next screen indicates if you must attach a statement from your doctor, based on your answer to the first question.

6. Click **Continue**. TurboTax transfers your entries to Schedule R, calculates your qualifying tax credit (if any), and records any tax credit on form 1040.

# Additional Credits for Mortgage Interest and Low-income Housing

If you own a home in the low-rent district or you've made low-income housing available, you might qualify for additional credits to help you pay your mortgage interest or offset the costs for providing low-income housing. If you received a mortgage interest credit certificate from a state or local agency, you qualify for the mortgage interest credit, as explained in the following section. If you have buildings that qualify as low-income housing units, you can claim the low-income housing credit, as discussed in "Low-income Housing Credits," later in this chapter.

## *The Mortgage Interest Credit*

When you apply for a mortgage or home-improvement loan, you might qualify for a mortgage interest credit of up to $2,000. If you qualified for this credit, you should have received a certificate for mortgage interest credit indicating the amount of the credit. You can claim that amount of mortgage interest as a credit rather than listing it as an itemized expense. For example, if your certificate states that you qualify for mortgage interest credit of $1,250 and you paid $6,000 in mortgage interest, you claim $1,250 as a mortgage interest credit and list the remaining $4,750 on Schedule A as a deduction.

To claim your mortgage interest credit, take the following steps:

1. In the Interview Navigator, click **Mortgage interest credit**. (If "Mortgage interest credit" is not listed, click **Personal credits**, click **Mortgage interest credit**, and click **Continue**.)
2. Type the amount of your mortgage interest credit, as shown on your certificate.
3. Click in the **How much is your MCC credit rate?** text box and type the credit rate. Click **Done**.
4. If you have any unused mortgage interest credit that was disallowed in previous years, enter the amount. Click **Continue**.
5. If your current address differs from the address of the home whose mortgage interest qualifies for the credit, click **No** and type the address of the home for which you are claiming the mortgage interest credit. Click **Continue**.

## *Low-income Housing Credits*

If you provided low-income housing for your tenants, you might be able to claim a credit to offset your expenses. The new tax laws provide three credits:

➤ New construction and improvements—You can claim a 9% credit (maximum) for up to three years for expenses you paid to build new rental properties and refurbish older buildings.

*If you received a mortgage interest credit certificate, be sure to take the credit.*

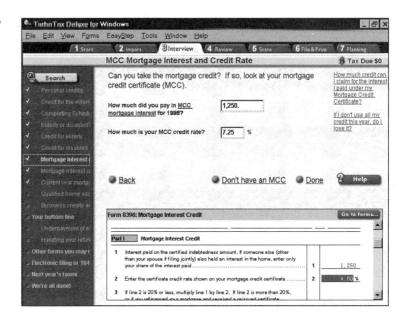

➤ New construction financed by federal subsidies—You can claim a 4% credit (maximum) for up to 10 years for expenses paid to build new rental properties and refurbish older buildings, even though some of the cost was covered by federal subsidies.

➤ Acquisition of existing property—If you acquired existing rental property, you can claim a credit for the cost of that property at 4% (maximum) for up to 10 years.

To qualify for these credits, your expenses must meet several conditions. For instance, refurbishing (technically known as "rehabilitating") a building must consist of some major reconstructive surgery: $3,000 per rental unit or 10% of the adjusted basis of the building, whichever is more. Check out the TurboTax help system for additional restrictions and limits.

To enter the information that TurboTax needs to calculate your credit for low-income housing, click **Low-income housing credit** in the Interview Navigator, and follow the instructions. (If "Low-income housing credit" is not listed, click **Personal credits**, click **Low-income housing credit**, and click **Continue**.

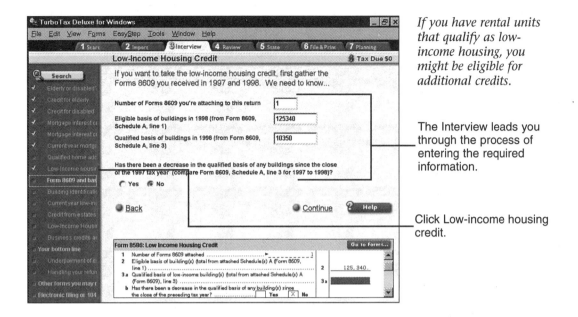

*If you have rental units that qualify as low-income housing, you might be eligible for additional credits.*

The Interview leads you through the process of entering the required information.

Click Low-income housing credit.

# Credits for Business Owners Only

If you own a business, you might start to wonder if the government wants you to stay in business. You pay income tax, self-employment tax, taxes on the wages you pay to your employees, inventory tax, sales tax, and other miscellaneous taxes throughout the year that take a huge bite out of your earnings.

Fortunately, there are a few credits that can help reduce your income tax:

➤ Federal taxes paid on fuels—If you paid federal taxes on fuels used for machinery to run your business or for vehicles used on your farm, you can list those taxes as a credit. The credit you receive depends on how you used the fuel (for instance, for farming or off-highway business use) and on the amount of alcohol in the fuel.

➤ Alternative minimum tax—If your business credits were limited by the alternative minimum tax in a previous year, you can carry over those credits to your 1998 return or to future returns until you have exhausted those credits. For instance, say your 1997 tax bill came to $15,000, you claimed business credits of $8,000 (dropping your tax bill to $7,000), and the AMT kicked in and said you owe $12,000. You lost out on $5,000 of your business credits. You can carry this amount over to your 1998 return.

➤ Investment tax credit—If you invested in restoring historical landmarks, making use of solar or geothermal energy in your business, reforestation, or other related activities or property, you might qualify for the investment tax credit.

➤ General business credits—This consists of a bunch of business credits that are lumped together and reported on form 3800, General Business Credit. These credits include credits for welfare-to-work (giving a person who is on welfare a job), alcohol fuels, investment carryovers, disability access, social security, empowerment zone employment, and enhanced oil recovery.

➤ Passive activity credits—These credits include most of the credits mentioned earlier in this list, including credits for alcohol-based fuels, welfare-to-work, low-income housing, and disability access. However, these credits apply only to passive activities, such as partnerships and S corporations. You might have already entered this information when you entered details from your 1099s or K-1s earlier in the Interview.

To determine if your business qualifies for any of these credits and enter the information TurboTax needs to perform the calculations, click in the Interview Navigator and click **Business credits and more personal credits**. Click the check box next to each item that pertains to your business, click **Continue**, and follow the Interview. The steps vary considerably, depending on the check boxes you selected.

*TurboTax displays a long list of business credits for which you might be eligible.*

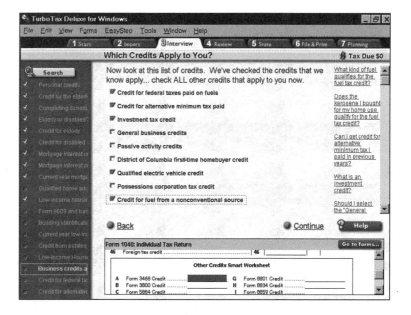

# Still on Track?

Every dollar you claim as a credit is a dollar in your pocket, so make sure you haven't overlooked any eligible credits:

➤ The child tax credit gives you $400 per kid. See "Parents Only: The Child Tax Credit," on page 212.

➤ The child and dependent care credit gives you back 20-30% of what you paid in childcare. See "Child and Dependent Care Credit," on page 215.

➤ The Hope Scholarship and Lifetime Learning Credits can give you back up to $1,500 of expenses for higher education and training. See "It Pays to Be Smart: Education Credits," on page 216.

➤ The credit for the elderly and disabled gives you back some of the taxes on money you received in disability payments. See "Credits for the Elderly and Disabled," on page 217.

➤ The mortgage interest credit returns up to $2,000 to your bank account. See "The Mortgage Interest Credit," on page 219.

➤ Low-income housing credits reimburse you for expenses you paid to make low-income housing available. See "Low-income Housing Credits," on page 219.

➤ Business credits offer plenty of incentives to use alternative fuels, conserve resources, move people off welfare, and carry over credits from previous years. See "Credits for Business Owners Only," on page 221.

# Part 4

# Reviewing and Filing Your Tax Return

*An unexamined tax form is not worth submitting.*

> *—Socrates*

*Okay, I took some liberties with this particular quote, but the spirit of "An unexamined life is not worth living," is quite true of your tax return. Without a thorough examination of your return, you risk submitting a form riddled with errors and becoming a prime target for a full-fledged audit. Even worse, you might pay more taxes than you have to.*

*Fortunately, TurboTax has some powerful tools that comb the bugs right out of your tax return and highlight deductions and credits you might have overlooked. And after you've completed the review, TurboTax has the tools you need to either immediately submit your tax return via modem, or print a copy to mail later. This part shows you just how to finish, review, and submit your final return.*

...CARRY OVER THE FOUR...

# Chapter 18

# Auditing and Reviewing Your Return with TurboTax

## In This Chapter

➤ Take a quick glance at the bottom line

➤ Make TurboTax check for missing forms and information

➤ Trim your tax bill with additional deductions and credits

➤ Perform a mock audit and iron out the wrinkles that could trigger a real audit

➤ Take a look at the average tax return for taxpayers in your bracket

➤ Kick yourself this year and learn how to save more next year

You've plodded through that long Interview, answering every question TurboTax shoved in your face and shuffling through your records to find the requested numbers. Now it's time to put TurboTax to work and take advantage of its professional expertise.

This chapter shows you how to use the high-tech tools built right into TurboTax to check your tax return for errors, dig up additional deductions, perform a pre-audit, determine if you've beat the averages, and learn a few strategies that can help you save taxes for years to come.

## Summary On-the-Go

Consider leaving the Tax Summary window open while you work on your return. As you change information on your tax return, the effects of those changes immediately show up in the Tax Summary.

# Ouch! Viewing Your Tax Summary

As you type entries for your income, deductions, and credits, TurboTax keeps a running tally and automatically updates the formulas that work behind the scenes to calculate your refund or taxes due. Just above the area where you enter information is a yellow bar, and on the right end of that bar, TurboTax displays the *Refund/Tax Due monitor*, which shows the amount you currently owe in taxes or the amount of refund you can expect. To expand the summary and display additional information, take one of the following steps:

➤ Rest the mouse pointer on the Refund/Tax Due monitor to display a pop-up window showing a brief summary of your tax return.

➤ Click the Refund/Tax Due monitor to display the Tax Summary window, which provides additional details.

➤ Open the **Tools** menu and choose **Tax Summary** (or press **Ctrl+T**) to display the Tax Summary window. (If you are in Forms view, this is the only way to make the Tax Summary window pop up.)

Click the Refund/Tax Due monitor to display the Tax Summary window.

Point to the Refund/Tax Due monitor to display a brief overview.

*For a quick overview of your income, deductions, credits, and refund or taxes due, display the Tax Summary.*

Tax Summary pop-up window

The Tax Summary displays additional details.

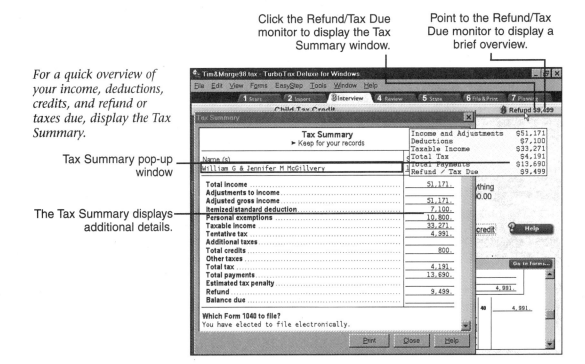

# Reviewing Your Tax Return for Missing Forms and Entries

As you're working through the Interview, it's easy to omit essential entries, such as your kid's social security number or a tax shelter ID number, and make a few typos. In addition, if your return is fairly complex and requires several supporting forms and schedules, you might fail to fill one out. In most cases, TurboTax immediately informs you of any major omissions, typos, and missing paperwork. However, it doesn't always catch these errors right away.

After you've answered all the questions and done everything you could possibly do to make your tax return complete and correct, you should have TurboTax perform a final check. TurboTax checks your return for the following errors and omissions and displays a screen for each problem, allowing you to skip or correct the problem in the Interview:

**Eliminate Errors**

Skipping an error doesn't remove the flag that TurboTax stuck on it. The error might prevent you from filing your return electronically or filing the simple 1040PC. Try your best to figure out why TurboTax is questioning an entry and fix the problem. (Overrides are not considered to be "errors," so TurboTax will allow you to file electronically or print a 1040PC that has overrides.)

➤ Inconsistent entries—If you typed an entry that contradicts a related entry somewhere else in the return, TurboTax questions it.

➤ Incomplete entries—An eight-digit social security number, incomplete phone number, or other odd-looking entry might warrant a flag.

➤ Overrides—In many cases, TurboTax drags a number from one form or worksheet and inserts it on a line or in a box on another form or worksheet. If you replace a number that TurboTax carried over, it questions the override. (TurboTax usually warns you before allowing you to override an entry.)

➤ Excessive amounts—If you entered an amount for an income, deduction, or credit that is far beyond the average, the error check questions it.

Take the following steps to check for and correct errors in your tax return:

1. Click the **Review** tab. TurboTax informs you that if you haven't yet updated TurboTax, you should do so now.

2. If you haven't updated TurboTax recently, click **Update TurboTax** and follow the onscreen instructions. (See "I Just Bought TurboTax. Now I Have to Update It?" in Chapter 1, "TurboTax Nickel Tour," for details.) Otherwise, click **Skip update** and proceed to step 3. TurboTax displays a list of checks it will perform.

### Get the Form

TurboTax doesn't have a built-in Interview sequence for correcting every error it turns up. You may need to switch to Forms view to correct the error directly on one of your forms or schedules. See "Plodding Through the Federal Tax Forms," in Chapter 4, "Okay, Let's Get Started," for details.

3. If **Error Check** is not checked, click it to place a check mark in its check box. Click any of the other check boxes, as desired.

4. Click **Run selected reviews**. TurboTax displays a little background information about the error check feature.

5. Click **Next**. If TurboTax locates an error, it displays a description of the error and returns you to the Interview, so you can correct it. In some cases, TurboTax might return you to a place in the Interview that's before the actual error; just click **Next** to move forward.

6. Type the missing entry or correct the entry, as necessary, and click **Next**.

*TurboTax describes the error and prompts you to correct it.*

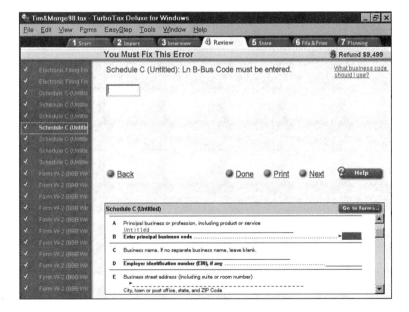

7. Proceed with the error checking process until you have entered all missing information and corrected all errors. At the end of the error check, TurboTax informs you that it will now search for any additional deductions.

# Make TurboTax Sniff Out Additional Deductions

You worked through Part 3 and are pretty sure you have accounted for all the deductions you qualified for, but your tax bill still looks pretty high to you. Maybe you missed something. When you were gathering your records, perhaps you forgot the folder that includes all your receipts for charitable donations. Perhaps you forgot to even consider looking at your medical expenses.

Never fear. If you missed anything, TurboTax can trip your memory switch and give you a few additional ideas for deductions you might have overlooked. To enlist TurboTax's aid in tracking down additional deductions, take the following steps:

**Return to the Beginning**

If you have trouble getting the list of checks to pop up on the Review tab, start over. Open the **Tools** menu and click **Final Review**. If TurboTax asks whether you want to update the program, click **Skip Update**.

1. Click the **Review** tab if it's not already front and center.

2. Make sure **Deduction Finder** is checked. (Remove the check mark next to Error Check, unless you want to run the error check again.)

3. Click **Run selected reviews**. TurboTax displays a little introduction describing the service it is about to perform.

4. Click **Next**. If TurboTax finds a deduction for which you might be eligible, it displays a description of the deduction. Don't expect all the deductions to pertain to your situation; TurboTax fishes pretty deep to find some of these.

5. To print the deduction for future reference, make sure your printer is on (and is loaded with paper), and click **Print**.

6. When you're done with this deduction, click **Next** to view the next deduction.

7. Repeat steps 5 and 6 until you have exhausted TurboTax's deductions, or until it has exhausted you.

*The TurboTax displays screen after screen of possible deductions.*

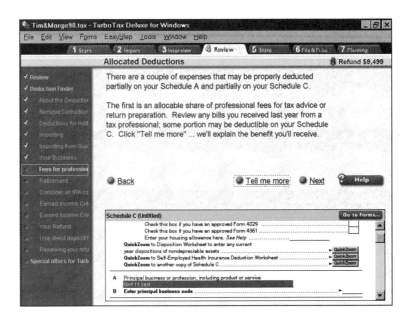

Although the Deduction Finder is a pretty cool idea in theory, it's not the greatest at locating deductions. You'll do better by opening Schedule A and flipping through it line by line yourself. To display Schedule A, press **Ctrl+M** and double-click **Schedule A**. If you don't have a Schedule A, you're not itemizing, and that might be the reason why you have so little in deductions. To create a Schedule A, press **Ctrl+A**, and double-click **Schedule A: Itemized Deductions**. You can then complete the form yourself or go back to the Interview. For details about deductions, see Chapter 12, "Income Reduction Through Deductions."

# Locate the Trouble Spots with TurboTax's Auditor

Except for a few sadists and a handful of anti-government protesters left over from the '60s, few taxpayers look forward to an audit. We want our tax returns to slide through the IRS like a quarter in a slot machine. And then we want to hear the sound of quarters dropping when we hit the tax refund jackpot. Even though the IRS audits a low percentage of tax returns each year, most of us dread the thought of any sort of audit.

**Deductions and Credits**

The Deduction Finder focuses mainly on deductions listed on Schedule A. If you're self-employed, check for additional deductions on Schedule C. You should also check for any credits that you may qualify for, as explained in Chapter 17, "Making the Most of the IRS Tax Credits."

To help you file your tax return with confidence, TurboTax can perform a mock audit of your return, examining your return for any entries that are likely to trigger an audit. In many cases, there's nothing you can do to rectify the situation, short of removing a deduction you know you're entitled to, but it's good to have a heads-up that the IRS might question an entry.

### No Guarantees

Intuit makes no guarantees that your return will not be audited if it passes inspection or that your return will be audited if it has some odd entries.

To have TurboTax audit your return for you, take the following steps:

1. If you checked all the boxes to have TurboTax perform all checks, just click **Next** to move to the next stage of the review. Otherwise, open the **Tools** menu, click **Final Review**, click **Skip update**, click **Audit Alerts**, and click **Run selected reviews**. TurboTax displays a brief introduction to the Audit Alert feature.

2. Click **Next**. TurboTax scans your return for entries that could trigger an audit and displays the first potential problem. Many of the potential audit triggers are not serious, so use your own common sense when responding.

3. If TurboTax points out a possible audit trigger, and you decide to correct it, click the **Interview** tab, click the topic in the Interview Navigator that relates to this issue, and enter your correction. Otherwise, click **Next** to move on to the next potential problem.

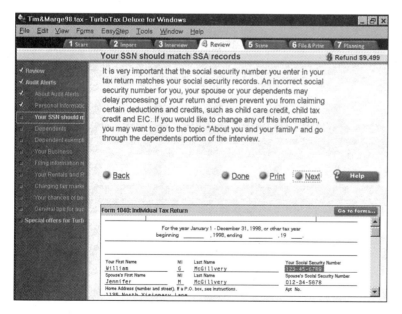

*TurboTax displays any entries that could trigger an audit.*

4. Continue through the audit check, skipping or fixing potential problems, until you reach the screen named **Common Questions About Audits**. Here, you can find answers to all your audit questions and become really paranoid.

5. Continue clicking **Next** and reading whatever interests you. When you reach the end, TurboTax gives you the option of running the review again or skipping it. I'll give you another option—do nothing and move on to the next section.

# Check Out the U.S. Averages for Income and Deductions

The trouble with taxpayers is that we're not an organized, unified group. The tax code has made us competitors. We work on our tax returns in secret, trying to outdo our neighbors and relatives. We might secretly slip out to talk with an accountant or read books and magazines in the hope that these resources will give us an edge over the competition. We're afraid that if we tell someone how much we earn and how much we pay in taxes, they'll turn us in to the IRS or laugh at our stupidity. But we always wonder what those other people earn and what *they* pay in taxes.

Well, now you can take a peek at what other people earn, contribute, deduct, invest, and pay in taxes... or at least check out the averages for your income bracket. To pull back the curtain and satisfy your curiosity, take the following steps:

**Infuriating?**

When checking out national averages, it's easy to lose your cool. You might see that the average taxpayer making the same amount of money that you are making is paying half the taxes. Just keep in mind that the average person might be much more in debt than you. Averages can be very deceiving.

1. If you checked all the boxes to have TurboTax perform all checks, just click **Next** to move to the next stage of the review. Otherwise, open the **Tools** menu, click **Final Review**, click **Skip update**, click **U.S. Averages**, and click **Run selected reviews**. TurboTax displays a brief introduction to the U.S. Averages feature.

2. Click **Next**. TurboTax informs you that it will begin by funding the range in which your income falls.

3. Click **Next**. TurboTax first displays your AGI and shows you the percentage of returns last year that reported AGI in the same bracket.

4. Click **Next** and follow the analysis to its conclusion. There's nothing tricky here. Just keep clicking **Next** and reading the screens.

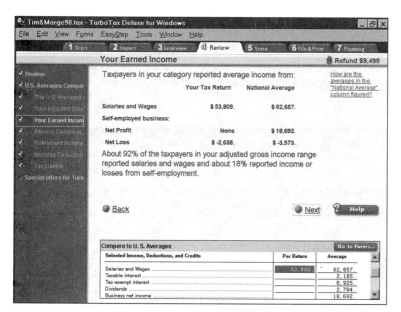

*TurboTax lets you check out the national averages for your income bracket.*

# Learn How to Save on Taxes Next Year

Your tax bill hit you hard this year. You made more money than you had anticipated, had less withheld from your pay, and your deductions and credits were minimal. Short of digging up some money and throwing it in an IRA at the last minute, you can't do much about this year's taxes. But what about 1999? What about the year 2000? TurboTax can create a Tax Report to help you plan ahead for the future, so you'll never have another tax year as bad as this one.

TurboTax doesn't just slap together a generic tax report. Instead, it analyzes your return to determine strategies that pertain to the information you entered on your return. You can then print the report for future reference or step through the strategies one-by-one.

If you checked all the boxes telling TurboTax to give your tax return a complete review, continue on through the review by clicking **Next**. After TurboTax displays the U.S. averages, it displays the introductory screen for the Tax Report. If you quit the review or chose not to run all the checks, take the following steps to view the Tax Report:

1. Open the **Tools** menu and click **Final Review.**
2. If prompted to update TurboTax, click **Skip update**.
3. Click **Tax Report** and click **Run selected reviews**. TurboTax displays a brief introduction to the Tax Report feature.

4. Take one of the following steps:

➤ To print your personalized Tax Report, click **Print**, click **Print Tax Report**, and click the **Print** button.

➤ To step through the tax-saving tips and strategies one by one, click **Next**. (You can print the report at any time or click **Done** to stop.)

*TurboTax creates a custom Tax Report containing tax-saving tips that apply to your situation.*

Click Done at any time to stop.

Click Print to print this tip or the entire report.

Click Next to view the next tip.

# Still on Track?

When you're done dropping in the numbers, it's great to have a second pair of eyes check your return, especially the professional eyes built into TurboTax. Before you even think of filing your tax return with the IRS, make sure you've done the following:

➤ Glanced at the bottom line and checked out the numbers that contribute to it. See "Ouch! Viewing Your Tax Summary," on page 228.

➤ Checked your return for missing or invalid entries, including social security numbers, and missing forms. See "Reviewing Your Tax Return for Missing Forms and Entries," on page 229.

➤ Unleashed TurboTax to help you track down additional deductions you might have overlooked. See "Make TurboTax Sniff Out Additional Deductions," on page 231.

236

➤ Performed a mock audit of your tax return and fixed any problems that could trigger a real audit (or decided that the fix wasn't needed). See "Locate the Trouble Spots with TurboTax's Auditor," on page 232.

➤ Determined what other taxpayers in your bracket were reporting on their own returns, and wondered where they came up with *their* numbers. See "Check Out the U.S. Averages for Income and Deductions," on page 234.

➤ Picked up a few tax-saving strategies that you think you might be able to use in 1999. See "Learn How to Save on Taxes Next Year," on page 235.

# Chapter 19

# Submitting Your Tax Return

## In This Chapter

➤ Make a tactical decision to file now or wait

➤ Got a modem? File electronically for a quick refund

➤ Take advantage of the Paperwork Reduction Act with the 1040PC

➤ Print the complete, unedited 1040 and stuff it in an envelope

➤ Make it official by adding your signature

➤ File for an extension if you're running behind

You have done everything possible to minimize your taxes and maximize your refund. You've gone through your stacks of W-2s, 1099s, 1098s, and the year-end statements from your mutual funds and dutifully reported every penny of income you received in 1998. You've tracked down every penny you paid in mortgage interest, every check you wrote to a charitable organization, and every receipt from your doctor and pharmacy. You're absolutely sure that you've missed nothing. Now it's time to bite the bullet and file your return with the IRS.

TurboTax provides three ways to file your income tax return: electronically (via modem), printing and sending the 1040PC (the short form), and printing and sending a standard 1040. This chapter provides instructions for all three methods, but you must first decide which method is best for you:

➤ File electronically by April 10, 1999—If you have a modem and a credit card, file electronically. TurboTax charges you $9.95 for the service, but it's worth it. By filing electronically, you receive your refund much earlier (if you're due for a refund), your return can't get lost in the mail, and you reduce the chances of errors being introduced by overworked data entry clerks at the IRS (hence reducing your chances of being audited). See "Filing Electronically for Quick Rebates," later in this chapter, for instructions. File by April 10 to give Intuit time to process your return and get it to the IRS by April 15.

### Copy to a Floppy

After you file your return, use the **File**, **Save As** command to save a duplicate copy of your return to a floppy disk and file the disk with a printed copy of the full 1040. This gives you a duplicate electronic copy of your return, so you won't have to hunt for it next year.

➤ Print and mail the abbreviated 1040PC—If you don't have a modem, print and file the 1040PC, an abbreviated 1040. When the IRS receives a 1040PC, it uses a scanner to transform the printout into a digital form. Because no data-entry clerk is retyping the numbers, this reduces the chance of introducing errors into your return. See, "Streamlining Your Return with the 1040PC," later in this chapter, to learn how to print your 1040PC.

➤ Print and mail the full 1040—If you don't have a modem or if your tax return has entries that disqualify it from being submitted as a 1040PC, print your full 1040 and mail it. You should also print a full 1040 for your own records. See "Going the Standard Route with the Full 1040," later in this chapter, for details.

## Should I Wait or Send It Right Now?

For many people, the question of whether to file now or wait till April 15 is moot. If you've put off doing your taxes until April 14 or 15, you have no choice. Others might have their taxes done by early March or even February. The decision to file now or later is based on the kind of taxpayer you are:

➤ The procrastinator—Procrastinators never know how much they'll need to pay or how much of a refund they'll receive, and they really don't care. Filing a tax return is just another bothersome chore. These folks file at the last minute.

➤ The overpayer—Overpayers have too much withheld in income taxes, so they can get a big, fat refund check in May and blow it on summer vacation. These people want to file as early as possible.

➤ The underpayer—Underpayers hate the idea of the government holding their money for any length of time. They have too little withheld from their paychecks and then owe money at the end of the year. These people want to file as late as possible, so they can hold onto the money a little longer.

➤ The strategist—Strategists worry about audits. There's something risky on their tax returns, and they're afraid the IRS is going to close in on their racket. They like to file as close to twelve o'clock midnight on April 15 as possible, on the premise that this lowers their chances of being audited.

# Filing Electronically for Quick Rebates

Filing your tax return electronically is definitely the best option, especially if the government owes you a refund. By filing electronically, you streamline the steps the IRS takes to process your return and can expect to see your refund check three to six weeks earlier than if you had mailed in your return. Even if you're not expecting a refund, filing electronically benefits you, because it reduces the chances that an overworked IRS clerk will make a typo that triggers an audit.

**Avoid Overpaying**

Ideally, you should have just enough money withheld from your pay (or pay just enough in estimated taxes) to cover your tax bill. By overpaying, you give the government an interest-free loan, something you should reserve only for yourself and your closest friends.

To file electronically, you must have a computer with a 9600bps or faster modem and a credit card. If you have an external modem, make sure it's turned on, and then take the following steps:

1. Perform a final review of your return, as explained in Chapter 18, "Auditing and Reviewing Your Return with TurboTax." Make any corrections, as suggested by TurboTax. If your return has errors, TurboTax won't allow you to file electronically.

2. Click the **File & Print** tab.

3. Click **File electronically**. (If you like menus, open the **File** menu, point to **Electronic Filing**, and click **File Electronically**.)

4. Read the instructions on filing electronically and click **Continue**. TurboTax prompts you to download or install your state program so you can file your state income tax return electronically at the same time.

5. To immediately file your federal income tax return, click **No, file just my federal return.**

6. Follow the remaining onscreen instructions to complete the filing process.

When you file your tax return electronically, it is sent to Intuit's Electronic Filing Center and then forwarded to the IRS. Wait 24 to 48 hours and then verify that your return has been accepted:

*Click the File electronic-ally option.*

Click the File & Print tab.

Click to file electronically.

**IRS e-file**

If the IRS selected you for its e-file pilot program, you may have received a postcard with an e-file number, which you can use to sign your return electronically. TurboTax will prompt you for this number during the filing process. By using your e-file customer number, you avoid having to send in form 8453-OL with your handwritten signature, or any copies of your W-2s, 1099s, or other forms typically required.

1. If you have an external modem, make sure it is turned on.

2. Run TurboTax and open the tax return you filed electronically.

3. Open the **File** menu, point to **Electronic Filing**, and click **Check Electronic Filing Status**.

4. Click **Connect now to get status**. TurboTax connects to Intuit's Electronic Filing Center and retrieves any information about the tax return you filed. If all went well, you should receive a message indicating that the IRS accepted your return. If your return was rejected, a description of the problem should appear. Correct your return and file it again (no charge).

5. Click **Next** to view instructions on how to complete the filing process.

After the IRS accepts your tax return, you still have some work to do. You might need to send additional forms (and a check, if you owe them some money). After you learn that the IRS has accepted your return, take the following steps:

➤ Complete form 8453-OL in TurboTax, print it, sign it, and send it to the specified address with any additional forms or documents requested by the IRS. Read the onscreen instructions that appear after your return is accepted to find out exactly what the IRS needs. If you fail to mail form 8453-OL within 24 hours of acceptance, the IRS might not allow you to file electronically next year.

➤ If you owe federal income taxes, print and mail form 1040-V along with a check for the amount due to the specified address. You cannot mail this form along with form 8453-OL, because it goes to a different IRS office. You must send the payment by April 15, 1999.

# Streamlining Your Return with the 1040PC

Do you seriously think that the IRS wants all those forms and schedules it made you fill out? It doesn't. The IRS only wants the key numbers, the bottom line, and form 1040PC gives the IRS exactly what it wants. 1040PC is a low-fat version of form 1040 that the IRS can scan into its system rather than having a data-entry clerk type the numbers.

To print your 1040PC, take the following steps:

1. Make sure your printer is on and has paper.
2. Click the **File & Print** tab.
3. Click **Print my return to mail it**.
4. Click **1040PC format** to place a check in its box. (You can also click the **1998 US Form 1040: Individual Income Tax Return** check box to print a complete tax return for your records.)
5. Click **Print**.

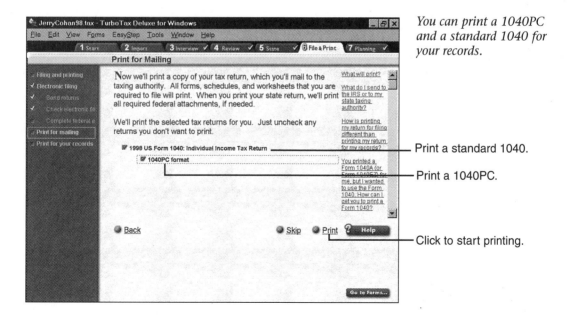

*You can print a 1040PC and a standard 1040 for your records.*

Print a standard 1040.

Print a 1040PC.

Click to start printing.

**Use the Right Paper**

If you print your return, use 8.5-by-11-inch, white, medium-weight (at least 20-lb.) paper. Don't get fancy with the ink, either; black-on-white is all the IRS accepts.

After you print your 1040PC, sign and date it (if you're married, have your spouse sign and date the return as well). You must then attach your W-2s, 1099s, and a check for any payment due to your 1040PC and mail it to the IRS (use a paper clip to attach the required forms and check, DO NOT staple). Don't attach any other schedules or tax forms. See "Preparing and Signing Your Printed Return," later in this chapter, for details.

If you owe taxes, TurboTax prints a 1040-V that you must send separately, along with a check for the taxes due, to an address other than the address you to which you send your return.

# Going the Standard Route with the Full 1040

If your tax return is fairly complex or has some overrides that TurboTax finds unacceptable, TurboTax might not allow you to file electronically or file a 1040PC. In such cases, you must print a complete 1040 along with supporting schedules and forms. You might also want to print a complete 1040 to file with your own records.

To print a full 1040, take the following steps:

1. Make sure your printer is on and has paper.
2. Click the **File & Print** tab.
3. Click **Print my return to mail it**.
4. Click the **1998 US Form 1040: Individual Income Tax Return** check box.
5. Click **Print**.

*If necessary, print a complete form 1040 along with all required forms and schedules.*

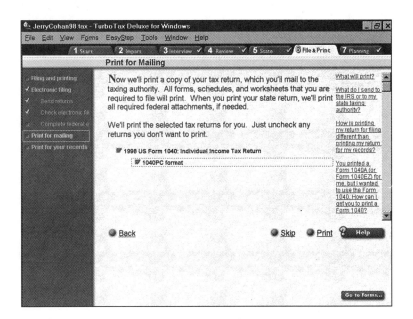

To take more control over which forms TurboTax prints, open the **File** menu and click **Print**. This displays the Printing dialog box, as shown in the following figure. Select one of the following options and click the **Print** button:

➤ Tax Return for Filing—This option prints your 1040 and all the schedules, forms, and supporting details the IRS requires.

➤ Tax Return for Your Records—This option enables you to choose to print only your tax return, your tax return and recommended worksheets, or your tax return and all related schedules, forms, and worksheets.

➤ Selected Forms—This option prints only the forms and schedules you specify. After selecting this option, click the **Choose** button, click the name of the form you want to print, and click **OK**.

➤ Form Name—This option prints only the current form. For example, if a form is displayed and you choose File, Print, the name of the form appears at the bottom of the Printing dialog box. Click the option button next to the form's name and click **Print** to print it.

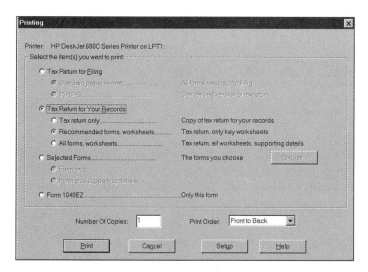

*For more control over what TurboTax prints, choose File, Print, and enter your preferences.*

# Preparing and Signing Your Printed Return

If you printed your tax return to mail to the IRS, you must take a few additional steps before you stuff the envelope and mail it off:

➤ Make sure the forms are in the proper order. TurboTax arranged the forms for you during printing. Unless you shuffled them, they should be in the proper order.

➤ If you received a barcoded label from the IRS, stick it to the designated area at the top of page 1 of form 1040. Although the label isn't required, it does help the IRS track your return.

➤ Sign and date your return. If you are married and filing a joint return, make sure your spouse signs and dates the return, too.

➤ Attach Copy B of forms W-2, W-2G, and 1099-R, and any other forms required by the IRS to the front of form 1040.

➤ Attach any other supporting statements referred to by an IRS form or schedule behind the form or schedule that references them. (TurboTax prints "Attach to Return" across the top of any supporting documents. Don't attach a worksheet unless it has "Attach to Return" printed on it.)

➤ If you owe taxes, make out a check to the Internal Revenue Service for the exact amount you owe. Make sure your social security number is written or printed on the front of the check and write "1998 form 1040" near the top of the check. (If you have a Discover card, you can charge your taxes, in which case, you don't have to attach a check.)

If you don't have an envelope from the IRS, use a standard business envelope to mail your return. To find the address of the IRS center for your region, open the **Forms** menu, click **Show My Return**, and double-click **Filing Instructions** (near the bottom of the list). Scroll down to view the address of your regional IRS office.

# It's April 15th and I'm Not Done!

All this information about filing your tax return is great—assuming your return is complete! If you're running behind schedule and you're nowhere near meeting that April 15th deadline, it's time for Plan 2—file an extension. Filing an extension is no big deal, but it doesn't give you an extension on *paying your taxes*. When you file an extension, you must pay any taxes that are due. So, what's the point? The extension simply gives you some extra time to collect your records and put the final touches on your return. When you file for an extension, the IRS automatically grants it.

To file for a four-month extension, you must file form 4868, Application for Automatic Extension. If you need additional time, file form 2688, Application for Additional Extension. To complete and print form 4868, take the following steps (these steps might vary slightly, depending on your filing status and other information on your return):

1. Click the **Interview** tab.
2. Click in the Interview Navigator and scroll down to **Other forms you may need**.
3. Click **Other forms you may need**.
4. Click the check box next to **Forms 4868 and 2688, extensions of time to file**. Click **Continue**.
5. Click **Continue**.
6. Click **Yes, I haven't filed for an extension yet**.
7. Click **No, start entering extension information**.

8. Click **Transfer information to my extension**. TurboTax transfers the necessary information from your tax return to the extension form.

9. Enter your name, social security number, and address, and then click **Continue**.

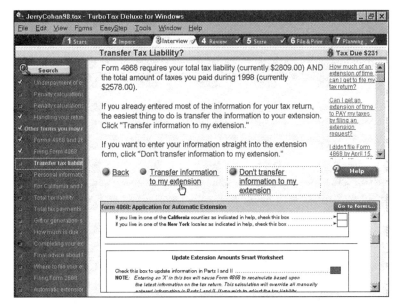

*TurboTax can transfer the required information from your return to form 4868.*

10. Enter the realistic amount of taxes you expect to have to pay in 1998. This is the total tax liability based on your income, deductions, and credits, not the amount you think you'll owe. Click **Continue**.

11. Enter the total amount you paid in taxes so far in 1998. This includes amounts withheld from your pay and reported on forms W-2 and 1099 along with any amounts you submitted in estimated tax payments. Click **Continue**.

12. If you need to file for an extension for a gift or generation-skipping transfer tax, click **Yes**, enter the amount of the tax, and click **Continue**. Otherwise, click **No**. TurboTax subtracts your payments from your tax liability and displays the amount you must submit with your extension. You can adjust the balance due, but when you actually get around to filing, the IRS might slap you with a penalty for late payment of the amount. Write a check for the amount you must pay and make the check out to Internal Revenue Service. Write your social security number on the front of the check and write "1998 form 4868" near the top.

13. Click **Continue**. TurboTax informs you that it has completed the request for an extension.

14. Click **Continue**. TurboTax displays the address to which you must send your extension request.

15. Open the **File** menu and click **Print**.

247

16. Click **Form 4868** (near the bottom of the Print dialog box) and click the **Print** button.

17. Mail form 4868 with a check for any balance due to the address displayed by TurboTax.

## Still on Track?

If you made it this far, you're essentially done and can officially ring in the new tax year. To celebrate, you might send in your first estimated tax payment for 1999. But first, make sure you've done all the following things required to get your 1040 to the IRS:

➤ Made the right decision of whether to file your return now or wait till the night of April 15. See "Should I Wait or Send It Right Now?," on page 240.

➤ Filed your tax return electronically via modem, if you wanted to. See "Filing Electronically for Quick Rebates," on page 241.

➤ Saved some paper by printing the 1040PC. See "Streamlining Your Return with the 1040PC," on page 243.

➤ Printed out a complete copy of your tax return, if TurboTax gave you no other option or you decided to keep a copy for your own records. See "Going the Standard Route with the Full 1040," on page 244.

➤ Checked your return one last time and signed it. See "Preparing and Signing Your Printed Return," on page 245.

➤ Filed an extension if you just couldn't make that April 15th deadline. See "It's April 15th and I'm Not Done!," on page 246.

# Paying Your State Income Taxes

After TurboTax has performed the calculations for your federal income tax return, you hardly need the state version. You just copy the key numbers from your 1040 to your state income tax return and make a few minor adjustments and calculations. However, using the state version helps you transfer numbers from your federal income tax return without a glitch. You won't wonder if you slipped up or missed an essential bit of information. TurboTax State grabs the required information, plugs the numbers into the right equations, and leads you through the process of entering any additional details.

This chapter shows you just what to do, covering everything from downloading and installing TurboTax State (if you don't already have it) to transferring information from your federal return and filing your state return electronically or producing a printed version for the mail. By the end of this chapter, you can wash your hands of the 1998 tax year and move on to bigger and better things—like spring break.

If you're fortunate enough to live in Alaska, Florida, Nevada, South Dakota, Texas, or Washington, you can skip this chapter. These states don't tax their residents' income. (I always wondered how those states got people to live there.) New Hampshire and Tennessee tax only interest and dividend income.

**$27.95**

TurboTax State costs $27.95. If your state has a simple tax return that grabs most of the numbers off the federal return, you can save yourself some money by transferring the numbers by hand. In most cases, the process is a breeze.

# Installing TurboTax State Software

If you ordered TurboTax State, you might have received your copy of it in the mail. It comes on a floppy disk in a little cardboard envelope, typically about one month after you receive the federal version. The wait can make you a little nervous, but be patient. If you didn't order it, you can pick it up on the Internet at Intuit's Web site, assuming that Intuit has finalized the version for your state. The following sections show you how to download your state version (if you have a modem) and install TurboTax State from the floppy disk or by running the downloaded file.

## *Downloading a Copy of TurboTax State*

In the past, I ordered TurboTax State and then twiddled my thumbs in March waiting for it to arrive in the mail. Then I got smart and decided that it wasn't worth the wait. I had a modem—I could get it myself the minute Intuit had worked the bugs out. The only drawback is that you end up paying a little more for the program than if you had ordered the two versions as a package. To get your own copy of TurboTax State, get your credit card, fire up your modem, and take the following steps:

1. Click the **State** tab in TurboTax.
2. Click **Buy and download state**. TurboTax connects you to the Internet, starts your Web browser, and connects you to the TurboTax State page.
3. Follow the instructions at Intuit's Web site to order and download TurboTax State for your state of residence.

One of the niftiest aspects of buying and downloading TurboTax State from Intuit's Web site is that the state program automatically installs itself after the download is complete. You can skip the next section and start working on your state return immediately.

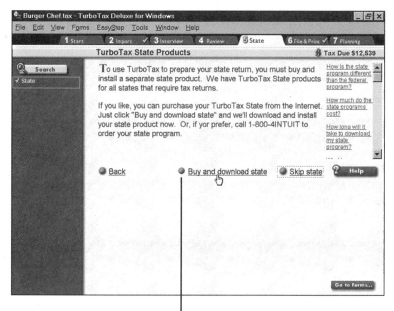

*You can order and download TurboTax State right when you download TurboTax.*

Click Buy and download state.

## *Installing TurboTax State from a Disk*

If you received TurboTax State on a floppy disk, take the following steps to install it:

1. Insert the floppy disk in your computer's floppy disk drive.
2. Open the Windows **Start** menu and click **Run**.
3. Type **a:setup** or **b:setup** (depending on which floppy drive the disk is in) and press **Enter**.
4. Follow the onscreen instructions to complete the installation.

# Starting Your State Income Tax Return

Before you even consider starting your state income tax return, make sure your federal income tax return is finished and in its final form. If you have not yet run an error check on your federal return, do it now. See Chapter 18, "Auditing and Reviewing Your Return with TurboTax," for details. Because TurboTax gets most of its information for your state return from your federal return, you want everything to be in order before you begin.

When you're sure that your federal income tax return is complete and correct, take the following steps to start your state income tax return:

1. Run TurboTax, as explained in Chapter 1, "TurboTax Nickel Tour." (TurboTax State becomes a part of TurboTax when you install it. You don't run a separate program.)

### Updating Your State Return

If you change any entries on your federal income tax return, you should update your state return. After making your changes, open the **File** menu and choose **Go to State**. If you have more than one state return, choose the return you want to open. TurboTax automatically updates your state return. Any entries you manually entered or chose to override in your state return are *not* changed.

### Married Filing Separately?

If you are married and filing your federal income tax return jointly, but want to file separate state income tax returns, use the **File**, **Save As** command to save your return under another name. Open the **File** menu, choose **Remove State**, select the state forms you want to remove, and click the **Remove** button. Click **OK**. Create a new state income tax return as explained in the previous section.

2. Open the federal income tax return on which you want to base your state return.

3. Click the **State** tab. TurboTax starts a new state income tax return for you and pulls all the required information from your federal return.

Yep, that's it. After TurboTax State is installed, all you have to do is click on the State tab, and you have an instant income tax return for your state. However, you will need to make a few minor adjustments and enter additional information as required by your state's revenue service.

## Making a Few Minor Adjustments

After you have the State tab front and center, the onscreen instructions guide you through the rest of the process. TurboTax's State Assistant provides the instructions and asks you a series of questions to supply any missing information. Just follow the Assistant's lead and type the requested entries. When you complete a step, click **Continue** to move on to the next series of questions.

At the end of the Interview, the Assistant leads you right into the review process and checks your return for any errors. Correct the errors and supply any additional information to ensure that your state return is complete and accurate.

## Printing Your State Tax Return

Most states give you the option of filing your tax return electronically or mailing in a printed version. Even if you decide to file electronically, you should print a copy of the tax return for your own records. To print your return, take the following steps:

1. In the Interview Navigator, click **Prepare 1998 State Name** (where *State Name* is the name of the state for which you are preparing the return).

2. Open the **File** menu and click **Print**.

3. Make sure **Tax Return for Filing** is selected.

4. If desired, click the **Supporting Details** check box to print additional schedules, forms, and worksheets that contain details about the entries on your state tax return.

5. Click the **Print** button.

**For the Record**

To create a copy of your state tax return for your own records, repeat these steps, but click **Tax Return for Your Records** in step 3.

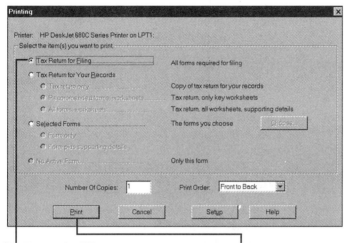

*You can print your state tax return to mail it.*

Click Tax Return for Filing.     Click the Print button to start printing.

# Preparing and Signing Your Return

After you have a printed copy of your state income tax return, take the following steps to prepare it to be mailed to your state revenue service:

➤ Make sure the forms are in the proper order. TurboTax arranged the forms for you during printing.

➤ If you received a barcoded label from the state, stick it to the designated area at the top of page 1 of your state return.

➤ Sign and date your return. If you are married and filing a joint return, make sure your spouse signs and dates the return, too.

➤ Attach any copies of W-2 forms and any other required forms to the front of your state tax return.

➤ If you owe taxes, make out a check to your state's revenue service for the exact amount you owe. Make sure your social security number is written or printed on the front of the check and write a description of the payment on the front of the check (for example, "1998 Indiana Income Tax").

If you don't have a barcoded envelope from your state's revenue service, use a standard business envelope to mail your return. To find the address of your state revenue service, see the Appendix, "State Tax Agencies: Addresses and Phone Numbers."

# Filing Your State Income Tax Return Electronically

Even the so-called "progressive states" have had a little trouble keeping up with the times. As late as 1997, few states allowed you to file your income tax return electronically. Fortunately, in 1998, most states are online and ready to support electronic filing.

The process for filing your state income tax return electronically mirrors the process for filing your federal income tax return:

1. Review your state income tax return, if you have not already done so. Make any corrections, as suggested by TurboTax. If your return has errors, TurboTax won't allow you to file electronically.
2. Click the **Interview** tab.
3. In the Interview Navigator, click **Electronic filing or 1040PC**.
4. Click **File Electronically-it's the fastest, most accurate way** and click **Continue**.
5. Open the **TurboTax supports electronic filing for...** drop-down list and click the name of your state. (If your state is not on the list, it doesn't support electronic filing.)
6. Make sure **Yes, I'll file my state return electronically** is selected and click **Continue**.
7. If you owe taxes, choose the preferred method of payment (automatic withdrawal, credit card, or check). If you are due to receive a refund, choose the option to specify whether you want the refund deposited directly into your bank account or you want to receive a check. Click **Continue**.
8. Enter any additional information to provide specific details about your bank account or credit card. Click **Continue**.
9. Follow the onscreen instructions to complete the electronic filing process. (These steps vary depending on whether you are submitting both your state and federal return or just your state return, and on the state in which you are filing your return.)

After filing your state income tax return electronically, you might need to mail a paper copy of your return along with your W-2s and other supporting documents to make it official. Follow the onscreen instructions to tie up any loose ends.

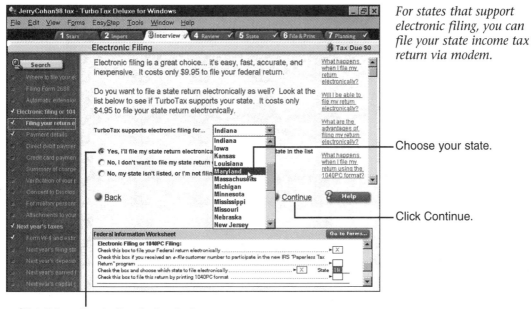

*For states that support electronic filing, you can file your state income tax return via modem.*

Choose your state.

Click Continue.

Click this option to file electronically.

## Still on Track?

At this point, both your federal and state income tax returns should be signed, sealed, and at least ready to deliver. To make sure that your state return is on its way to the proper authorities, you should have accomplished the following in this chapter:

➤ Purchased and downloaded the state version of TurboTax from Intuit's Web site, if you didn't already have it on disk. See "Downloading a Copy of TurboTax State," on page 250.

➤ Installed the state version of TurboTax on your hard drive. See "Installing TurboTax State from a Disk," on page 251.

➤ Ported the essential data from your federal income tax return to your state return. See "Starting Your State Income Tax Return," on page 251.

➤ Edited any values that were different on your state return and entered any additional information. See "Making a Few Minor Adjustments," on page 252.

➤ Printed a copy of your state return to file it or keep it for your records. See "Printing Your State Tax Return," on page 252.

➤ Signed and dated your state income tax return to make it official. See "Preparing and Signing Your Return," on page 253.

➤ If your state supports electronic filing, you should have filed your state income tax return electronically. See "Filing Your State Income Tax Return Electronically," on page 254.

# Part 5

# After the Fact: Amendments, Audits, and Future Plans

*People collect the money. It doesn't come over the transom without some effort to collect it.*

—Former IRS Commissioner, Donald Alexander

*You've just submitted your tax return. Congratulations! You can now kick back, relax, and wait for your refund, right? Well, not exactly. This tax thing is a year-long activity. If you recheck your return and notice errors, you might have to file an amended return. If the IRS has any questions, they might send you a notice that either asks you to submit additional information or notifies you of an audit. And even if your form slides through the IRS computers without a glitch, you really should start planning now for the 1999 tax year.*

*In this part, you learn how to tie up all the loose ends for 1998 and take some strategies to cut your 1999 tax bill. You learn how to file an amended return to correct errors on your 1998 tax return, prepare for and survive an IRS audit, and take steps early in 1999 to reduce your adjusted gross income and take advantage of additional tax credits. This part also includes a list of the 20 most common tax questions and answers to help out when you've hit a dead end.*

# Chapter 21

# Oops, I Made Some Honest Mistakes

## In This Chapter

➤ Try, try again with an amended return

➤ Understand the more common audit procedures

➤ Prepare for and respond to various types of IRS audits

➤ Know and exercise your rights as a taxpayer

➤ Appeal an audit when you disagree with the IRS

➤ Negotiate with the IRS for a better deal

By using TurboTax and filing your tax return electronically (or filing a 1040PC), you significantly reduce your chances of being audited. Because TurboTax performs the calculations for you, you reduce the risks of punching a wrong key on your calculator or performing the wrong calculation altogether. In addition, because no IRS data-entry clerk must key in your information again, you further reduce the risk of human error, which commonly triggers an audit.

However, using TurboTax does not completely eliminate potential errors and typos. For example, you might have mistyped your social security number, made a typo while transferring entries from your W-2 into TurboTax, or submitted your return too early—before you had received all of your W-2s and 1099s. In addition, you might have misinterpreted one of the more complicated tax rules and entered the wrong information.

If you discover the error right after submitting your tax return, you can file an amended return to correct the error. If the IRS discovers the error before you do, it might request an explanation or let you know that your tax return has been selected for an audit. Whatever the case, you must know how to file an amended return and how to prepare for and reply to an audit notification from the IRS.

# Filing an Amended Return

Although the IRS likes people to think that filing income tax returns is easy, it knows that the process is flawed, that forms and instructions can be confusing, and that people make mistakes. To help you report the errors and correct your income tax return, the IRS allows you to fix your own mistakes by filing form 1040X, Amended U.S. Individual Income Tax Return.

## *Rules and Time Limits*

You can use the 1040X to report any errors on your return, whether these errors increase or decrease your tax bill. If you took the standard deduction in the past and realized that you would have saved more by itemizing, file an amended return. If you had too much withheld in social security tax two years ago and just learned about the limits in this book, file an amended return to get some of that money back.

**Amend Now, Get Audited Later**

Filing an amended return slightly increases your chances of being audited. However, you're better off fixing an error right away, instead of waiting to see if the IRS will catch it. If you owe additional taxes because of the error, the IRS penalizes you by charging interest on the amount owed; by paying it early, you reduce or eliminate the penalty. If you're filing an amended return because the IRS owes you five bucks, just take the loss and forget about it.

However, there are some limitations for filing an amended return:

➤ You must have filed a 1040 for the tax year in question before you can file a 1040X for that year. Duh!

➤ You have three years to file an amended return. For instance, you can file an amended return for your 1995 tax return by April 15, 1998. You cannot file an amended return for your 1994 income tax return.

➤ You must file a separate 1040X for each tax return you want to amend. You can't lump three years together on a single 1040X.

If you file an amended return that shows you owe additional income tax, write a check for the amount you owe to the Internal Revenue Service. Write your social security number on the check and write "199? form 1040X" on the front of the check (where the question mark is the year of the return you are amending).

If you cannot pay the bill in full, complete and print form 9465, Installment Agreement Request, to request permission to pay over time.

## Preparing a 1040X in TurboTax

One of the best features of TurboTax is that it has all the obscure forms you need. You don't have to call the IRS or take a trip to the local library or post office in search of a form. TurboTax even has a 1040X. To display a new 1040X and fill in the blanks, take the following steps:

1. Open the **Forms** menu and click **Open a Form**.

2. Scroll down the list of forms and click **Form 1040X: Amended Tax Return**.

3. Click the **Open** button.

4. Enter the year for which you are filing this amended return. The year is printed at the top of the return you are amending.

**Amend Your State Income Tax Return**

Whenever you submit a 1040X to amend your federal income tax return, you should submit the required form to amend your state income tax return, as well.

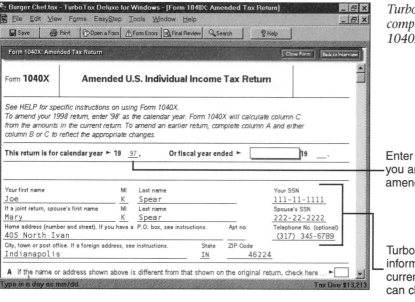

*TurboTax can help you complete and print a 1040X.*

Enter the year for which you are filing this amended return.

TurboTax lifts this information from your current return, but you can change it.

261

5. Press the **Tab** key. TurboTax automatically fills in most of the information at the top of the return using information you entered in the currently open return.

6. Tab to any of the fields in the personal information section and enter your changes, if any.

7. Click the check boxes below the personal information section to indicate any change of name, address, or filing status, or to specify if the original return has been or will be audited or changed by the IRS.

*Click the check boxes to answer these essential questions.*

Click your filing status on your original return.

Click the same filing status or the new filing status you want to use.

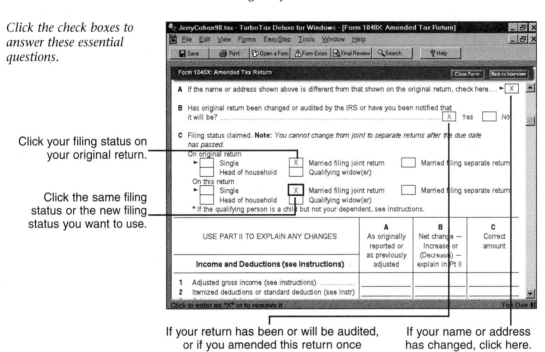

If your return has been or will be audited, or if you amended this return once already, click here.

If your name or address has changed, click here.

8. Scroll down to the Income and Deductions section.

9. For each item, enter the amount on your original return in Column A and then tab to Column B and type the net correction. (Type positive values as normal, and type negative values in parentheses.)

10. Repeat step 9 until you have entered all the requested information for income and deductions, tax liability, and tax payments.

11. On line 16, enter any amounts you paid in taxes by filing form 4868, 2688, or 2350.

12. On line 17, enter the total amount of tax paid on your original return, including any taxes you paid at the time you filed your return. TurboTax performs the requried calculations and shows whether you owe additional taxes or are due a refund.

13. Open the **File** menu and choose **Print**.
14. Make sure **Form 1040X** is selected and click the **Print** button.

After you print form 1040X, sign and date the form. If you are married filing jointly, have your spouse sign and date the form. If you owe taxes, attach your check, made payable to the Internal Revenue Service, to the front of your 1040X, and mail the form (and payment, if necessary) to your regional IRS office. See "Preparing and Signing Your Printed Return," in Chapter 19, "Submitting Your Tax Return," for details.

### Deadline for Changing Filing Status

If you submitted the original return as Married Filing Jointly, you cannot change to Married Filing Separately after the filing deadline for that year. If you filed your 1998 return in February or March of 1999 and you are filing this amended return before April 15, 1999, you can change your filing status. If you are filing any later than that, you must use the same filing status.

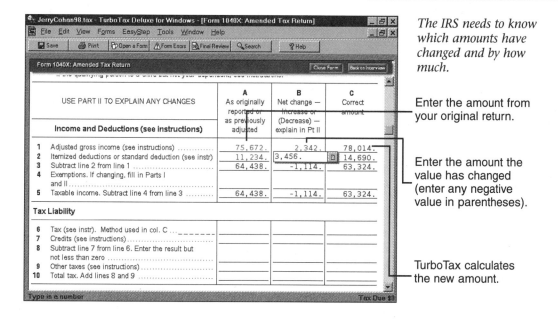

*The IRS needs to know which amounts have changed and by how much.*

Enter the amount from your original return.

Enter the amount the value has changed (enter any negative value in parentheses).

TurboTax calculates the new amount.

# IRS Audits: What Are My Chances?

I wish I could tell you that you have a better chance of getting hit by lightning than of having your tax return audited, but that wouldn't be quite true. The truth is that the IRS audits (or *examines*, in IRS lingo) about 1% of all tax returns submitted in any given year. Does this mean you have a 1% chance of having your tax return audited? Nope. The IRS carefully selects the tax returns it audits, looking for the following audit triggers:

➤ Hidden income—Income from cash businesses, transportation, retail sales, agriculture, restaurants, and any other type of business in which it is easy to hide income.

➤ High gross income, low AGI—If you have a bunch of money coming in but come up with enough deductions to warrant taxing only a quarter of it, the IRS might suspect something.

➤ Independent contractors and their employers—Some businesses might trim taxes by sending workers home and paying them as independent contractors. As an independent contractor, you lose, because you have to pay the self-employment tax. The IRS loses a portion of income tax, because you can claim half of your self-employment tax as a deduction. In short, the IRS doesn't like this type of setup.

➤ Conflicting claims—The IRS cross-checks the information it receives, comparing the amounts on the W-2s you received to the amounts you entered on your tax return. If the IRS finds conflicting information, the IRS will question it. In addition, if you're claiming a dependent that someone else is claiming on his tax return, the IRS might question both of you.

➤ Large deductions—The IRS knows that if you're earning $30,000 a year and you have four kids, it's unlikely that you donated $10,000 to charity. If any deductions or expenses seem out of line with your income, the odd entries might trigger an audit.

➤ Extravagant expenses—If your business is losing money, but you seem to be doing alright financially, the IRS might suspect that you're doing something shady.

➤ Alimony payments—If you are deducting alimony payments, you can expect the IRS to check your return against your ex-mate's return. If your ex isn't reporting your payments as income or vice versa, the IRS might haul you both in for questioning.

In addition, the IRS might choose to audit you because a neighbor, relative, or friend (I use the term loosely) squeals on you or because you filed a return with errors in the past. The IRS actually pays people to turn in tax evaders. And they call it a voluntary tax system.

### The Big, Bad IRS

Back in 1997, the IRS got hit with some pretty bad press. The papers made it sound as though the IRS was nothing more than the mafia with government stationery. Sure, a few IRS auditors got a little carried away, but when you think about it, the IRS *should* have the power to put a little pressure on tax evaders. Tax evaders are basically shoplifters—when they get something for nothing, the rest of us, honest taxpayers, have to foot the bill.

If the IRS does choose to audit your income tax return, what can you expect? Will they surround your house? Pull a van in the front drive with the official "IRS" logo painted on the side? An audit usually is not so dramatic, but if the IRS does decide to audit your tax return, the odds that you'll have to pay extra in taxes and penalties are fairly high. The following list introduces you to the three most common types of audits (and one document check that's not really an audit) along with data on the average amount the IRS nets from each type of audit:

➤ CP-2000—The CP-2000 isn't an audit; it's a computerized system that matches the information on your return with information that the IRS already has, including information from W-2s and 1099s. In most cases, if the computer finds a discrepency, it spits out a report asking you for additional documentation or an explanation. Assuming you clarify your claim over the phone or in writing to the satisfaction of the IRS, you should be able to avoid an audit.

### Keep Your Big Mouth Shut

When you first receive notice of an audit, don't announce it to the world. Neighbors, relatives, disgruntled employees, your ex, and even people you thought were your friends might offer to help the IRS successfully prosecute you.

➤ Office audit—The most popular audit is the office audit, which accounts for nearly 50% of all audits. This type of audit takes place in an IRS district or regional office in your area. More than 85% of office audits result in additional taxes and penalties averaging $2,500–$3,000.

**Statement of Changes to Your Account**

If the IRS discovers an error in your return, it might automatically correct the error and send you a form informing you of the correction, without auditing your return. If you disagree with the correction, you can file an appeal. See "Appealing the Audit," later in this chapter.

➤ Mail audit—Accounting for nearly 30% of all audits, the mail (correspondence) audit is carried out through the mail and is typically the least painful of the three types of audits. The IRS sends you a letter requesting a form or document that provides additional information or supports a deduction you claimed. More than 80% of mail audits result in additional taxes and penalties averaging $3,000–$3,500.

➤ Field audit—Accounting for nearly 20% of all audits, the field audit takes place at your business (or home office). This is the audit from hell. The auditor shows up at your business and starts poking around in your records. Your chances of escaping this audit with your savings intact are low; more than 90% of field audits result in additional taxes and penalties averaging over $13,000.

The following sections provide additional details on how to prepare for these various types of audits and properly reply to the IRS.

# Preparing for an Office Audit

When the IRS notifies you that your income tax return was selected for an audit, the notice will specify the date, time, and location of the meeting. The IRS should provide a brief explanation of the procedure and a list of questions concerning your tax return or a list of problems it has found. It might also specify a list of documents you should bring to the office.

When you're gathering the required documents, obtain only those documents that the IRS specifically requested. If the IRS requested that you bring receipts and cancelled checks for your cash donations to charitable organizations, bring only the receipts and cancelled checks for your cash donations. Don't bring receipts for non-cash donations, such as boxes of clothes. If you show the IRS anything it hasn't requested, the IRS then has the right to question you about those items.

The same rule holds for the actual audit interview—answer the questions and don't offer any additional information. The IRS has the right to question you only about the items on the list it sent you when it notified you of the audit. The IRS questions cannot stray from this list. If the IRS asks you a question concerning an issue that's not on the list, politely reply that the item is not on the list and you are not prepared to discuss it.

# Responding to the IRS Via Mail

Although people commonly accuse the government of being too impersonal, few people complain when the IRS asks them to reply to an audit question or issue by mail. The mail audit is the easiest and least stressful to deal with. The IRS sends its question or the list of supporting documentation it needs, and then you copy the requested documents, send them to the specified address, and get on with your life.

The best way to protect yourself in this type of audit is to do as little as possible. Don't write a four-page letter explaining yourself. You'll probably just incriminate yourself on some other issue. Send a terse reply and send only the requested documents or receipts.

**Be Polite, Yet Curt**

Don't get defensive or try to be friendly with your auditor. If you lose your cool, the person will probably try a little harder to nab you. If you strike up a conversation, you might say something that leads to additional questions. If you offer the auditor anything, it might be misinterpreted as a bribe. Stick to business and answer the questions.

# Preparing for a Field Audit

A field audit can run you ragged and interfere with your business. In a field audit, IRS auditors show up at your business and flip through your records. They might stay all day. They might come back the next day and the day after that. You'll feel obligated to fetch them lunch and coffee, all the while feeling compelled to kick them out.

The best way to deal with a field audit is to hire an accountant you trust, give the accountant Power of Attorney, ship the requested records to the accountant's office, and have the audit held at the accountant's place of business. That way, the audit doesn't interfere with your business, and you can focus on making money (and you'll need a lot of it after the audit). However, if you claimed business use of a portion of your home, the IRS may demand to inspect your home to ensure that the space qualifies for a deduction.

**Send a CPA**

If you're too busy to attend the audit or you're afraid you'll get violent, send an accountant in your place. You must sign a form to give the account Power of Attorney, so the IRS will have the right to discuss your tax return with that person. The IRS cannot discuss your tax return with anyone to whom you have not given Power of Attorney.

**Lost Receipts**

If you lost the receipts or other documentation the IRS asks you to produce, locate the best documentation you can find. For example, a credit card statement lists charges that might support your business deductions. Your bank might be able to supply cancelled checks. For charitable donations, contact the organization to determine if it has a record of your donation.

If you prefer to handle the field audit yourself, follow the same strategy explained in "Preparing for an Office Audit," earlier in this chapter. Provide only the requested books, forms, schedules, receipts, and other documentation, and provide direct answers to questions posed by the IRS auditors. Don't offer any information you're not specifically asked to provide. Be calm and polite without playing sycophant. And keep in mind the following two rules the IRS agent must follow:

➤ The agent may review your original books and records only one time. If the agent wants to review these books and records again, he or she must have a written statement indicating that a second review is necessary or you must request a second review.

➤ The agent cannot review any secondary records or other documentation that is not on the list of documents you originally received. If the agent requests to see secondary records, he must submit a revised list and provide you with additional time to gather the records.

## Knowing Your Rights

With standard crimes, such as robbery, murder, and rape, you're presumed innocent until proven guilty. With tax evasion, you're guilty until you can prove to the IRS that you're innocent. Without the right documentation, you might be subject to additional taxes and penalties, which you *must* pay. If you fail to pay, the IRS has the right to turn your life into a living hell by docking your wages, withdrawing money from your bank accounts, selling your stocks, taking your home and car, and seizing any other property you own.

Yes, the all-powerful IRS can make your life miserable, but Congress has recently limited some of the powers of the IRS and given taxpayers a little more control of their own destiny. Congress has done this by issuing the Taxpayer Bill of Rights. When you go into an audit, you should be aware of your rights:

➤ The IRS must explain your rights to you before the audit, which is typically done in writing.

➤ Audits must be held at a time and place that is convenient for you.

➤ You have the right to be treated with courtesy and to have your issues and questions addressed promptly. In short, the IRS has no right to be rude. You should be nice, too.

➤ You can refuse to provide documentation that the IRS has not specifically requested in writing.

➤ You may stop the examination at any time and request to consult with an accountant, lawyer, or tax advisor.

➤ You may ask the IRS to postpone the audit or change the site. (Give the IRS sufficient notice; don't request the change the day before the audit is scheduled to take place.)

➤ You may demand to talk with the IRS agent's supervisor. When you make this request, the agent must immediately stop the interview and let you talk with a supervisor.

➤ You can have a representative, accountant, or lawyer present at the audit.

➤ You may tape the interview or purchase the IRS recording.

➤ You may refuse to allow the IRS to inspect the non-business portion of your home.

➤ You may refuse to answer questions that might connect you to a crime. You can't take the Fifth Amendment concerning issues related to your tax return and you must answer questions about other people, but if the interview leads into questions that could connect you to a criminal investigation, stop the interview and talk to an attorney.

➤ If an IRS agent provided wrong or misleading information that resulted in your having to pay additional taxes or penalties (and you can prove it), you are excused from paying the additional tax and penalty. (You must prove not only that the IRS agent provided the wrong answer, but also that you worded your question clearly.)

➤ You have a 21-day grace period from the time you are notified of a tax debt before you are charged interest on that debt.

The Taxpayer Bill of Rights lists additional rights you have. For more information, check out the Taxpayer Bill of Rights at the IRS Web site (www.irs.ustreas.gov) or check out the *Money Income Tax Handbook* in TurboTax's help system.

# Appealing the Audit

After the examination, the auditor should mail you (or hand to you) a form 4549, Examination Report, indicating the recommended changes and any additional taxes and penalties you owe. If your audit proceeded smoothly and you agree with the auditor's changes to your tax return (or decide that the money you owe isn't worth fighting for), you sign form 870, Consent to Proposed Tax Adjustments, and mail it with your check to the specified address. Don't sign this form unless you agree with the changes.

If you disagree with the changes and want to file a complaint, you can appeal the audit. Take the following steps to appeal:

1. Contact the auditor with whom you disagree. Ask if you can provide any additional documentation to support your claim.

2. Contact the auditor's manager and tactfully state the disagreement you are having with the auditor. The auditor must provide information on how to contact his manager.

**Settle Quick**

It's in your best interest to settle any disagreements as quickly as possible. Every day your appeals process drags on, the IRS assesses penalties on the taxes you eventually have to pay. In addition, the further along the appeals process you go, the more likely it is that you'll need costly professional help. I'm not telling you to wimp out, but the odds are that you'll lose financially, even if you win the appeal.

3. Wait for the 30-day letter. If you don't sign form 870, the IRS will send you a 30-day letter, to which you must respond in 30 days or less. If you miss the deadline, you give up your right to appeal. When you receive the letter, write your own reply, make copies of both letters, and send the originals to the IRS. You'll get another interview with an auditor who's one rung higher up the ladder. Good luck.

4. Wait for the 90-day letter. If you don't pay the taxes the IRS says you owe or file an appeal within 30 days of receiving the 30-day letter, the IRS will send you a 90-day letter (also called a Statutory Notice of Deficiency). At this point, you have 90 days to pay the taxes due or petition with the U.S. Tax Court to hear your case. If you fail to petition the court within 90 days from receiving the notice, you must pay your taxes due in full and then sue for your refund later.

5. If you get a Notice of Tax Due and Demand for Payment, the IRS is getting serious. This is the first collection notice. Pay it, or the IRS will start feeding your life through its meat grinder. However, you can negotiate, as explained in the following section.

# Negotiating with the IRS

When Willie Nelson got into trouble with the IRS for tax evasion, they didn't throw him in jail or destroy his career. The IRS knew that if it did that, it would never see the money. They just came up with an easy-payment plan that let Willie pay a good chunk of his back taxes and penalties over a long period of time.

The point is that the IRS wants the money, or a good portion of the money, that it thinks you owe in taxes. The IRS wants to close the case and move on to other audits. It wants the matter settled. With that in mind, be prepared to negotiate. Here are your options:

➤ Survive the deadline—Pay as much as you think you can afford by the deadline. Contact the IRS immediately and negotiate a deal for paying the rest.

➤ Request an abatement for penalties—If you agree that you owe back taxes, but you owe penalties because your payment was late, the IRS may cancel the penalties if the delay was due to causes beyond your control: personal or family illness, catastrophic event (such as a fire or flood), bad advice from a tax consultant, and so on.

➤ Pitch a compromise—Contact the IRS and let them know that you cannot possibly afford to pay all the taxes you owe. Make a reasonable offer. Hey, it's worth a try. If back taxes are causing you serious hardship, you can contact the IRS Problem Resolution Office for help.

➤ Ask the IRS to postpone the deadline—If you don't have the money right now, but you will have it in six months, contact the IRS and ask to have the deadline postponed.

➤ Pay in installments—If you can't pay all at once, contact the IRS and ask if you can pay your bill in installments. You still must pay your back taxes, but you might be able to avoid penalties by paying your installments on time.

# Still on Track?

When you discover that you made a mistake or the IRS points out an error, you feel as though you've been derailed. To get back on track, take one of the following steps:

➤ Fix your mistakes before anyone else discovers them. See "Filing an Amended Return," on page 260.

➤ Get a pretty good idea of how likely it is that the IRS will audit your income tax return. See "IRS Audits: What Are My Chances?," on page 264.

➤ Get your records together and take a trip to the IRS office. See "Preparing for an Office Audit," on page 266.

➤ Reply to any audit through the mail. See "Responding to the IRS Via Mail," on page 267.

➤ Get your house in order before the IRS comes knocking at your door. See "Preparing for a Field Audit," on page 267.

➤ Memorize the Taxpayer Bill of Rights. See "Knowing Your Rights," on page 268.

➤ Question authority! Appeal that audit. See "Appealing the Audit," on page 269.

➤ Cut a deal with the IRS to get an easy payment plan. See "Negotiating with the IRS," on page 270.

# Chapter 22

# Tax Planning for 1999

## In This Chapter

➤ Map out an overall strategy for saving taxes in 1999

➤ Revise your W-4 to have your employer withhold just the right amount of taxes

➤ Make estimated tax payments to avoid penalties at the end of the year

➤ Maximize your income by taking advantage of your employer's tax-free benefits

➤ Save more for the future with tax-deferred investments

➤ Take advantage of low taxes on long-term capital gains

Those who pay less in taxes don't do it by frantically searching for deductions the night before their tax returns are due. For these savvy taxpayers, minimizing taxes is an ongoing process that began when they first realized that they were in charge of their own tax destiny.

Although you might not have reduced your 1998 tax bill significantly, the tips and tricks in this chapter should help reduce your *next* tax bill. This chapter shows you how to develop your own tax-saving plan, make the most of your tax-free benefits at work, save more for your golden years with tax-deferred investments, and even use investment returns as a source of low-tax income.

# The Overall Strategy

As you develop a strategy for saving taxes, you should understand the big picture, the overall goal, the plan of attack. It's pretty simple, actually—withhold just enough tax to cover your bill, reduce reported income, and increase deductions and credits.

Although simple, the plan is fairly complex when you start to examine the details. How do you estimate your taxes more accurately? How do you reduce your reported income without lying about it? What kind of deductions and credits will give you the most significant tax breaks? The following sections answer these questions and provide additional tips and tricks for trimming your tax bill.

## The Marriage Penalty

In a marriage in which both people earn approximately the same income, it's common for them to pay more taxes than if they were single. When filling out the W-4, make sure you fill out the Two-Earner/Two-Job worksheet on the back. This will give you a closer estimate of your withholding.

# Reviewing Your W-4s

Are you getting a whopping refund? Could the amount you owe in taxes support a family of four? Either scenario is undesirable. If you had too much withheld from your pay, you missed the opportunity to invest that money or use it to pay off your charge card balance. If you had too little withheld, the IRS probably hit you with a penalty in addition to your bill for back taxes. To avoid this situation, revise your W-4.

The W-4 is a document that helps you estimate the amount your employer should withhold in taxes. It indicates your filing status, number of dependents, average itemized deductions, and any additional amount you want your employer to withhold. It typically provides a fairly good estimate of withholdings, assuming you're single or that one person in the family is the primary wage earner. If you're married and you both earn nearly the same income, watch out. The estimated amount is rarely enough to cover your combined tax bill.

To revise your W-4, first contact your employer's accounting department and get a copy of your previous W-4. Without this document, you'll have no idea whether you should increase or decrease your withholding. With this document in hand, complete a new W-4. You can obtain a blank W-4 from your employer or take the following steps to open a W-4 in TurboTax:

1. Open the **Forms** menu and click **Open a Form**.
2. Scroll down to near the bottom and click **Form W-4-T: Withholding Allowance Certificate** or **Form W-4-S: Withholding Allowance Certificate**. (T stands for Taxpayer; S stands for Spouse.)
3. Click the **Open** button.
4. Follow the instructions on the W-4 worksheet to complete it.

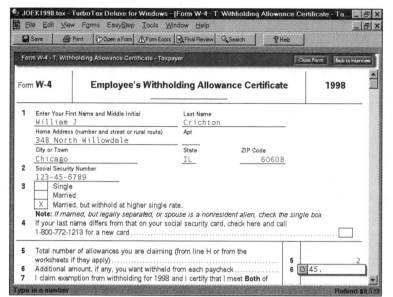

*Complete a new W-4 in TurboTax.*

You can also recalculate your withholding by using the TurboTax tax planner, as explained in "Drawing Up a Plan with TurboTax," later in this chapter. If you want the most accurate calculations, let TurboTax handle them.

The easiest way to increase your withholding is to complete the new W-4 using the same entries on the previous W-4 and choose to have an additional chunk of money withdrawn from each paycheck. For example, if you owed $1,200 in 1998 and you get paid every two weeks, have an additional $46 withheld per paycheck ($1,200/26 paychecks per year). If you are married, you can also increase withholding by choosing **Married, but withhold at higher, single rate**. However, basing your withholding on the amount you owed in 1998 should bring you closer to the target.

To have less withheld, perform the same steps in reverse. If you received a refund of $2,000, divide $2,000 by the number of paychecks you receive each year, and have your employer withhold that much less from each paycheck. Because the W-4 has no simple way to specify that you want less withheld, let TurboTax handle it for you, as explained in "Drawing Up a Plan with TurboTax," later in this chapter.

# Calculating and Paying Estimated Taxes

Are you self-employed? Do you have a good chunk of income from interest, investments, gambling, or other sources? If so, any amount withheld from your paychecks does not cover this other income. If you own your own business or act as an independent contractor, you have only one choice—send in estimated tax payments each quarter. If you have a regular job, you have two options: your employer can withhold additional money from your paycheck or you can send in estimated tax payments.

### 1040-ES Did Not Print

If you didn't print your 1040-ES forms, open the **File** menu and click **Print**. Click **Selected Forms** and click the **Choose** button. Click **1040-ES 1&2**, Ctrl+click **1040-ES 3&4** and click **OK**. Click the **Print** button.

If you're self-employed, TurboTax already calculated the amount you should send in each quarter and completed a set of four 1040-ES forms for submitting your estimated tax payments. TurboTax should have printed these forms along with your 1998 income tax return. Just complete the forms and send them in with a check for the specified amount by the date printed on the form. You must send your estimated payments on the 15th of April, June, and September of 1999, and January of the year 2000.

*TurboTax creates the form 1040-ES you need to submit estimated payments.*

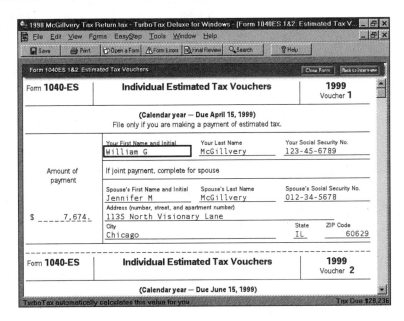

Ideally, the IRS wants you to send equal payments each quarter. Realistically, this isn't always possible. You might earn more money in one quarter than in another, and the IRS doesn't require you to pay estimated taxes on money you haven't received. To estimate your taxes for each quarter, take the following steps:

1. Divide your total tax bill for 1998 by your 1998 net earnings (gross income minus expenses). This gives you the percentage you paid in 1998.

2. For the current quarter, subtract your expenses from your gross earnings (to determine your net earnings for the quarter).

3. Multiply your net earnings for the quarter by the percentage you calculated in step 1. This gives you a rough estimate of the taxes you owe. Perform the same steps to calculate your state estimated tax payment.

It seems logical to base your estimates on your tax bracket. For instance, if you were in a 28% tax bracket, you would owe 28% in income tax plus 15.3% in self-employment tax for a total of 43.3% of your net income, right? Not quite. This calculation does not take into consideration your exemptions, deductions, and credits, including the deduction for half of your self-employment tax. If your net income from self-employment is $60,000, your spouse earns roughly the same amount, and you have a couple kids, you can expect your tax bill to come in at about 25-30%. So, if you're thinking of starting your own business and you consult with an accountant who performs a quickie calculation and tells you to be prepared to pay an enormous amount in taxes, it's probably not as bad as the accountant says it is.

## Maximizing Your Expenses

Some people (typically those who are not self-employed) have the misconception that if you purchase more equipment and supplies for your business, you make more money because you save so much in taxes. It's true that as your expenses rise, your tax bill sinks, but so does your net income, your profit, the amount that goes in *your pocket.* Never purchase something for your business because you think that the taxes you save will miraculously increase your profit.

However, when you consider purchasing essential equipment, keep in mind that you will save some money on taxes. If you pay estimated federal and state taxes of 40%, every dollar you spend on a qualifying expense actually costs you only sixty cents. When you're making a purchasing decision, keep that in mind. For instance, if you purchase a $3,000 computer and list it as a Section 179 expense, the computer will cost you only $1,800, because you'll save $1,200 in taxes. With the amount you save in taxes, you might be able to purchase equipment of higher quality that will save you money in the long run.

### Don't Need It? Don't Buy It!

Always remember that you're not earning money by spending more—even though you might save a great deal in taxes when you purchase an expensive piece of equipment, that expense is reducing your profit. If you don't need it, don't buy it.

# Making the Most of Tax-free Benefits

Vigilance and endurance. That's what it takes to save taxes. If your employer offers a 401(k) plan, and you don't know about it or you fail to contribute to it regularly, you lose. If your employer offers a cafeteria plan, and you think it's too much of a hassle to turn in receipts to be reimbursed for medical expenses, you lose again. When you work for a company that offers tax-saving programs, take advantage of them:

➤ Cafeteria plan (or flexible spending account)—With a cafeteria plan, also called a flexible spending account (FSA), non-taxed dollars are placed in your account with each paycheck. You then pay your medical insurance premiums, doctor and dentist bills, prescriptions, and qualifying child and dependent care expenses with funds from your account. It's a hassle, but if you're in a 28% tax bracket, you save 28 cents on every dollar you spend. (Don't contribute too much to the plan—you lose any money that's left in the account at the end of the year.)

➤ Medical savings account—Like a cafeteria plan, a medical savings account (MSA) enables you to contribute pre-tax dollars to a special account and pay your insurance premiums and medical bills with money from the account. With an MSA, you earn interest on the money in your account and you get to keep any money that's left over at the end of the year. However, there are stiff penalties for withdrawing the money early.

➤ Tax-deferred retirement account—If your employer offers a 401(k), sign up for it. In most cases, the employer contributes matching contributions of 50 cents or more on every dollar, and you contribute non-taxed money into your account. You can watch your retirement nest egg grow and save on taxes at the same time.

➤ Incentive stock options—An incentive stock option (ISO) enables an employee to purchase stocks from the company at a discounted price. Typically, the employee is subject to tax on those stocks only when the employee sells them.

➤ Deferred compensation—For some high-income positions, companies might offer deferred compensation plans. The company pays you less in regular salary and sets aside a portion of your salary to be paid when you leave the company or retire. You pay tax on that money only when you receive it, hopefully at a lower tax rate. This is a little risky—tax rates might jump or the company might fold before you see your money.

**Balancing Wages and Benefits**

If you're in a union or in a position to negotiate a contract with your employer, don't focus only on wages. A $100 boost in a tax-free benefit is worth more than a $100 raise.

# Deferring Taxes Through Retirement Investments

As the social security system teeters on the brink of collapse, it's important for you to secure your future by developing your own retirement plan. Fortunately, you can sock away loads of money into a retirement plan and save on taxes at the same time. Every dollar you contribute to a qualifying plan is tax-free till the day you start withdrawing from the plan. If you do not contribute to a tax-deferred retirement account, start now. The following list explains your options:

➤ Company-sponsored plans—Many companies offer their own retirement plans to their employees in the form of a 401(k), SIMPLE, Keogh, tax-deferred annuity (TDA), or other plan. Some companies offer matching contributions up to a certain percentage of your salary; for example, a company might offer matching contributions of fifty cents on a dollar, up to 6% of your salary. Try to contribute the maximum percentage to take full advantage of your company's plan.

➤ Individual retirement account (IRA)—If your company does not offer its own retirement plan, you can contribute up to $2,000 per year to an IRA. To learn more about IRAs and their limitations, see the section "Traditional IRAs: Save Now, Pay Later," in Chapter 14, "Getting a Tax Break with Retirement Investments."

➤ Self-employed plans—The complexities and limitations of IRAs make them an impractical choice for the self-employed. If you are self-employed, consult a financial advisor or mutual fund company about setting up your own SEP or Keogh plan. For details about SEP, Keogh, and SIMPLE plans, see the section "401(k), SEP, Keogh, and SIMPLE Retirement Contributions," in Chapter 14.

# Taking Advantage of the Tax Reduction for Capital Gains

Although tax-deferred accounts are great for retirement, when you're thirty years old, you might not see a great benefit of being a millionaire when you turn sixty. You see your income being heavily taxed, and you're working overtime just to keep up. The only way to get ahead is to invest—use your savings to earn money.

Given the current low tax rates for long-term capital gains, you get to keep a higher percentage of the money you earn from investments than from your labor, especially if you're self-employed. For instance, you might pay 35% in income tax and self-employment tax combined, but only 20% tax on long-term capital gains. Here are the brackets about which you need to know:

➤ Short-term investments—Gains from investments you held for less than 12 months are taxed at the same rate as your income. There's no cap on short-term capital gains tax—if your income falls in the 31% tax bracket, your short-term capital gains are taxed at 31%.

**Buy and Hold**

Most financial advisors recommend against buying and selling investments in panic mode. With long-term capital gains being taxed at such low rates, it makes even more sense now to hold your investments for at least 18 months before selling them.

➤ Long-term investments held between 12 and 18 months—Gains from investments you held for more than 12 months but less than 18 months are subject to a maximum 28% long-term capital gains tax. If you are in a lower income-tax bracket, your gains are taxed at the lower rate.

➤ Long-term investments held more than 18 months—Gains from investments you held for more than 18 months are subject to a maximum 20% long-term capital gains tax or 10% if your income falls in the 15% tax bracket.

When you invest outside a tax-deferred retirement account, you should consider buying into tax-free investments, such as state and municipal bonds. Although your return on these investments might not equal the return you might see from stocks, the interest you see is not subject to federal income tax.

# Drawing Up a Plan with TurboTax

To help you develop a foolproof tax-saving program, TurboTax can walk you through an Interview to develop a custom tax plan. You just need to start the Interview and answer a few questions:

1. Make sure your 1998 income tax return is open in TurboTax, so the tax planner can lift data from your current return.

2. Open the **EasyStep** menu and click **Planning**. If you're already on the Interview screen, click the **Planning** tab.

3. Click **Run planners**. TurboTax displays a little blurb about the recent tax changes that might help you save taxes.

4. Click **Tax Planner**.

5. Under Plan 1, click **1998**. Under Plan 2, click **1999**. Click **Continue**. (You may choose 1999 for both plans to compare the results of two different tax-saving strategies.)

6. Enter your filing status for both years and enter the number of dependents you plan on claiming for both years. (For example, if you're expecting twins, bump up the number of planned exemptions by two.) Click **Continue**.

7. Click the check box next to each area you want your tax plan to examine. Click **Continue**.

8. For each plan, enter the percentage increase you expect to receive in wages, or edit the number in the Wages text box to reflect your expected wages. Click **Continue**.

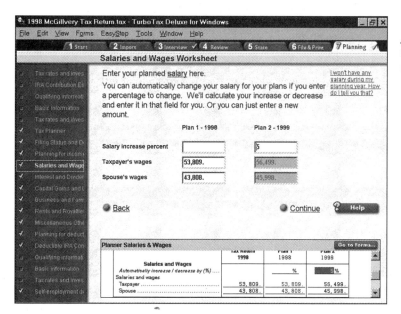

*The TurboTax tax planner gathers the information it needs to help you develop a custom tax plan.*

**9.** Continue answering the questions posed in the Interview until you have completed it. The steps vary depending on the types of income and deductions you reported on your 1998 income tax return and on the check boxes you selected in step 7.

At the end of the Interview, TurboTax leads you through the process of reviewing your plan and making changes to it. The Interview also leads you through the process of updating your W-4s, preparing a set of 1040-ES forms for paying estimated taxes, and printing your plan and any related forms.

# Still on Track?

Just when you thought you could stop thinking about taxes, you need to start planning for the next round of taxes. As you look forward to 1999, make sure you've developed a strategy and flagged the big tax breaks:

➤ Understand the strategy behind maximizing income and minimizing taxes. See "The Overall Strategy," on page 274.

➤ Update your W-4s to ensure that your employer doesn't withhold too much or too little in taxes from your paycheck. See "Reviewing Your W-4s," on page 274.

➤ Calculate your quarterly estimated tax payments and print the forms required for submitting your payments. See "Calculating and Paying Estimated Taxes," on page 276.

➤ Buy what you need to make money, and write it off as an expense. See "Maximizing Your Expenses," on page 277.

➤ Set up a meeting with your personnel manager at work, and see what your employer has to offer. See "Making the Most of Tax-free Benefits," on page 278.

➤ Earn some income from investments and pay less tax on it than if you had actually worked for it. See "Taking Advantage of the Tax Reduction for Capital Gains," on page 279.

➤ Create a foolproof tax-saving plan for 1999. See "Drawing Up a Plan with TurboTax," on page 280.

# Chapter 23

# Top 20 Tax Facts, Questions, and Answers

---

### In This Chapter

➤ Discover the five most common filing errors, so you don't repeat them

➤ Determine if you should expect to pay a penalty

➤ Learn how you can help reduce the national debt, assuming you want to

➤ Find out how to check on your refund when it's late

➤ Learn what tortures the IRS can perform if you refuse to pay

➤ Claim a bounty for turning in your friends, neighbors, and relatives for tax evasion

---

What should you do if you missed the April 15 filing deadline? How long should you keep your old tax returns and records? What are the most common filing errors? Where do your tax dollars go? What can the IRS do to you if you decide not to pay taxes? How do you check the status of your refund? If the IRS audits you, how far back can they go to check your records?

This chapter provides answers to these common tax questions and many more, addressing the concerns of all taxpayers, while providing some interesting facts and figures that can make you a tax-trivia expert. The question-and-answer format used in this chapter helps you test your own tax knowledge and brush up on the facts.

# 1. What Are the Five Most Common Filing Errors?

As the IRS processes returns, it also keeps statistics on everything from the average salaries of physicians to the average deductions for charitable contributions. One of the more interesting statistics is the list of the five most common filing errors:

### What if TurboTax Has a Bug?

In the past, TurboTax has had minor bugs that caused the program to make some errors. However, Intuit fixed these bugs and offered free program updates. Before you finalize your tax return, make sure you have the latest updates installed. See "I Just Bought TurboTax. Now I Have to Update It?!" in Chapter 1, "TurboTax Nickel Tour." If a miscalculation in TurboTax results in a penalty, and you are a registered TurboTax user, Intuit will pay the penalty.

1. Taxpayer inserted the incorrect amount of tax from the tax table. (Because TurboTax looks this up for you, the risk of having this error in the tax return you filed is virtually zero.)

2. Taxpayer miscalculated the amount for qualifying child or dependent care credit or earned income credit. (TurboTax performs the required calculations for you, so you don't have to worry about this one either.)

3. Taxpayer entered the income tax withheld and estimated tax payments on the wrong line on form 1040. (Because TurboTax automatically transfers withholdings from your W-2s to the proper line on form 1040, you're not at risk for this error.)

4. Taxpayer entered an incorrect social security number for himself, a spouse, or a child. (Although TurboTax can verify that a social security number is valid, it cannot verify that it is correct. Double-check the social security numbers you enter against your records.)

5. Taxpayer miscalculated the total of income, deductions, or credits. (Because TurboTax performs the calculations, the only way your return can have an error is if you entered the wrong numbers.)

# 2. How Long Should I Keep My Records?

Over the years, you can pack a couple standard filing cabinets with all your old tax returns and supporting documents, including canceled checks, receipts, bank statements, and other forms. Use the following list as your guide of what to pitch and what to keep:

➤ You can pitch most records that are more than three years old. The IRS can audit a return only up to three years from the date the return was due or filed, or two years from the date you paid the taxes (whichever is later).

➤ If you filed a return in which you under-reported your income by over 25%, the IRS has six years from the date the return was due or filed to audit it.

➤ If you filed a false or fraudulent return, or filed no return at all, the six-year audit limit does not hold for that return. The IRS can demand your records for as far back as it deems necessary. A false or fraudulent return is one that contains intentionally false information.

➤ Don't pitch the whole file. It might include some records you might need later, such as records showing the purchase of your home or other property, and the costs of improvements to the home or property. You will need these records if you ever sell the property and claim a gain or loss.

**12-18 Months**

The IRS typically informs a taxpayer that his return has been selected for an audit within 12 to 18 months of when he filed the return. If he receives no notice after 18 months, it is highly unlikely that the IRS will audit that return.

## 3. Will the IRS Penalize Me for Having Too Little Withheld?

In general, you are subject to an underpayment penalty only if you owe more than $1,000 at the end of the year. However, the IRS provides plenty of exceptions to this rule:

➤ You didn't owe taxes at the end of 1997. The IRS is basically giving you a free year to correct your mistake. Revise your W-4 or start making estimated tax payments to avoid the penalty next year.

➤ The amounts withheld or submitted in estimated payments equal at least 90% of your total tax bill. For instance, if your total bill is $15,000 and you paid $14,000 in withholding and estimated payments, you paid 93% of your tax bill, so you're safe.

➤ The amounts withheld or submitted in estimated payments in 1998 equal 100% of the total income tax you paid in 1997. However, if your 1997 income exceeds $150,000, the 1998 payments must equal 110% of the income tax you paid in 1997.

➤ You became disabled or you retired at the age of 62 or later and have reasonable cause for underpaying your taxes.

# 4. I Just Filed My Return and Received Another W-2. What Should I Do?

Don't panic. Simply file an amended return and attach Copy B of the W-2 to your 1040X. See "Filing an Amended Return," in Chapter 21, "Oops, I Made Some Honest Mistakes," for details.

# 5. Oops, I Forgot to Attach My W-2s. Now What?

Don't do anything. *Do not* file an amended return. The IRS will send a request in writing within six weeks of the date that you filed your income tax return. When you receive the request, follow the instructions to submit the missing forms.

# 6. Can I Help Reduce the National Debt?

Congress is kidding right? The same people who tripped over themselves to find ways to spend the 70 billion dollar budget surplus in 1998 have set up a way for citizens to contribute money to reduce the national debt.

If you're that much of a sucker, here's what you do: Enclose a separate check with your income tax return. Make the check payable to the "Bureau of the Public Debt." You can also send the check separately to the Bureau of the Public Debt, Department G, Washington, DC 20239-0601. If you itemize your deductions, you might be able to claim your contribution as a deduction. Whoopee!

# 7. What's the Interest Rate on Late Payments?

Late payment penalties can be pretty stiff. The IRS currently charges 9% annually on late payments. It determines the percentage based on the federal short-term interest rate and adds 3%. In addition, if you filed your return on time, but did not pay the taxes owed at that time, you must pay one half of 1% on the tax owed each month, not to exceed 25%. If you received several bills from the IRS and then received a notice of intent to levy, the IRS boosts the penalty 1% each month. If you filed late and paid late, the penalty is even stiffer: 5% of the tax owed each month, not to exceed 25%. If your return is more than 60 days late, the *minimum* penalty is the smaller of $100 or 100% of the tax owed.

To avoid the harshest penalties, be sure you file your income tax return on time or at least file a request for an extension. If you cannot pay the taxes due, contact

**No Late Filing Fee**

If you file your tax return late and are due a refund, the IRS does not charge a late fee. Penalties consist of interest on unpaid taxes.

the IRS immediately and inquire about available payment options. If you just sit back and wait for the IRS to act, the penalties can significantly increase your debt.

## 8. The IRS Docked My Refund. What Gives?

You were waiting for that $2,000 refund for six weeks. When it finally arrived, it was only $500. What happened to the rest?

If your tax return contained errors, the IRS might have taken it upon itself to correct those errors and issue a refund check that was less than what you had expected. The IRS should issue you a Statement of Changes to Your Account, explaining the errors and corrections. If you disagree with a correction, contact the IRS. See "Appealing the Audit," in Chapter 21 for details.

The IRS may also dock your return if you owe money for child support, taxes, or student loans. State and federal agencies commonly share information with the IRS about taxpayers who are delinquent in their payments. The IRS may then deduct any amounts you owe from your refund and use it to pay off your debts.

## 9. I Filed Two Months Ago, and I Still Haven't Received My Check!

If you filed your tax return electronically, you should receive your refund check in three weeks. If you mailed your return, expect to wait at least six weeks.

If the check still has not arrived, get out your copy of your return and call the Automated Refund Service at 1-800-829-4477. The automated service will request the first social security number on your return, the filing status, and the exact whole dollar amount of your refund. If the service does not have information about your refund, check back in seven days.

## 10. I'm in College. Do I Have to File a Return?

When you're in college, you typically have just enough money to get by and have a couple pizza parties each month. Assuming you're studying full time, your parents are footing the bill (along with some financial aid), and you're not earning much money, you don't have to file an income tax return. However, you might need to file a return if any of the following describes your situation:

➤ You must file a return if you can be claimed as a dependent on someone else's return (for instance, on your parents' return), you had *any* unearned income (from interest, dividends, capital gains, or trusts), and your total income is over $650.

➤ If you are listed as a dependent on someone else's return, you must file a return only if your gross income exceeds your standard deduction.

For more information on how to deal with taxes on the income of children (even older college kids), see "Paying Your Children's Taxes: The Kiddie Tax," in Chapter 16, "More Taxes (As If You Weren't Paying Enough)."

# 11. My Kid's in College. Can I Claim Him as a Dependent?

Just look at the bill from the college for a quick answer to that question. Sure, your college kids are still your dependents, unless they have disowned you, decided to pay their own way through college, and are filing their own income tax returns and claiming themselves as exemptions. If there is any dispute about whether the parent or kid gets the exemption, the parent gets it.

# 12. My Rich Uncle Just Gave Me $1,000. Should I Report It as Income?

No. Your rich uncle paid taxes on that money already. It's a gift, and as such it is typically not treated as income. However, if your rich uncle gives you a rental property and you make some money off that property, that money is taxed.

# 13. The Legal Fees for My Divorce Are Astronomical. Can I Deduct Them?

No, the government won't help you pay your legal fees for a divorce. You pay those fees out of your own pocket and cannot claim them as a deduction. However, if you have to take your ex to court to collect taxable income, such as alimony, those expenses are deductible.

# 14. If I Refuse to Pay Income Tax, What Can the IRS Do About It?

Plenty. The IRS has all sorts of ways to get its hands on the money you owe. The IRS can automatically withdraw money from your bank account, sell your stocks and bonds, seize your house and car, sell your valuables, and even garnish your wages. However, the IRS must follow the proper procedure and send you timely notifications of your tax debt before it starts looting your land.

Sound bad? Well, before the Taxpayer Bill of Rights, it was even worse. In one horror story, the IRS set up a meeting with a taxpayer under the pretense of interviewing the person. When the person showed up for the interview, the IRS seized the person's car!

# 15. My Neighbor Brags About How Little He Pays in Income Tax. Can I Turn Him In?

Nobody likes to snitch, but when you're an honest taxpayer seeing 30 to 40% of your money float away in taxes while some cheat is getting rich by fudging on his tax return, it can drive you crazy.

If you believe that someone is violating the federal tax laws by failing to report significant amounts of income or taking non-qualifying deductions, you can turn the person's name in to the IRS by calling 1-800-829-1040 for the Criminal Investigation Hotline in your area. You need not identify yourself, but if you want to receive a bounty, provide your name, address, and phone number, so the IRS can get in touch with you. The IRS keeps this information confidential. However, when the IRS shows up to seize your neighbor's property, you might want to stay inside.

# 16. I Earned Nearly Nothing from the Sale of My Home. Do I Need to Report the Sale?

Yes. Whenever you sell a home, you must complete form 2119, Sale of Your Home. It doesn't matter how much you made or lost from the sale. The IRS keeps these records on file to help determine if you qualify for tax breaks on the sale of future homes. For instance, if you live in a home for at least two years before selling it, you pay no income tax on up to $500,000 of the profit from the sale. If the IRS has records that you had purchased and sold the home before the two-year period, it can deny your claim. In short, the IRS needs the information, even if you didn't profit from the sale of your home.

# 17. I'm Married Filing Separately and My Spouse Is Itemizing. Can I Take the Standard Deduction?

No. If your spouse itemizes, you must itemize. This gives you one more thing about which to disagree.

# 18. I Moved from One State to Another. Do I Need to File Two State Income Tax Returns?

Yes. If you lived and worked in two or more states in 1998, you must file a state income tax return for each state in which you worked. Of course, there are a few states that do not tax the income of their residents.

# 19. What Percentage of Income Tax Collected Goes Toward Paying Interest on the National Debt?

In 1999, the United States will use 14% of its revenues to pay interest on the national debt. Here's where the rest of the money goes:

➤ Social security: 23%

➤ Non-defense discretionary spending, including education, training, science, technology, housing, transportation, and foreign aid: 17%

➤ National defense: 15%

➤ Medicare: 12%

➤ Medicaid: 6%

➤ Means-tested entitlements, including benefits for low-income families, food stamps, earned income credits, and veterans' pensions: 6%

➤ Additional entitlements, including federal retirement and insurance programs and payments to farmers: 6%

➤ Reserve for social security: 1%

**Deficit Versus Debt**

Don't confuse the *federal deficit* or *surplus* with the *national debt*. A deficit or surplus relates to the annual budget. If the government spends more than it collects in revenue in a given year, the government has a deficit. If the government collects more than it spends in a given year, it has a surplus. The national debt refers to the amount that the government has borrowed from itself and from the public to cover its deficits. That's why politicians are able to brag about a $70 billion surplus, even when the nation debt is nearly $6 trillion.

As you can see, that 14% in interest is a huge chunk, and with no funds going to pay off the national debt, the interest will continue to grow. On average, the national debt grows by $628 million per day. (This makes the $40 million that Ken Starr spent on investigating Clinton seem like pocket change.)

**Don't Worry, Be Happy**

Compared to the deficits in other developed countries, including Canada, France, Italy, England, Japan, and Germany, the national debt of the United States isn't that bad.

# 20. Why Do I Feel as Though I'm Being Ripped Off?

The problem with taxes is that nobody wants to pay them, but people enjoy the benefits of costly programs. We want everyone to receive a good education and quality healthcare, to live in safe neighborhoods and be relatively free from foreign threats, to have our savings secured through tough times, and to be assured that we can retire comfortably when that time comes. All these programs cost money, and the government levies taxes to pay for them.

The only way to successfully lower taxes without increasing the national debt is to cut spending. Unfortunately, Democrats and Republicans cannot agree on where to cut spending. Traditionally, Republicans have attempted to increase spending for defense, while the Democrats have sought additional funding for education, health, and environmental programs. The voters push for their pet programs, and we all pay more in taxes.

In short, you're being ripped off by a system that has grown too fat, but we have all contributed to creating this beast.

# State Tax Agencies: Addresses and Phone Numbers

If you decided not to file your state income tax return with TurboTax State, or you printed your state income tax return and you need more information, the following list contains the contact information you need:

**Alabama Department of Revenue**
Income Tax Forms
P.O. Box 327410
Montgomery, AL 36132-7410
(334) 242-1000
www.ador.state.al.us

**Alaska Department of Revenue**
State Office Building
P.O. Box 110420
Juneau, AK 99811-0420
(907) 465-2320
www.revenue.state.ak.us

**Arizona Department of Revenue**
P.O. Box 29002
Phoenix, AZ 85038-9002
(602) 542-4260
www.revenue.state.az.us

**Arkansas Department of Finance and Administration**
Revenue Division
P.O. Box 3628
Little Rock, AR 72203
(501) 682-1100
www.state.ar.us/revenue/

**California Franchise Tax Board**
Tax Forms Request
P.O. Box 942840
Sacramento, CA 94240-0040
(800) 852-5711
www.ftb.ca.gov

**Colorado Department of Revenue**
1375 Sherman Street
Denver, CO 80261
(303) 232-2416
www.state.co.us

**Connecticut Department of Revenue**
State Tax Department
25 Sigourney Street
Hartford, CT 06106-5032
(800) 382-9463
www.state.ct.us/drs

**Delaware Department of Finance**
Division of Revenue
Delaware State Building
820 North French Street
Wilmington, DE 19801
(302) 577-8200
www.state.de.us/revenue

**District of Columbia Department of Finance and Revenue**
Room 1046
300 Indiana Avenue, N.W.
Washington, D.C. 20001
(202) 727-6170
www.dccfo.com

**Florida Department of Revenue**
104 Carlton Building
Tallahassee, FL 32399-0100
(850) 488-5050
www.fcn.state.fl.us/dor/

**Georgia Department of Revenue**
507 Trinity-Washington Building
Atlanta, GA 30334
(404) 656-4188
www2.state.ga.us/Departments/DOR/

**Hawaii Department of Taxation**
830 Punchbowl Street
P.O. Box 259
Honolulu, HI 96809-0259
(800) 222-3229
www.state.hi.us/tax/tax.html

**Idaho State Tax Commission**
800 Park Boulevard, Plaza IV
Boise, ID 83722
(800) 972-7660
www2.state.id.us/tax/forms.htm

**Illinois Department of Revenue**
Willard Ice Building
101 W. Jefferson
Springfield, IL 62702
(800) 732-8866
www.revenue.state.il.us

**Indiana Department of Revenue**
100 North Senate
Room N105
Indianapolis, IN 46204-2253
(317) 233-4018
www.state.in.us/dor/

**Iowa Department of Revenue and Finance**
Hoover State Office Building
Des Moines, IA 50319
(800) 367-3388
www.state.ia.us/government/drf/

**Kansas Department of Revenue**
Docking State Office Building
915 S.W. Harrison
Topeka, KS 66612
(785) 296-0222
www.ink.org/public/kdor/

**Kentucky Revenue Cabinet**
200 Fair Oaks Lane
Frankfort, KY 40620
(502) 564-4581
www.state.ky.us/agencies/revenue/revhome.htm

**Louisiana Department of Revenue**
8490 Picardy Avenue
Building 600
Baton Rouge, LA 70809-3684
(225) 925-4611
www.rev.state.la.us

**Maine Bureau of Taxation**
Income Tax Section
State Office Building
Station 24
Augusta, ME 04332
(207) 624-7894
janus.state.me.us/revenue

**Maryland Comptroller of the Treasury**
Revenue Administration
Division
Annapolis, MD 21411-0001
(800) 638-2937
www.comp.state.md.us

**Massachusetts Department of Revenue**
Customer Service Bureau
P.O. Box 7010
Boston, MA 02204
(800) 392-6089
www.state.ma.us/dor/dorpg.htm

**Michigan Department of the Treasury**
Revenue Administration
Services
The Treasury Building
430 West Allegan Street
Lansing, MI 48922
(800) 367-6263
www.treas.state.mi.us

**Minnesota Department of Revenue**
Mail Station 7704
10 River Park Plaza
St. Paul, MN 55146-7704
(800) 652-9094
www.state.mn.us/ebranch/mdor/

**Mississippi Department of Revenue**
State Tax Commission
P.O. Box 1033
Jackson, MS 39215-3338
(601) 923-7000
www.mstc.state.ms.us/revenue/

**Missouri Department of Revenue**
P.O. Box 3022
Jefferson City, MO 65105-3022
(800) 877-6881
dor.state.mo.us

**Montana Department of Revenue**
Income Tax Division
P.O. Box 5805
Helena, MT 59604-5805
(406) 444-3674
www.mt.gov/revenue/rev.htm

**Nebraska Department of Revenue**
Nebraska State Office Building
301 Centennial Mall South
P.O. Box 94818
Lincoln, NE 68509-4818
(800) 742-7474
www.nol.org/revenue

**Nevada Department of Taxation**
Capitol Complex
Carson City, NV 89710-0003
(702) 687-4892

**New Hampshire Department of Revenue**
P.O. Box 457
Concord, NH 03302-0457
(603) 271-2191
www.state.nh.us/revenue/
revenue.htm

**New Jersey Division of Taxation**
P.O. Box 269
Trenton, NJ 08646-0269
(609) 588-2200
www.state.nj.us/treasury/
taxation

**New Mexico Taxation and Revenue Department**
P.O. Box 630
Santa Fe, NM 87504-0630
(505) 827-2206
www.state.nm.us/tax/
trd_form.htm

**New York Department of Taxation and Finance**
Taxpayer Service Bureau
West Averell Harriman Campus
Albany, NY 12227
(800) 462-8100
www.tax.state.ny.us

**North Carolina Department of Revenue**
P.O. Box 25000
Raleigh, NC 27640
(919) 715-0397
www.dor.state.nc.us/DOR

**North Dakota**
Office of the State Tax
Commissioner
State Capitol
600 East Boulevard Avenue
Bismark, ND 58505-0599
(701) 328-2770
www.state.nd.us/taxdpt

**Ohio Department of Taxation**
Income Tax Division
P.O. Box 530
Columbus, OH 43266-0030
(614) 433-7750
www.state.oh.us/tax/

**Oklahoma Tax Commission**
Income Tax Division
P.O. Box 26800
Oklahoma City, OK 73126-0800
(405) 521-3160
www.oktax.state.ok.us

**Oregon Department of Revenue**
955 Center St., N.E.
Salem, OR 97310
(503) 378-4988
www.dor.state.or.us

**Pennsylvania Department of Revenue**
711 Gibson Boulevard
Harrisburg, PA 17104-3200
(888) 728-2937
www.revenue.state.pa.us

**Rhode Island Division of Taxation**
One Capitol Hill
Providence, RI 02908-5800
(401) 222-1111
www.tax.state.ri.us

**South Carolina Tax Commission**
Individual Income Tax Division
301 Gervais Street
P.O. Box 125
Columbia, SC 29214
(800) 763-1295
www.dor.state.sc.us

**South Dakota Department of Revenue**
445 E. Capitol Avenue
Pierre, South Dakota 57501
(800) 829-9188
www.state.sd.us/state/
executive/revenue/revenue.
html

**Tennessee Department of Revenue**
Andrew Jackson State Office Building
500 Deaderick Street
Nashville, TN 37242
(615) 741-4465
www.state.tn.us/revenue

**Texas Comptroller of Public Accounts**
111 East 17th Street
Austin, TX 78774
(512) 463-4600
www.window.texas.gov

**Utah State Tax Commission**
210 North 1950 West
Salt Lake City, UT 84134
(800) 662-4335
www.tax.ex.state.ut.us

**Vermont Department of Taxes**
109 State Street
Montpelier, VT 05609-1401
(802) 828-2865
www.state.vt.us/tax

**Virginia Department of Taxation**
Taxpayers Assistance
P.O. Box 1115
Richmond, VA 23218-1115
(804) 367-8031
www.state.va.us/tax/
tax.html

**Washington Department of Revenue**
General Administration Building
P.O. Box 47478
Olympia, WA 98504-7478
(800) 647-7706
www.wa.gov/DOR/wador.htm

**West Virginia State Tax Department**
Taxpayer Service Division
P.O. Box 3784
Charleston, WV 25337-3784
(304) 558-3333
www.state.wv.us/taxrev

**Wisconsin Department of Revenue**
P.O. Box 8933
Madison, WI 53708-8933
(608) 266-1961
www.dor.state.wi.us

**Wyoming Revenue Department**
Herschler Building, 2nd Floor West
122 West 25th Street
Cheyenne, WY 82002-0110
(307) 777-7961
www.state.wy.us

# Glossary of IRS Technobabble

The IRS is populated by accountants and tax lawyers who have developed their own unique language. When you need a plain English translation of a particularly obscure term, here's where you'll find it.

**401(k) plan**  A tax-deferred retirement savings plan offered by many companies to their employees. Any money you contribute to the plan is not taxed, and your investments grow untaxed. The money is taxed only when you start taking it out.

**1040**  The unabridged U.S. Individual Income Tax Return, which you fill out if you choose to complicate your life and save some money by itemizing your deductions.

**1040A**  The simplified U.S. Individual Income Tax Return for those who have a taxable income below $50,000 from only wages, salaries, tips, scholarships, fellowships, IRA distributions, pensions, annuities, unemployment checks, social security benefits, dividends, and interest. The 1040A does not allow you to itemize deductions; however, it does allow you to adjust income for IRA contributions and gives you tax credits for child and dependent care, earned income, and the elderly and disabled.

**1040EZ**  The quick and easy U.S. Individual Income Tax Return for those who file as single or married filing jointly with no dependents, no deductions, no adjustments to income, and income only from wages, interest, and unemployment compensation.

**accelerated cost recovery system (ACRS)**  An outdated method of depreciating assets, which enables you to claim a higher depreciation for the asset during the first years you own it. ACRS was replaced by the modified accelerated cost recovery system (MACRS) back in 1987. See also *modified accelerated cost recovery system (MACRS).*

**accelerated depreciation**   Any depreciation method that enables you to claim a higher percentage of depreciation for an asset in the first years you own it, and a lower percentage in later years. Contrast to *straight-line depreciation*.

**accrual method**   A method of accounting in which you record income in the year in which you bill or invoice a customer and record expenses in the year in which you receive the bill. This is in contrast to the *cash method*, in which you record income in the year you actually receive it and record expenses in the year you actually pay them.

**adjusted basis**   The cost of an asset plus the cost of improvements to the asset minus the asset's depreciation. The adjusted basis reflects what you have invested in the asset over its life, so that when you sell the asset, you can more accurately report your profit from the sale.

**adjusted gross income (AGI)**   Your gross income from wages, salaries, tips, and other sources, minus any adjustments to your income (IRA contributions, student loan interest, alimony payments, and so on). The IRS uses your AGI to determine limits for itemized deductions and credits.

**after-tax contribution**   Contributions to a tax-deferred retirement account that exceed the amount that you are allowed to contribute with pre-tax dollars. This excess is subject to income tax, but it is allowed to grow tax-free until you withdraw money from the account.

**alimony**   Payments you make to your ex-spouse as ordered by the court. Alimony does not include any legal expenses or property settlements agreed to at the time of the separation. It applies only to regular payments. The payer can use alimony to reduce his AGI and receive a tax break. The recipient must report the alimony received as income.

**alternative minimum tax (AMT)**   A separate tax for those with high gross income whose net income on paper is significantly lower. The AMT is intended to close some of the income tax loopholes that enable those with high income to avoid paying taxes.

**amended return**   An income tax return that you can submit to correct errors in a tax return you filed previously. You can file a 1040X to amend a return.

**annuity**   An investment product typically offered by insurance companies that enables your investments to grow tax-deferred until you sell them.

**assessment**   A bill that the IRS sends you for additional tax due. In most cases, the IRS cannot collect the assessment until it has sent you several notices and you have had the option of appealing the IRS' claims.

**assets**  Stuff. Assets consist of anything of value that you own, except money. Assets include cars, equipment, mutual funds, stocks, and anything else from which you could profit by selling.

**at-risk**  The state of potentially experiencing a loss from an activity. The IRS uses at-risk rules to determine the limitations for claiming losses. If you are a partner in a business and have only $10,000 invested in that business, the IRS uses the at-risk rules to prevent you from claiming losses in excess of the amount you are personally at risk of losing.

**audit**  An IRS examination of your income tax return. An audit typically consists of an interview in which an IRS agent asks you to produce records to back up your claims on the amount of income you earned and the deductions you listed on a return.

**backup withholding**  Income tax that is automatically withheld from payments if you fail to provide the payer with your social security number or taxpayer identification number. The IRS requires the payer to withhold 20% of the payment in taxes, to ensure that the IRS receives its cut of the proceeds.

**bad debt**  Money that someone owes you and you will probably never see. Some bad debt might be deductible as a loss.

**basis**  The value of a property that is used to determine the profit or loss on its sale, depreciation, casualty loss, or other deduction. See also *adjusted basis*.

**beneficiary**  The designated recipient of money from a trust, estate, insurance policy, or retirement plan.

**business asset**  Property that belongs to your business and that your business uses to generate income. By depreciating a business asset, you claim a deduction for the asset's loss of value over time.

**capital gain**  The profit you see from the sale of an asset, such as a home, business equipment, stocks, or mutual fund. To determine the capital gain from a transaction, you subtract the adjusted basis of the asset from the sale price. Capital gains are subject to income tax, but they are taxed at a lower rate than income you earn by working. Capital gains from transactions in a retirement account are not taxed until you withdraw money from the account. See also *dividend*.

**capital loss**  The financial loss you experience from the sale of an asset. Capital losses are deductible only if you have enough capital gains to offset the losses. If your capital losses in any given year exceed your capital gains for that year, you may carry the losses over to later years.

**carryover**   An amount carried over from a past tax return to the current return or a future return. If your deductions for a certain category exceed the limits for this year, you might be able to carry over the excess to future income tax returns to take advantage of the tax break in later years.

**cash method**   An accounting method in which you report income when you receive it and report expenses when you pay them. This is in contrast to the *accrual method*, in which you report income when you bill a customer and report expenses when you receive your bills.

**casualty**   A loss caused by forces beyond your control, including tornadoes, fires, hurricanes, and earthquakes. The cause must be sudden and unexpected. If carpenter ants disassemble your home over 20 years, the loss is not considered a casualty and is not deductible.

**charitable contribution**   A donation of cash, belongings, or valuable property to a nonprofit organization. By itemizing deductions, you can deduct your charitable contributions.

**child and dependent care credit**   A chunk of money you can lop off the bottom line of your tax bill for child or dependent care expenses you paid so you could work or seek employment.

**child support**   Payments that the court orders you to make to financially support a child you brought into this world. Unlike alimony payments, child support payments cannot be listed as adjustments to income.

**consumer interest**   Money you pay to borrow money for buying consumer products, such as a car, washing machine, or clothes. The interest you pay on your Visa balance is consumer interest. This interest is nondeductible. The only interest that is deductible is *mortgage interest*. That's why it makes sense for some people to refinance their mortgage or use money from a home-equity loan to pay off their credit card bills and other consumer debt.

**correspondence audit**   The least painful of all audits, this type of audit is carried on through the mail.

**cost basis**   The amount you paid for an asset, including the cost of the asset, sales tax, shipping, and setup costs.

**credit**   A dollar-for-dollar reduction of your tax bill. Unlike a deduction, which reduces your tax bill only by a percentage of each dollar based on your income tax bracket, each dollar in credit is like a dollar in your pocket. The most significant credits are the $400 child tax credit and the $1,500 Hope Scholarship Credit.

**deduction**　A qualifying expense that the IRS allows you to subtract from your Adjusted Gross Income to reduce the amount of income that's subject to income tax. You can choose to itemize deductions or take the standard deduction for your filing status. See also *itemize* and *standard deduction*.

**deferred gain**　The profit from a sale of a home that is rolled over to the next, more expensive home. In the past, when you sold your home, the money from the profit of the sale was subject to income tax. However, if you purchased a more expensive home, you could choose to defer the gain indefinitely until you purchased a less expensive home and actually received the profit. Recent changes to the tax code exempt up to $500,000 profit from taxes, making it unlikely that you will benefit from a deferred gain.

**dependent**　A person (typically one of your children) you financially support and whom you can claim as an exemption on your tax return. Financial support includes providing food, shelter, education, and other living necessities.

**dependent care credit**　See *child and dependent care credit*.

**depletion**　A deduction allowed for the decrease in a depletable resource, such as gas, oil, coal, or minerals.

**depreciation**　A deduction allowed for the amount an asset decreases in value over time. You commonly depreciate office equipment or machinery you use in your business to give yourself a deduction in each year you use the equipment or machinery to generate income. In many cases, you can choose to deduct the entire cost of the equipment in the year you purchased it by claiming it as a Section 179 expense. See also *Section 179 expense*.

**dividend**　Income from stocks, mutual funds, or corporations that are paid to shareholders as their share of the company's profits. This is in contrast to a *capital gain*, which is income from the increased value of shares of stock or mutual funds.

**earned income**　Money that you make by working, as opposed to money you make through investments. Earned income entitles you to contribute to a tax-deferred retirement account and is one of the essential conditions for qualifying for the *earned income credit*.

**earned income credit**　A dollar-for-dollar reduction of taxes for low-income workers. With the earned income credit, the IRS might actually pay *you* when you file a tax return.

**effective tax rate**　The percentage of your taxable income that you pay in taxes. For example, if you and your spouse have taxable income of $62,490 and pay $12,297 in income tax, your effective tax rate is $12,297 divided by $62,490, or 19.6%. So, why doesn't that match up neatly with the 15% or 28% tax bracket? Because the IRS taxes the income at different rates. For example, if you're married filing jointly, the first $40,000 of income is taxed at 15%; the next $60,000 is taxed at 28%; and the next $50,000 is taxed at 31% (I rounded the numbers a bit). Using my rounded numbers, here's how it works:

| | | |
|---|---|---|
| $40,000 at 15% | = | $6,000 |
| $22,490 at 28% | = | $6,297 |
| Total tax | = | $12,297 |
| Effective tax rate | = | 19.6% |

**equity**   The difference between what an asset is worth and what you owe on the asset. For instance, if you own a $150,000 home and owe $100,000 on it, your equity in that home is $50,000.

**estate**   Your net worth when you die. An estate's value is based on the value of savings and assets minus debts.

**estimated payment**   A quarterly tax payment for the self-employed that takes the place of withholding. To avoid paying penalties, your estimated payments must equal or exceed 90% of your total tax bill.

**exemption**   An amount specified by the current tax code that you can claim as a deduction for yourself, your spouse, and any qualifying dependents.

**expense**   Money you pay for a product or service. By deducting business expenses from your gross receipts, you can lower your reported profit and pay less tax. Unfortunately, most personal expenses are not deductible.

**fair market value (FMV)**   The current value of an asset as determined by the amount you could sell it for today. For a valuable asset, you can hire an appraiser to determine the asset's fair market value.

**federal income tax**   The money you pay the U.S. government to support social security, Medicare, national defense, education, and other programs. This tax is based on a percentage of the money you receive from being gainfully employed, making intelligent investments, gambling successfully, leasing and selling property, and performing any other activities that make money.

**fiduciary**   A person or group given the responsibility of managing someone else's assets. Fiduciaries include executors of wills and trustees of estates.

**field audit**   An on-site, IRS examination of a business's financial records. A field audit is the mother of all audits and can be quite intrusive. IRS agents show up at your business, flip through your records, and ask lots of questions. You might be able to avoid such an audit by hiring an accountant and giving the accountant Power of

Attorney to represent you. The accountant may then request that the audit be held at his office instead of at your business.

**filing status**   The category the IRS uses to determine income tax rates for taxpayers in various situations: single, married filing jointly, married filing separately, head of household, or qualifying widower. Taxes hit single people the hardest, so get married and have a kid or two.

**fiscal year**   A twelve-month period that a business uses for its record-keeping. The fiscal year must end on the last day of any month but need not match the calendar year—January 1 to December 31. If you're an independent contractor or small-business owner, you can avoid headaches by aligning your fiscal year with the calendar year.

**gain**   A fancy word for "profit."

**gross income**   The total amount of money you made before you start figuring in adjustments and deductions.

**gross receipts**   The total amount of money that a business receives for its products and services before subtracting materials, returns, salaries, and other expenses.

**head of household**   A filing status for those who are unmarried but living with a qualifying dependent. For example, if you're divorced and you support a child or other qualifying dependent, you can file as head of household and pay much less in taxes than if you were to file as single.

**hobby**   An activity that's not motivated by profit, even if you make a profit doing it. Why is the IRS interested in your hobbies? You are required to report the profit from your hobby as income, but any losses cannot exceed the profit you make. The IRS becomes a little testy if you try to treat a hobby as a small business, so you can have fun and claim a loss for it.

**holding period**   The time you own an asset, measured from the time you purchase the asset until the time you sell it. The IRS uses holding periods to determine if any profit or loss from the sale of an asset is a long-term or short-term capital gain or loss. See also *long-term capital gain.*

**home office**   A place in your home that is used exclusively for business purposes. The home office deduction enables you to claim a percentage of your home's mortgage interest, property taxes, and maintenance and utility bills as expenses, assuming you are self-employed or working for a company that requires you to work out of your home. However, the IRS has some fairly strict rules on claiming the home office deduction.

**incentive stock options (ISO)**   Stocks that an employer sells to its employees at a bargain. No tax is due on the growth of the stock until the employee chooses to sell it.

**income**   Money you make by working, investing, leasing property or equipment, gambling, or performing any other gainful activity. Most income is taxable.

**independent contractor**   A person who is employed by various companies but is considered self-employed. To qualify as an independent contractor, a person generally must work for more than one company, maintain a work area (such as a home office), and have control over the process used to perform the job as well as the work hours.

**individual retirement account (IRA)**   A tax-deferred holding that allows you to contribute up to $2,000 per year and avoid paying income tax on that money. You must be employed and cannot be a participant in an employer-sponsored plan. Several other conditions might prohibit you from contributing to an IRA or limit your tax-deferred contributions.

**information return**   Forms that the IRS requires from those who pay salaries, interest, dividends, pension distributions, and other types of payments. The IRS uses information returns to cross-check the information provided on tax returns. For instance, if you claim to have made $50,000 in income, but your W-2s show that you made $100,000, the IRS can quickly determine that you're lying and audit your return.

**installment agreement**   A deal you might be able to work out with the IRS to pay back taxes over time.

**installment sale**   A sales transaction in which the seller of an asset agrees to let the buyer pay for the asset over time rather than paying for it all at once.

**interest**   Money you pay to borrow money or money you earn from loaning money.

**Internal Revenue Service (IRS)**   An arm of the U.S. government that collects federal taxes, enforces the tax laws, and tirelessly defends its reputation.

**itemize**   The process of adding up qualifying expenses to exceed the standard deduction and cut your tax bill. If you have significant qualifying expenses (mortgage interest, charitable contributions, medical expenses, property taxes, and so on), you may deduct these expenses from your income rather than taking the standard deduction and save yourself some money. See also *standard deduction*.

**joint return**   A tax return filed by a married couple. In most cases, married people can reduce their taxes by choosing the filing status of married filing jointly. In some cases, however, the couple might pay more by filing jointly than if they were single. This is known as the *marriage penalty*.

**Keogh plan**   A tax-deferred retirement plan for the self-employed, which enables you to contribute gobs more than you could with an IRA.

**kiddie tax**   Additional tax that parents must pay on the first $1,300 of their children's unearned income, for children under the age of 14. The kiddie tax was designed to discourage parents from shifting investments to their children to avoid paying taxes on the income.

**levy**   To forcefully collect taxes by legal authority. If you fail to reply to the IRS when you receive a Notice of Levy for back taxes, the IRS uses whatever means it has available to collect those taxes and any additional penalties. The IRS may garnishee your wages, place a lien on your home, or seize your car or other personal property.

**lien**   A legal claim that the IRS can place on property that prevents the owner from selling or transferring the property until the owner pays back taxes and penalties. For example, if the IRS places a lien on your home, you can't sell it unless the IRS gives its approval and devises a plan to get the back taxes and penalties before you see any profit from the sale.

**like-kind exchange**   An exchange of similar assets of equal value that produces no net gain or loss for either party. Assuming the exchange meets the requirements, no taxes are due.

**long-term capital gain**   The profit made on the sale of an asset held for over 18 months. The maximum tax on long-term capital gains is 20% (10% if your income falls in the 15% tax bracket).

**lump-sum distribution**   A withdrawal of the entire amount saved in a tax-deferred retirement account. Lump-sum distributions are typically made if you leave the company, retire, become disabled, or pass away (in which case the lump-sum is distributed to your beneficiary). If you leave the company before age 59½, you should roll over your investments into another account to avoid any penalties associated with lump-sum distributions.

**marginal tax rate**   The highest income tax rate that applies to your income. The IRS taxes your income at different rates. For example, if you're married filing jointly, the first $40,000 of income is taxed at 15%; the next $60,000 is taxed at 28%; and the next $50,000 is taxed at 31% (I rounded the numbers a bit). The highest tax rate you pay is your marginal tax rate. The percentage you actually pay is called the effective tax rate. For an example, see *effective tax rate*.

**marriage penalty**   A bug in the tax code that might cause two married people to pay more income tax by filing a joint return than if they filed as single. The problem is that the tax rates are graduated—the higher your income, the higher percentage you pay in taxes. When you and your spouse combine your incomes, you boost yourself into a higher tax bracket and pay a higher percentage than you would by filing separately.

**married filing separately**   A filing status commonly used by couples who are separated but not divorced and choose to keep their finances separate. If you're a victim of the marriage penalty, as explained earlier, filing separately can help reduce the penalty by taxing each income at a lower rate. In addition, if you and your spouse have widely differing income and deduction levels, filing separately might be beneficial.

**materially participate**   To take an active role in managing a business from which you receive income or experience a loss. If you are your only employee, you materially participated in the business. If you have additional employees and you put in more hours than anyone else, or you put in at least 500 hours, you materially participated. If you just stood by, watched, and counted the money, you didn't materially participate.

**medical expense**   A deductible cost for healthcare, including expenses for health insurance, doctor visits, dental care, and prescriptions. For you to benefit from the medical expense deduction, your medical expenses must exceed 7.5% of your AGI (or the combined AGI of you and your spouse, if you are married filing jointly).

**modified accelerated cost recovery system (MACRS)**   A method of depreciating assets that enables you to claim a higher depreciation for the asset during the first years you own it. MACRS replaced ACRS back in 1987. MACRS is a slightly less accelerated cost recovery system, forcing you to depreciate the asset over a longer period. See also *accelerated cost recovery system (ACRS)*.

**mortgage interest**   Money you pay to a bank or mortgage company to borrow money for purchasing a home. Currently, mortgage interest is the only interest that is deductible. That's why so many people refinance their homes or take out home-equity loans to pay off their auto loans and high-interest credit card balances.

**mutual fund**   An investment option that enables you to buy a diversified set of stocks or bonds by purchasing shares of the fund. Mutual funds are typically managed by professional investors and make it easy for novice investors to create a balanced investment portfolio.

**net income**   The amount of money that's left after your business pays its expenses.

**net operating loss (NOL)**   A business loss in excess of any other income you received in a given year from sources including wages, tips, interest, and investments. Basically, an NOL indicates that not only did your business lose money, but it lost so much money that you personally suffered a loss. Deductions for NOLs are severely limited, but you can carry the NOL back three years and forward to future years to help offset income from previous or upcoming tax returns.

**office audit**   An IRS examination that takes place at a local or regional IRS office. The IRS notifies you of the place and time of the audit and provides a list of records it wants to see. You must then show up, hand over the requested records, and answer any relevant questions.

**original issue discount (OID)**   Bonds that you can purchase at a discount that increase in value over time. The discount (your savings) are considered income and must be claimed as such as the bond's value rises.

**partnership**   A business that's not subject to income taxes. Although a partnership does not have to pay taxes, whatever it pays to the partners or shareholders is taxable income.

**passive activity**   A business activity in which you did not materially participate. See also *materially participate*. You can claim losses from passive activities only to off-set gains from other passive activities. If you have only one passive activity, your loss is *your* loss.

**penalty**   A monetary amount that the IRS charges for failing to pay taxes on time or for underpaying estimated taxes or withholding. Penalties are charged as interest on the money you owe the IRS, so if you file your return late and don't owe taxes, you won't have to pay a penalty.

**pension**   An employer-sponsored retirement plan that pays retirement benefits based on the number of years you worked for the company.

**personal exemption**   A set amount that you can deduct from your income for yourself, your spouse, and each child or other qualifying dependent. The personal exemption is a small way of accounting for the fact that it costs money to live.

**personal property**   Stuff you own that's typically not used for business purposes, including your car, boat, personal jet, Waverunner, or Winnebago. Although the federal government doesn't tax these possessions, your state and local governments might, and you might be able to deduct these taxes as itemized deductions.

**points**   Interest paid up-front to secure a loan. Points are typically paid for mortgage and home-equity loans and are deductible.

**principal**   The loan amount, or the amount on which interest is charged.

**profit-sharing plan**   An employer-sponsored retirement plan in which each employee's contribution to the plan might vary from year to year based on the employer's profits.

**qualified plan**   A tax-deferred retirement plan that's approved by the government. Types of qualified plans include 401(k), Keogh, SEP, SIMPLE, and employer-sponsored pension plans.

**qualifying widow(er)** A filing status that enables a surviving spouse with dependents to take advantage of the income tax rates available for couples who are married filing jointly.

**quarterly payment** See *estimated payment*.

**real property** Buildings, land, and other types of real estate.

**receipt** A piece of paper that proves you purchased what you claim to have purchased.

**refund** Money that the IRS returns to you at the end of the year when you paid too much withholding or estimated taxes during the year.

**roll over** To move money from one investment account directly into another without touching the money yourself. Rolling over funds is a much less complicated way of transferring funds than if you were to withdraw and then deposit the funds. Rolling over also helps you avoid early withdrawal penalties.

**royalty** Money you receive from licensing or selling intellectual property, such as books, movies, and patents. You may also receive royalty income from leasing property rights for mining depletable resources, such as oil and gas.

**S corporation** A sly business setup that enables the business to run tax free. Payments from the S corporation to its shareholders are taxable.

**schedule** An attachment to your tax return that provides supporting details for income, expenses, deductions, or credits reported on your tax return.

**Section 179 expense** An exception that enables business owners to deduct up to $18,000 in business assets as an expense in the year they purchased the assets, rather than having to depreciate the asset over several years. See also *depreciation*.

**self-employment tax** Taxes that the self-employed pay to cover their share of social security and Medicare. This tax is 15.3% of your net income from self-employment. For those who are not self-employed, the employer pays half of social security and Medicare, so the employee pays only 7.65%.

**short-term capital gain** The profit realized by selling an asset that you held for less than 12 months. See also *long-term capital gain*.

**SIMPLE plan** A tax-deferred retirement plan for businesses that employ fewer than 100 workers.

**Simplified Employee Pension (SEP) plan** A tax-deferred retirement plan for the self-employed that allows you to contribute up to 15% of your net business profit annually. An SEP is easy to set up and provides higher limits than are available with IRAs. See also *individual retirement account (IRA)*.

**single**   The only filing status available for single people. Filing as single qualifies you to pay the highest income tax rates.

**standard deduction**   An optional deduction for those who choose not to itemize deductions. See also *itemize*. The standard deduction is based on your filing status:

| | |
|---|---|
| Married filing jointly | $7,100 |
| Qualified widow(er) | $7,100 |
| Head of household | $6,250 |
| Single | $4,250 |
| Married filing separately | $3,350 |

**statute of limitations**   The period beyond which a person or organization is allowed by law to perform a given action. The IRS typically has three years from the date your return was due to audit your return and 10 years to collect assessments. Likewise, you have three years from the time you filed your return to file an amended return.

**straight-line depreciation**   A way of depreciating assets that results in deducting the same amount each year. Calculating straight-line depreciation is easy—you divide the cost of the asset by its useful life. See also *modified accelerated cost recovery system (MACRS)*.

**tax liability**   The amount of tax you owe.

**tax shelter**   Any investment that allows you to deduct expenses that exceed your investment. The IRS frowns on tax shelters because they enable you to reduce your taxable income when you're not really experiencing a loss.

**tax-sheltered annuity**   An investment product designed specifically for nonprofit organizations to offer tax incentives for contributions to the annuity. Although tax-sheltered annuities can help you save money, their fees are typically higher than the fees for standard mutual funds.

**taxable income**   The amount of money that's subject to income tax after you subtract all adjustments, exemptions, and deductions from your gross income.

**Taxpayer Bill of Rights**   A statement penned by Congress that lays out your rights as a taxpayer, including your right to demand to speak with an IRS agent's supervisor and the right to stop an audit at any time and seek professional counsel. The Taxpayer Bill of Rights is intended to keep the IRS from overstepping its boundaries.

**trust**   Something you shouldn't do during an IRS audit. Also, a legal arrangement in which the ownership of assets is passed from one person to another.

**useful life**   The average life span of a business asset. For example, according to the IRS, the useful life of a computer is five years. You use the useful life of an asset to determine the amount you can deduct for depreciation each year. See also *depreciation*.

**W-2**   A form sent to you and the IRS by your employer to report your annual income, withholdings, contributions to tax-deferred retirement accounts, and other financial information.

**wages**   Regular income you receive as an employee.

**withholding**   Money that your employer automatically deducts from your paycheck and sends to the government to pay your taxes. Ideally, your withholding should equal your total tax at the end of the year, so you owe no taxes and receive no refund. However, this rarely happens, so you must fill out a tax return at the end of the year to square everything with the IRS.

# Index

for elderly and disabled, 217
low-income housing credits,
    219-220
mortgage interest credit, 219

# D

damage deposits, rental income,
    122
data
    entering
        into EasyStep Interview, 65
        into W-2 forms, 66
    importing
        from other personal
            finance programs, 40
        from QuickBooks,
            38-40
        from Quicken, 34
daycare, 54-55
debt
    versus deficit, 290
    *see also* national debt
deceased persons, W-2 forms, 63
deducting fuel, farmers, 115
Deduction Finder, 231-232
deductions
    401(k)s, 27
    automobile license fees, 157
    business expenses for non-
        business owners,
        164-167
    businesses, 98, 149
    capital gains, 279-280
    car expenses, 164
    casualties, 169
    charitable contributions,
        155-157
    dental expenses, 24-25
    depletion deduction, 121
    divorce, 288
    employee business deductions,
        25-26
    foreign taxes, 158
    gambling, 68
    home offices, 26-27,
        95-97
    homes, 148
        entering into TurboTax,
            150-151
    interest, 24
        student loans, 216

investments, 167-169
IRAs, 27, 174-175
itemized, 148, 289
medical expenses, 24-25,
    152-153
moving expenses,
    170-171
natural disasters, 170
net operating loss (NOL), 172
paperwork, for kids, 25
points, 149-150
property taxes, 23, 149, 157
retirement investments,
    investing beyond the
    deductible amount, 177
royalties, 120-121
SEPs (Simplified Employee
    Pension plan), 27
SOHO, 95-97
standard, 148
state income taxes, 158
tax-deferred retirement
    accounts, 27-28
    maximizing, 65
taxes you've already paid,
    157-159
thefts, 169-170
tracking down with TurboTax,
    231-232
uniforms, 164
union dues, 164
deferred compensation
    tax-free benefits, 278
    W-2 forms, 63
deferring
    payments, farmers, 114
    taxes through retirement
        investments, 279
deficit versus debt, 290
Delaware Department of Finance,
    294
deleting forms, 48
dental expenses, deductions,
    24-25
dependent care benefits,
    W-2 forms, 62
dependents
    college students, 288
    qualifications, 53
    qualified medical
        expenses, 55
depletion deduction, royalties
    (exhaustible resources), 121

depreciating
    assets, 102
        cars, Section 179, 105
        computers, 102
        descriptions for,
            106-107
        farms, 115-116
        leasing, 104
        livestock, 117
        transferring data from pre-
            vious year, 107
    business assets, 93
    land, 128
    methods, 104
    rental property, 127
    Section 179, 104-105
descriptions for depreciating
    assets, 106-107
direct expenses, home offices,
    96-97
direct sales, 186-188
disabled credits, 217
District of Columbia Department
    of Finance and Revenue, 294
dividends, 74
divorce, 160
    deductions, 288
    *see also* alimony
donations, 22
downloading TurboTax State, 250

# E

earned income credit (EIC), 213
    1099-G form, 77
EasyStep Interview, 44-45
    data, entering, 65
    information about children,
        53-54
    personal information, enter-
        ing, 48-50
    switching to forms
        view, 46
editing forms, 47
education
    credits, 216
    grants, 139
    IRAs, 178-179
EIC, *see* earned income
    credit

**315**